Hacking the Hacker

Hacking the Hacker

Learn from the Experts Who Take Down Hackers

Roger A. Grimes

WILEY

Hacking the Hacker: Learn from the Experts Who Take Down Hackers

Published by
John Wiley & Sons, Inc.
10475 Crosspoint Boulevard
Indianapolis, IN 46256
www.wiley.com

Copyright © 2017 by John Wiley & Sons, Inc., Indianapolis, Indiana

Published simultaneously in Canada

ISBN: 978-1-119-39621-5
ISBN: 978-1-119-39623-9 (ebk)
ISBN: 978-1-119-39622-2 (ebk)

Manufactured in the United States of America

V007408_060518

For general information on our other products and services please contact our Customer Care Department within the United States at (877) 762-2974, outside the United States at (317) 572-3993 or fax (317) 572-4002.

Wiley publishes in a variety of print and electronic formats and by print-on-demand. Some material included with standard print versions of this book may not be included in e-books or in print-on-demand. If this book refers to media such as a CD or DVD that is not included in the version you purchased, you may download this material at http://booksupport.wiley.com. For more information about Wiley products, visit www.wiley.com.

Library of Congress Control Number: 2017934291

I dedicate this book to my wife, Tricia. She is truly the woman behind the man in every sense of the saying.

(ISC)² books published by Wiley provide aspiring and experienced cybersecurity professionals with unique insights and advice for delivering on (ISC)²'s vision of inspiring a safe and secure world.

(ISC)² is an international nonprofit membership association focused on inspiring a safe and secure cyber world. Best known for the acclaimed Certified Information Systems Security Professional (CISSP) certification, (ISC)² offers a portfolio of credentials that are part of a holistic, programmatic approach to security. (ISC)²'s membership is made up of certified cyber, information, software and infrastructure security professionals who are making a difference and helping to advance the industry.

About the Author

Roger A. Grimes has been fighting malicious computer hackers for three decades (since 1987). He's earned dozens of computer security certifications (including CISSP, CISA, MCSE, CEH, and Security+), and he even passed the very tough Certified Public Accountants (CPA) exam, although it has nothing to do with computer security. He has created and updated computer security classes, been an instructor, and taught thousands of students how to hack or defend. Roger is a frequent presenter at national computer security conferences. He's been paid as a professional penetration tester to break into companies and their web sites, and it has never taken him more than three hours to do so. He's previously written or co-written eight books on computer security and nearly a thousand magazine articles. He's been the *InfoWorld* magazine computer security columnist (http://www.infoworld.com/blog/security-adviser/) since August 2005, and he's been working as a full-time computer security consultant for more than two decades. Roger currently advises companies, large and small, around the world on how to stop malicious hackers and malware. And in that time and those experiences, he's learned that most malevolent hackers aren't as smart as most people believe, and they are definitely not as smart as most of the defenders.

Credits

Project Editor
Kelly Talbot

Production Editor
Barath Kumar Rajasekaran

Copy Editor
Kelly Talbot

Production Manager
Kathleen Wisor

**Manager of Content
Development & Assembly**
Mary Beth Wakefield

Marketing Manager
Carrie Sherrill

**Professional Technology
& Strategy Director**
Barry Pruett

Business Manager
Amy Knies

Executive Editor
Jim Minatel

Project Coordinator, Cover
Brent Savage

Proofreader
Nancy Bell

Indexer
Johnna VanHoose Dinse

Cover Designer
Wiley

Cover Image
©CTRd/Getty Images

Acknowledgments

I would like to thank Jim Minatel for greenlighting this book, which has been living in my head for 10 years, and Kelly Talbot for being the best book editor I've had in over 15 years of book writing. Kelly is great at fixing the problems while not changing the voice. I want to thank Microsoft, my employer for over 10 years, for being the best company I've worked for and pushing us to recognize the strength that diversity brings to the table. I want to thank Bruce Schneier for his unofficial mentoring of me and everyone else in the industry. Kudos to Brian Krebs for his great investigative reporting and pulling back the curtain on the big business that cybercrime has become. Thanks to Ross Greenberg, Bill Cheswick, and other early authors who wrote so interestingly about computer security that I decided to make a career of it as well. Lastly, I wouldn't be who I am today without my twin brother, Richard Grimes, the better writer of the family, encouraging me to write over 20 years ago. To everyone in our industry, thanks for your help on the behalf of all of us.

Contents at a glance

Contents

Foreword

Roger Grimes has worked in the computer security industry for nearly three decades, and I've had the pleasure of knowing him for roughly half that time. He's one of a select few professionals I've met who clearly has security in his bones—an intuitive grasp of the subject that, coupled with his deep experience catching bad guys and rooting out weaknesses in security defenses, makes him uniquely qualified to write this book.

Roger first began writing for *InfoWorld* in 2005 when he sent an email criticizing the work of a security writer, a critique that carried so much weight we immediately asked him to contribute to the publication. Since then he has written hundreds of articles for *InfoWorld*, all of which exhibit a love of the subject as well as a psychological understanding of both malicious hackers and the people who defend against them. In his weekly "Security Adviser" column for *InfoWorld*, Roger shows a unique talent for focusing on issues that matter rather than chasing ephemeral threats or overhyped new technologies. His passion for convincing security defenders and their C-suite bosses to do the right thing has been steadfast, despite the unfortunate inclination of so many organizations to neglect the basics and flock to the latest shiny new solution.

In this book, Roger identifies the ethical hackers in this industry who have made a difference. Their tireless efforts help hold the line against a growing hoard of attackers whose objectives have shifted over the years from destructive mischief to the ongoing theft of precious intellectual property and millions of dollars from financial institutions and their customers. We owe these people an enormous debt. In providing a forum for the likes of Brian Krebs, Dr. Dorothy Denning, and Bruce Schneier, Roger pays tribute to their efforts while delivering a fascinating compendium that entertains as well as informs. It's essential reading for anyone interested in computer security and the people who strive against all odds to keep us safe.

Eric Knorr
Editor-in-chief, *InfoWorld*

Introduction

The intent of this book is to celebrate the world of computer security defenders by profiling some of the world's best whitehat hackers, defenders, privacy protectors, teachers, and writers. It's my hope that you'll walk away with a greater appreciation of the behind-the-scene efforts it took to give us the fantastic world of computers we live in today. Without all the good people on our side fighting against those who would do us harm, computers, the Internet, and everything connected to them would not be possible. This book is a celebration of the defenders.

I want to encourage anyone contemplating a career in computers to consider a career in computer security. I also want to encourage any budding hackers, especially those who might be struggling with the ethics of their knowledge, to pursue a career in computer security. I've made a good life fighting malicious hackers and their malware creations. I've been able to explore every single hacking interest I've had in an ethical and law-abiding way. So, too, do tens of thousands of others. Computer security is one of the hottest and best paying careers in any country. It has been very good to me, and it can be for you, too.

For most of this book, I provide a chapter that summarizes how a particular style of hacking is accomplished, and then I follow it with one or more profiles of computer security defenders lauded in that field. I've tried to pick a variety of representative industry legends, luminaries, and even some relatively unknowns who are brilliant for what they have accomplished even if they are obscure outside their industry. I tried to choose a good cross-section of academics, corporate vendors, teachers, leaders, writers, and private practitioners located in the United States and around the world. I hope readers interested in computer security careers can find the same motivation I did to help to make computing significantly safer for all of us.

Go fight the good fight!

1

What Type of Hacker Are You?

Many years ago, I moved into a house that had a wonderful attached garage. It was perfect for parking and protecting my boat and small RV. It was solidly constructed, without a single knot in any of the lumber. The electrical work was professional and the windows were high-quality and rated for 150 mph winds. Much of the inside was lined with aromatic red cedar wood, the kind that a carpenter would use to line a clothing chest or closet to make it smell good. Even though I can't hammer a nail straight, it was easy for me to see that the constructor knew what he was doing, cared about quality, and sweated the details.

A few weeks after I moved in, a city official came by and told me that the garage had been illegally constructed many years ago without a permit and I was going to have to tear it down or face stiff fines for each day of non-compliance. I called up the city to get a variance since it had been in existence for many years and was sold to me as part of my housing purchase. No dice. It had to be torn down immediately. A single day of fines was more than I could quickly make selling any of the scrap components if I took it down neatly. Financially speaking, the sooner I tore it down and had it hauled away, the better.

I got out a maul sledge hammer (essentially a thick iron ax built for demolition work) and in a matter of a few hours had destroyed the whole structure into a heap of wood and other construction debris. It wasn't lost on me in the moment that what had taken a quality craftsman probably weeks, if not months, to build, I had destroyed using my unskilled hands in far less time.

Contrary to popular belief, malicious hacking is more maul slinger than craftsman.

If you are lucky enough to consider a career as a computer hacker, you'll have to decide if you're going to aspire to safeguarding the common good or settle for pettier goals. Do you want to be a mischievous, criminal hacker or a righteous, powerful defender? This book is proof that the best and most intelligent hackers work for the good side. They get to exercise their minds, grow intellectually, and not have to worry about being arrested. They get to work on the forefront of computer security, gain the admiration of their peers, further human advancement in the name of all that is good, and get well paid for it. This book is about the sometimes unsung heroes who make our incredible digital lives possible.

> **NOTE**   Although the terms "hacker" or "hacking" can refer to someone or an activity with either good or bad intentions, the popular use is almost always with a negative connotation. I realize that hackers can be good or bad, but I may use the terms without further qualification in this book to imply either a negative or a positive connotation just to save space. Use the whole meaning of my sentences to judge the intent of the terms.

Most Hackers Aren't Geniuses

Unfortunately, nearly everyone who writes about criminal computer hackers without actual experience romanticizes them all as these uber-smart, god-like, mythical figures. They can guess any password in under a minute (especially if under threat of a gun, if you believe Hollywood), break into any system, and crack any encryption secret. They work mostly at night and drink copious amounts of energy drinks while littering their workspaces with remnants of potato chips and cupcakes. A school kid uses the teacher's stolen password to change some grades, and the media is fawning on him like he's the next Bill Gates or Mark Zuckerberg.

Hackers don't have to be brilliant. I'm living proof of that. Even though I've broken into every single place where I've ever been hired to do so, I've never completely understood quantum physics or Einstein's Theory of Relativity. I failed high school English twice, I never got higher than a C in math, and my grade point average of my first semester of college was 0.62. That was composed of five Fs and one A. The lone A was in a water safety class because I had already been an oceanfront lifeguard for five years. My bad grades were not only because I wasn't trying. I just wasn't that smart and I wasn't trying. I later learned that studying and working hard is often more valuable than being born innately intelligent. I ended up finishing my university degree and excelling in the computer security world.

Still, even when writers aren't calling bad-guy hackers super-smart, readers often assume they are because they appear to be practicing some advanced black magic that the rest of the world does not know. In the collective psyche of the world, it's as if "malicious hacker" and "super intelligence" have to go together. It's simply not true. A few are smart, most are average, and some aren't very bright at all, just like the rest of the world. Hackers simply know some facts and processes that other people don't, just like a carpenter, plumber, or electrician.

Defenders Are Hackers Plus

If we do an intellectual comparison alone, the defenders on average are smarter than the attackers. A defender has to know everything a malicious hacker does plus how to stop the attack. And that defense won't work unless it has almost no end-user involvement, works silently behind the scenes, and works perfectly (or almost perfectly) all the time. Show me a malicious hacker with a particular technique, and I'll show you more defenders that are smarter and better. It's just that the attacker usually gets more press. This book is an argument for equal time.

Hackers Are Special

Even though I don't classify all hackers as super-smart, good, or bad, they all share a few common traits. One trait they have in common is a broad intellectual curiosity and willingness to try things outside the given interface or boundary. They aren't afraid to make their own way. Computer hackers are usually life hackers, hacking all sorts of things beyond computers. They are the type of people that when confronted with airport security are silently contemplating how they could sneak a weapon past the detectors even if they have no intention of actually doing so. They are figuring out whether the expensive printed concert tickets could be easily forged, even if they have no intention of attending for free. When they buy a television, they are wondering if they can access its operating system to gain some advantage. Show me a hacker, and I'll show you someone that is questioning status quo and exploring at all times.

NOTE   At one point, my own hypothetical scheme for getting weapons past airport security involved using look-alike wheelchairs with weapons or explosives hidden inside the metal parts. The wheelchairs are often pushed past airport security without undergoing strong scrutiny.

Hackers Are Persistent

After curiosity, a hacker's most useful trait is persistence. Every hacker, good or bad, knows the agony of long hours trying and trying again to get something to work. Malicious hackers look for defensive weaknesses. One mistake by the defender essentially renders the whole defense worthless. A defender must be perfect. Every computer and software program must be patched, every configuration appropriately secure, and every end-user perfectly trained. Or at least that is the goal. The defender knows that applied defenses may not always work or be applied as instructed, so they create "defense-in-depth" layers. Both malicious hackers and defenders are looking for weaknesses, just from opposite sides of the system. Both sides are participating in an ongoing war with many battles, wins, and losses. The most persistent side will win the war.

Hacker Hats

I've been a hacker my whole life. I've gotten paid to break into places (which I had the legal authority to do). I've cracked passwords, broken into networks, and written malware. Never once did I break the law or cross an ethical boundary. This is not to say that I haven't had people try to tempt me to do so. Over the years, I've had friends who asked me to break into their suspected cheating spouse's cellphone, bosses who asked me to retrieve their boss's email, or people who asked to break into an evil hacker's server (without a warrant) to try to stop them from committing further hacking. Early on you have to decide who you are and what your ethics are. I decided that I would be a good hacker (a "whitehat" hacker), and whitehat hackers don't do illegal or unethical things.

Hackers who readily participate in illegal and unethical activities are called "blackhats." Hackers who make a living as a whitehat but secretly dabble in blackhat activities are known as "grayhats." My moral code is binary on this issue. Grayhats are blackhats. You either do illegal stuff or you don't. Rob a bank and I'll call you a bank robber no matter what you do with the money.

This is not to say that blackhats can't become whitehats. That happens all the time. The question for some of them is whether they will become a whitehat before having to spend a substantial amount of time in prison. Kevin Mitnick (https://en.wikipedia.org/wiki/Kevin_Mitnick), one of the most celebrated arrested hackers in history (and profiled in Chapter 5), has now lived a long life as a defender helping the common good. Robert T. Morris, the first guy to write and release a computer worm that took down the Internet (https://en.wikipedia.org/wiki/Morris_worm), eventually became an Association for Computing Machinery Fellow (http://awards.acm.org/award_winners/morris_4169967.cfm) "for contributions to computer networking, distributed systems, and operating systems."

Early on the boundary between legal and illegal hacking wasn't as clearly drawn as it is today. In fact, most early illegal hackers were given superhero cult status. Even I can't help but be personally drawn to some of them. John Draper (a.k.a. "Captain Crunch") used a toy whistle from a box of Cap'n Crunch cereal to generate a tone (2600 Hz) that could be used to steal free long-distance phone service. Many hackers who released private information for "the public good" have often been celebrated. But with a few exceptions, I've never taken the overly idealized view of malicious hackers. I've had a pretty clear vision that people doing unauthorized things to other people's computers and data are committing criminal acts.

Years ago, when I was first getting interested in computers, I read a book called *Hackers: Heroes of the Computer Revolution* by Steven Levy. In the dawning age of personal computers, Levy wrote an entertaining tale of hackers, good and mischievous, embodying the hacker ethos. Most of the book is dedicated to people who improved the world through the use of computers, but it also covered the type of hackers that would be arrested for their activities today. Some of these hackers believed the ends justified the means and followed a loose set of morals embodied by something Levy called "hacker ethics." Chief among these beliefs were the philosophies that any computer could be accessed for any legitimate reason, that all information should be free, and to distrust authority. It was a romanticized view of hacking and hackers, although it didn't hide the questionable ethical and legal issues. In fact, it centered around the newly pushed boundaries.

Steven Levy was the first author I ever sent a copy of his own book to and asked him to autograph my copy and send it back (something others have done to me a few times now that I'm the author of eight previous books). Levy has gone on to write or become the technical editor for several major magazines, including *Newsweek*, *Wired*, and *Rolling Stone*, and he has written six other books on computer security issues. Levy continues to be a relevant technology writer to this day. His book, *Hackers*, introduced me to the wonderful world of hacking in general.

Later on, other books, like Ross Greenberg's *Flu-Shot* (long out of print) and John McAfee's *Computer Viruses, Worms, Data Diddlers, Killer Programs, and Other Threats to Your System* (https://www.amazon.com/Computer-viruses-diddlers-programs-threats/dp/031202889X) introduced me to fighting malicious hackers. I read these books and got excited enough to make a lifelong career out of combating the same threats.

Along the way, I've learned that the defenders are the smartest hackers. I don't want to paint all malicious hackers with the same brush of mediocrity. Each year, a few rogue hackers discover something new. There are a few very smart hackers. But the vast majority of malevolent hackers are fairly average and are just repeating something that has worked for twenty years. To be blunt, the average malicious hacker doesn't have enough programming talent to write a simple notepad application, much less discover on their own how to break into some place, crack encryption, or directly successfully guess at passwords—not without a lot of help from other hackers who previously did the real brain work years before.

The irony is that the uber-smart people I know about in the computer world aren't the malicious hackers, but the defenders. They have to know everything the hacker does, guess at what they might do in the future, and build a user-friendly, low-effort defense against it all. The defender world is full of PhDs, master's degree students, and successful entrepreneurs. Hackers rarely impress me. Defenders do all the time.

It is common for defenders to discover a new way of hacking something, only to remain publicly silent. It's the job of defenders to defend, and giving malicious hackers new ways to hack something before the defenses are in place won't make anyone else's life easier. It's a way of life for defenders to figure out a new hack and to help with closing the hole before it gets discovered by the outside world. That happens many more times than the other way around (such as the outside hacker discovering a new hole).

I've even seen defenders figure out a new hack, but for cost efficiency or timing reasons, the hole didn't get immediately fixed, and later on, some outside hacker gets credit as the "discoverer." Unfortunately, defenders don't always get immediate glory and gratification when they are doing their day jobs.

After watching both malicious hackers and defenders for nearly three decades, it's clear to me that the defenders are the more impressive of the two. It's not even close. If you want to show everyone how good you are with computers, don't show them a new hack. Show them a new, better defense. It doesn't require intelligence to find a new way of hacking. It mostly just takes persistence. But it does take a special and smart person to build something that can withstand constant hacking over a long period of time.

If you want to impress the world, don't tear down the garage. Instead, build code that can withstand the hacker's mauling axe.

2 How Hackers Hack

The most enjoyable career activity I do is penetration testing (also known as pen testing). Pen testing is hacking in its truest sense. It's a human against a machine in a battle of wits. The human "attacker" can use their own ingenuity and new or existing tools as they probe for weaknesses, whether they be machine- or human-based. In all my years of pen testing, even though I am usually given weeks to conduct a test, I have successfully hacked my target the majority of the time in around one hour. The longest it has ever taken me is three hours. That includes every bank, government site, hospital, and corporate site that has ever hired me to do so.

I'm not even all that good as a pen tester. On a scale 1 to 10, with 10 being the best, I'm about a 6 or a 7. On the defender side, I feel like I'm the best person in the world. But as an attacker, I'm very average. I've been surrounded by awesome pen testers—men and women who think nothing of writing their own testing tools or who don't consider their testing a success unless they did not generate a single event in a log file that could have caused an alert. But even the people I consider to be 10s usually think of themselves as average and admire other pen testers that they think are tens. How good must those hackers be?

But you don't have to be extremely good to be a very successful hacker. You don't even have to actually break in for the customer that hired you (I'm assuming you're being paid for a lawful assignment to pen test) to be happy with your work. In fact, the customer would absolutely be thrilled if you were not successful. They could brag that they hired some hackers and their network withstood the attack. It's a win-win for everyone involved. You get paid the same and they get to brag that they are impenetrable. It's the only job I know where you cannot have a bad outcome. Unfortunately, I know of no pen tester who has *ever* not successfully broken into *all* of their targets. I'm sure there must be hackers who fail, but the vast majority of pen testers "capture their prize."

NOTE If your pen testing doesn't find any weaknesses and soon afterward your client is compromised by real attackers, you aren't going to look good. If this happens several times, word will get around and you'll probably be looking for a new career. The weaknesses are there. Find them.

Usually pen testers will do something extra to impress their target's senior managers, such as taking a clandestine picture of the CEO at his desk using his own computer's camera or embedding the domain administrator's password in the picture of a pirate flag that shows up on the security administrator's screensaver. A picture is worth a thousand words. Never underestimate how much one goofy picture can increase your customer's satisfaction with your job. They'll be talking about the picture (and bragging about you) years after you've finished the job. If you can, always finish with a flourish. I'm giving you "consultant gold" with this recommendation.

The Secret to Hacking

If there is a secret to how hackers hack, it's that there is no secret to how they hack. It's a process of learning the right methods and using the right tools for the job, just like an electrician, plumber, or builder does. There isn't even one way to do it. There is, however, a definitive set of steps that describe the larger, encompassing process, and that includes all the steps that a hacker could possibly have to perform. Not all hackers use all the steps. Some hackers only use one step. But in general, if you follow all the steps, you're likely to be very successful at hacking. You can skip one or more of the steps and still be a successful hacker. Malware and other hacking tools often allow hackers to skip steps, but at least one of the steps, initial penetration foothold, is always required.

Regardless of whether you're going to make a career out of being a (legal) hacker, if you're going to fight malicious hackers, you have to understand the "hacking methodology" or whatever it is being called by the person or document describing it. The models can vary, including the number of steps involved, the names of the steps, and the specific details of each step, but they all contain the same basic components.

The Hacking Methodology

The hacking methodology contains the following progressive steps:
1. Information Gathering
2. Penetration
3. Optional: Guaranteeing Future Easier Access
4. Internal Reconnaissance
5. Optional: Movement
6. Intended Action Execution
7. Optional: Covering Tracks

Information Gathering

Unless a hacker tool is helping the hacker to randomly access any possible vulnerable site, the hacker usually has a destination target in mind. If a hacker wants to penetrate a specific company, the first thing the hacker does is start researching everything they can about the company that might possibly help them break in. At the very least, this means accessible IP addresses, email addresses, and domain names. The hacker finds out how many potential sites and services they can access that are connected to the company. They use the news media and public financial reports to find out who the senior executives are or to find other employee names for social engineering. The hacker looks up news stories to see what big software the target has bought recently, what mergers or divestitures are happening (these are always messy affairs often accompanied by relaxed or missed security), and even what partners they interact with. Many companies have been compromised through a much weaker partner.

Finding out what digital assets a company is connected to is the most important part of information gathering in most hacker attacks. Not only are the main (public) sites and services usually identified, but it's usually more helpful to the attacker to find the less popular connected sites and services, like employee and partner portals. The less popular sites and servers are more likely to have a weakness compared to the main sites that everyone has already beat on for years.

Then any good hacker starts to gather all the software and services hosted on each of those sites, a process generally known as *fingerprinting*. It's very important to learn what operating systems (OS) are used and what versions. OS versions can tell a hacker what patch levels and which bugs may or may not be present. For example, they might find Windows Server 2012 R2 and Linux Centos 7.3-1611. Then they look for software programs and versions of those software versions (for the same reason) running on each OS. If it's a web server, they might find Internet Information Server 8.5 on the Windows server and Apache 2.4.25 on the Linux server. They do an inventory of each device, OS, application, and version running on each of their intended targets. It's always best to do a complete inventory to get an inclusive picture of the target's landscape, but other times a hacker may find a big vulnerability early on and just jump into the next step. Outside of such a quick exploit, usually the more information the hacker has about what is running, the better. Each additional software and version provides additional possible attack vectors.

NOTE Some hackers call the general, non-technical, information gathering *footprinting* and the OS and software mapping *fingerprinting*.

Sometimes when a hacker connects to the service or site it helpfully responds with very detailed version information so you don't need any tools. When that isn't the case, there are plenty of tools to help with OS and application fingerprinting. By far the number one used hacker fingerprinting tool is Nmap (https://nmap.org/). Nmap has been around since 1997. It comes in several versions including Windows and Linux and is a hacker's Swiss Army knife tool. It can perform all sorts of host scanning and testing, and it is a very good OS fingerprinter and an okay application fingerprinter. There are better application fingerprinters, especially when they are focused on a particular type of application fingerprinting, such as web servers, databases, or email servers. For example, Nikto2 (https://cirt.net/Nikto2) not only fingerprints web servers better than Nmap, but also performs thousands of penetration tests and lets you know which vulnerabilities are present.

Penetration

This is the step that puts the "hack" in "hacker"—gaining initial foothold access. The success of this step makes or breaks the entire cycle. If the hacker has done their homework in the fingerprinting stage, then this stage really isn't all that hard. In fact, I've never not accomplished this stage. There is always old software being used, always something left unpatched, and almost always something misconfigured in the collection of identified software.

NOTE   One of my favorite tricks is attacking the very software and devices that the defenders use to defend their networks. Often these devices are *appliances*, which is simply another word for running a computer with harder-to-update software. Appliances are notorious for being years out of patch compliance.

If by chance all the software and devices are perfectly secured (and they never are), then you can attack the human element, which is always the weakest part of the equation. But without the initial penetrating foothold, all is lost for the hacker. Fortunately for the hacker, there are lots of ways to penetrate a target. Here are the different techniques a hacker can use to break into a target:

- Zero-days
- Unpatched software
- Malware
- Social engineering
- Password issues
- Eavesdropping/MitM
- Data leaks
- Misconfiguration
- Denial of service
- Insider/partner/consultant/vendor/third party
- User error
- Physical access
- Privilege escalation

Zero-days   Zero-day (or 0-day) exploits are rarer than every-day vulnerabilities, which vendors have usually long ago patched. A zero-day exploit is one for which the targeted software is not yet patched against and the public (and usually the vendor) isn't aware of. Any computer system using software with a zero-day bug is essentially exploitable at-will, unless the potential victim uninstalls the software or has put in place some sort of other mitigation (for example a firewall, an ACL list, VLAN segmentation, anti-buffer overflow software, and so on).

Zero-days are not as common as known exploits because they can't be widely used by an attacker. If an attacker overused a zero-day, the coveted exploit hole would be discovered and patched by vendors and placed in anti-malware signatures. These days most vendors can patch new exploits within a few hours to a few days after discovery. When zero-days are used, they are either used very broadly against many targets all at once for maximum exploitation possibility or used "low and slow," which means sparingly, rarely, and only used when needed. The world's best professional hackers usually have collections of zero-days that they use only when all else has failed and even then in such a way that they won't be especially noticed. A zero-day might be used to gain an initial foothold in an especially resistant target, and then all traces of it will be removed and more traditional methods used from that point onward.

Unpatched Software   Unpatched software is always among the top reasons why a computer or device is exploited. Each year there are thousands (usually between 5000 and 6000, or 15 per day) of new publicly announced vulnerabilities among all popularly used software. (Check out the stats reported in each issue of Microsoft's *Security Intelligence Report*, http://microsoft.com /sir.) Vendors have generally gotten better at writing more secure code and finding their own bugs, but there are an ever-increasing number of programs and billions of lines of code, so the overall number of bugs has stayed relatively stable over the last two decades.

Most vendors do a fairly good job of patching their software in a timely manner, especially after a vulnerability becomes publicly known. Unfortunately, customers are notoriously slow in applying those patches, even often going so far as disabling the vendor's own auto-patching routines. Some moderate percentage of users never patch their system. The user either ignores the multiple patch warnings and sees them as purely annoying or is completely unaware that a patch needs to be applied. (For example, many point-of-sale systems don't notify cashiers that a patch needs to be applied.) Most software exploits happen to software that has not been patched in many, many years.

Even if a particular company or user patches critical vulnerabilities as quickly as they are announced, a persistent, patient hacker can just wait for a patch to be announced that is on their target's fingerprint inventory list and launch the related attack before the defender has time to patch it. (It's relatively easy for a hacker to reverse engineer patches and find out how to exploit a particular vulnerability.)

Both zero-days and regular software vulnerabilities come down to insecure software coding practices. Software vulnerabilities will be covered in Chapter 6.

Malware   Malicious programs are known as malware, and the traditional types are known as viruses, Trojan horse programs, and worms, but today's malware is often a hybrid mixture of multiple types. Malware allows a hacker to use an exploit method to more easily attack victims or to reach a greater number of victims more quickly. When a new exploit method is discovered, defenders know that malware writers will use automated malware to spread the exploit faster in a process known as "weaponization." While any exploit is something to be avoided, it is often the weaponization of the exploit that creates the most risk to end-users and society. Without malware, an attacker is forced to implement an attack one victim at a time. With malware, millions of victims can be exploited in minutes. Malware will be covered in more detail in Chapter 9.

Social Engineering   One of the most successful hacking strategies is social engineering. Social engineering, whether accomplished manually by a human adversary or done using automation, is any hacker trick that relies upon tricking an end-user into doing something detrimental to their own computer or security. It can be an email that tricks an end-user into clicking on a malicious web link or running a rogue file attachment. It can be something or someone tricking a user into revealing their private logon information (called *phishing*). Social engineering has long been in the quiver of attacks used by hackers. Long-time whitehat hacker, Kevin Mitnick, used to be one of best examples of malicious social engineers. Mitnick is profiled in Chapter 5, and social engineering is covered in more detail in Chapter 4.

Password Issues   Passwords or their internally stored derivations can be guessed or stolen. For a long time, simple password guessing (or social engineering) was one of the most popular methods of gaining initial access to a computer system or network, and it still is. But credential theft and re-use (such as pass-the-hash attacks) has essentially taken over the field of password hacking in a big way over the past half decade. With credential theft attacks, an attacker usually gains administrative access to a computer or device and retrieves one or more logon credentials stored on the system (either in memory or on the hard drive). The stolen credentials are then used to access other systems that accept the same logon credentials. Almost every major corporate attack has involved credential theft attacks as a common exploit component, so much so that traditional password guessing isn't as popular anymore. Password hacks are covered in Chapter 21.

Eavesdropping/MitM   Eavesdropping and "man-in-the-middle" (MitM) attacks compromise a legitimate network connection to gain access to or maliciously participate in the communications. Most eavesdropping occurs due to flaws in network or application protocols, but it can also be accomplished due to human error. These days the biggest eavesdropping attacks occur on wireless networks. Network attacks will be covered in Chapter 33, and wireless attacks will be covered in Chapter 23.

Data Leaks   Leaks of private information can be an outcome from one of the other forms of hacking or can result from an unintentional (or intentional) human action. Most data leaks occur because of inadvertent (and underprotected) placement or because some hacker figured out a way to access otherwise private data. But insider attacks where an employee or contractor intentionally steals or uses private information are also a common form of hacking. Several of the chapters in this book apply to preventing data leakages.

Misconfiguration   It is also common for computer users and administrators to (sometimes inadvertently) implement very weak security choices. I can't tell you how many times I've gone to a public web site to find that its most critical files are somehow marked with Everyone or World permissions—and those permissions are exactly what they look like. And when you tell the entire world that they can access any file they like, your site or the files stored on it are not going to stay private for very long. Secure operating systems and configurations are covered in Chapter 30.

Denial of Service   Even if no one made a single error or had a single piece of unpatched software, it's still possible to take nearly any web site or computer off the Internet. Even if you are perfect, your computers rely on one or more services, not under your control, that are not perfect. Today, huge distributed denial of service (DDoS) attacks can take down or significantly impact nearly any web site or computer connected to the Internet. These attacks often contain billions of malicious packets per second, which overwhelms the targeted site (or its upstream or downstream neighbors). There are dozens of commercial (sometimes illegal) services that anyone can use to both cause and defend against huge DDoS attacks. DDoS attacks are covered in Chapter 28.

Insider/Partner/Consultant/Vendor/Third Party   Even if your network and all its computers are perfect (which they aren't), you can be compromised by a flaw in a connected partner's computer or by insider employees. This category is fairly broad and crosses a range of other hacker methods.

User Error   This penetration category also crosses a range of other hacker methods. For example, a user can accidentally send private data to an unauthorized user by putting a single mistyped character in an email address. The user can accidentally miss patching a critical server or can accidentally set the wrong permission. A frequent user error is when someone replies to an email thinking they are replying privately to one person or a smaller list of people but they accidentally are actually replying to the larger list or even to a person they are talking disparagingly about. I point out user error separately here only because sometimes mistakes happen and hackers are ready to take advantage of them.

Physical Access   Conventional wisdom says that if an attacker has physical access to an asset, they can just steal the whole thing (poof, your cell phone is gone) and destroy it or eventually bypass all protections to access private data. And this perception has proven pretty accurate so far, even against defenses that are explicitly meant to protect against physical attacks. For example, many disk encryption programs can be defeated by the attacker using an electron microscope to identify the protected secret key by identifying the individual electrons that compose the key. Or RAM can be frozen by canned air to reveal the secret encryption key in plaintext because of a fault in the way memory physically stores data.

Privilege Escalation   Each hacker uses one of the various penetration methods described in the previous sections to initially exploit a target system. The only question after gaining access is what type of security access they get. If they exploit a software program or service running in the user's own security context, they initially only have the same access privileges and permissions as the logged on user. Or they may get the Holy Grail on that system and get complete administrative system access. If the attacker only gets regular, non-privileged access permissions, then they generally execute a second, privilege escalation attack to try and obtain higher privileged access. Privilege escalation attacks run the gamut, essentially duplicating the same approaches as for penetration, but they begin with the higher starting point of already having at least some access. Privilege escalation attacks are generally easier to perform than the initial exploits. And since the initial exploits are almost always guaranteed to succeed, the privilege escalation is just that much easier.

Guaranteeing Future Easier Access

Although it's optional, once an attacker has obtained the initial foothold access, most hackers then work on implementing an additional method to ensure that they can more easily access the same asset or software faster the next time around. For many hackers, this means placing a "listening" backdoor program that they can directly connect to next time. Other times it means cracking passwords or creating new accounts. The attacker can always use the same exploits that worked successfully last time to gain the initial foothold, but usually they want some other method that will work even if the victim fixes the issue that worked the previous time.

Internal Reconnaissance

Once most hackers have penetrated the system, they start executing multiple commands or programs to learn more about the target they have gained access to and what things are connected to it. Usually that means looking in memory, on the hard drive, for network connectivity, and enumerating users, shares, services, and programs. All this information is used to better understand the target and also as a launching point for the next attack.

Movement

It is the rare attacker or malware program that is content to break into one target. Nearly all hackers and malware programs want to spread their range of influence over more and more targets. Once they gain access to the initial target, spreading that influence within the same network or entity is pretty easy. The hacker penetration methods listed in this chapter summarize the various ways they can do it, but comparing it to the initial foothold efforts, the subsequent movement is easier. If the attacker moves to other similar targets with similar uses, it is called lateral movement. If the attacker moves from devices of one privilege to a higher or lower privilege, it's called vertical movement.

Most attackers move from lower to high levels of privilege using vertical movement techniques (again, using the hacker penetration methods described in this chapter). For example, a very common hacker methodology is for the attacker to first compromise a single, regular end-user workstation. They use that initial foothold to search for and download local administrative account passwords. Then, if those local administrative credentials are shared among more machines (which they often are), they then move horizontally and repeat the process until they can capture very privileged account access. Sometimes this is done immediately during the first break-in because the logged on user or system already has very high privileges. They then move to the authentication server and capture every user's logon credentials. This is the standard modus operandi for most hacker groups these days, and moving from the initial compromise to complete network ownership (or pwning in hacker terminology) can be less than an hour.

In my personal experience, and remember I'm just an average hacker, it usually takes me about one hour to gain the initial foothold and another hour to capture the centralized authentication database. So for me, an average hacker, it takes about two hours to completely own a company. The longest it has taken me is three hours.

Intended Action Execution

After access is guaranteed and asset ownership is taken, hackers then accomplish what they intended to do (unless the action of breaking in revealed something new to do). Every hacker has intent. A legitimate penetration tester has a contractual obligation to do one or more things. A malicious hacker might spread malware, read or steal confidential information, make a malicious modification, or cause damage. The whole reason for the hacker to compromise one or more systems is to do something. In the old days (two or three decades ago), simply showing off that they had hacked a system would have been enough for most hackers. Today, hacking is 99% criminally motivated, and the hacker is going to do something malicious to the target (even if the only damage they do is to remain silently infiltrated for some potential, future action). Unauthorized access without any direct damage is still damage.

Covering Tracks

Some hackers will try to cover their tracks. This used to be what almost all hackers did years ago, but these days computer systems are so complex and in such great numbers that most asset owners don't check for hacker tracks. They don't check the logs, they don't check the firewall, and they don't look for any signs of illegal hacking unless it hits them in the face. Each year, Verizon's *Data Breach Investigations Report* (http://www.verizonenterprise.com/verizon-insights-lab/dbir/) reports that most attackers go unnoticed for months to years, and over 80% of the attacks would have been noticed had the defenders bothered to look. Because of these statistics, most hackers don't bother to cover their tracks anymore.

Hackers need to cover their tracks even less these days because they are using methods that will never be detected using traditional hacker-event detection. Or what the hacker uses is so common in the victim's environment that it is nearly impossible to distinguish between legitimate and illegitimate activity. For example, after breaking in, a hacker usually performs actions in the security context of a legitimate user, often accessing the same servers and services as the legitimate user does. And they use the same tools (such as remote access software and scripting languages) that the admins do. Who can tell what is and isn't malicious? The field of intrusion detection is covered in Chapter 14.

Hacking Is Boringly Successful

If you want to know how hackers hack, there you go. It's all summarized throughout this chapter. The only thing left to do is add tools, curiosity, and persistence. The hacking cycle works so well that many penetration testers, after getting over the initial excitement of being paid to be a professional hacker, get bored and move on to something else after a few years. Could there be a bigger testament to how well the cycle works? And it is within this framework and understanding that defenders need to fight against attackers.

Automated Malware as a Hacking Tool

When malware is involved, the malware can accomplish one or more of the steps, automating everything, or hand over manual control once the target is acquired and pwned. Most hacking groups use a combination of social engineering, automated malware, and human attackers to accomplish their objectives. In larger groups, the individual hackers may have assigned roles and specialties. Malware may execute a single penetration step and be successful without ever trying any of the other steps. For example, the fastest malware program in history, SQL Slammer, was just 376 bytes big. It executed its buffer-overflowing payload against SQL UDP port 1434 regardless of whether the target was running SQL. Since most computers aren't running SQL, you might think it would be very inefficient. Nope, in 10 minutes it changed the world. No malware program has ever come close to infecting as many hosts in as short of a time.

> **NOTE**   If I've missed a step in the hacker methodology or missed a penetration method, I apologize. Then again, I told you I was only an average hacker.

Hacking Ethically

I would like to think that my readers are ethical hackers who make sure they have the legal right to conduct hacking on any target they have fixed their sights on. Hacking a site you do not have the predefined and expressed authority to hack is unethical and often illegal. It is even unethical (if not also illegal) to hack a site and let them know of a found vulnerability for no money. It is unethical and often illegal to find a vulnerability and then ask the site to hire you as a pen tester. This latter scenario happens all the time. I'm sorry, there is no way to tell someone that you have found a way to hack their sites or servers and ask for a job or money without it being seen as extortion. I can tell you that almost all sites receiving such an unsolicited request do not think you're being helpful and do not want to hire you. They see you as the enemy, and lawyers are always immediately called.

The rest of this book is dedicated to describing specific types of hacking, particular penetration methods, how defenders fight those methods, and experts in their field at fighting hackers at their own game. If you want to hack for a living or fight hackers, you'll need to understand the hacker methodology. The people profiled in this book are the giants in their field, and you can learn a lot from them. They led the way. A great place to start is with Bruce Schneier, who is profiled in Chapter 3 and is considered by many to be the father of modern computer cryptography.

3 Profile: Bruce Schneier

Bruce Schneier is one of those people with so much experience and expertise that many introductions refer to him using the words "industry luminary." Starting out as what many people called the "father of modern day computer cryptography," Schneier transcended his early cipher-focus to ask the bigger questions about why computer security is not significantly better after all these decades. He speaks with authority and clarity on a wide range of computer security topics. He is frequently invited as an expert on national television shows and has testified several times in front of the United States Congress. Schneier writes and blogs, and I have always considered his teachings to be my informal master's degree in computer security. I would not be half the computer security practitioner I am today without his public education. He is my unofficial mentor.

Schneier is famous for saying disarmingly simple things that get to the heart, and sometimes gut, of a previously held belief or dogma. For example, "If you are focused on SSL attacks, then you're doing better in computer security than the rest of the world." He meant that there are so many other, more often successfully exploited things to be worried about, that if you were truly worried about a rarely used SSL exploit, you must have solved all the other more likely, more important, things first. In other words, we need to prioritize our computer security efforts instead of reacting to every newly announced (and sometimes never exploited) vulnerability.

Another example of something he has commented on is computer security workers getting upset when employees don't treat password security seriously. Instead, many employees use weak passwords (when allowed), use the same password across many unrelated web sites (that's just asking to be hacked), and often give their passwords away to friends, co-workers, and even strangers. We get frustrated because we know the possible consequences to the business but end-users don't understand the risk to the company from using poor password policies. What Schneier taught is that the end-user is evaluating passwords based on the personal risk to themselves. Employees rarely get fired for using bad password policies. Even if a hacker steals the end-user's banking funds, usually they are immediately replaced. Schneier taught us that it's us, the computer security professionals, who don't understand the real risk. And until the real risk actually causes the end-user harm, they won't voluntarily change their behavior. How's that for thinking you were the expert on a subject and it turns out the end-user understood the risk better?

He is the author of over 12 books, including such early books as 1996's *Applied Cryptography: Protocols, Algorithms and Source Code in C* (https://www.amazon.com/Applied-Cryptography-Protocols-Algorithms-Source/dp/1119096723). He wrote a few other books on cryptography (including a couple with Niels Ferguson), but Schneier also began to follow his long-time interest in the larger reasons why computer security was not being improved. The result was a series of books, each exploring the non-technical reasons (trust, economics, sociology, and so on) for the continued weakness. They are filled with easy-to-understand theory and elucidated by example stories. Here are my favorite general-interest Schneier books:

- *Secrets and Lies: Digital Security in a Networked World* (https://www.amazon.com/Secrets-Lies-Digital-Security-Networked/dp/0471453803)
- *Beyond Fear: Thinking Sensibly About Security in an Uncertain World* (https://www.amazon.com/Beyond-Fear-Thinking-Sensibly-Uncertain/dp/0387026207)
- *Liars and Outliers: Enabling the Trust that Society Needs to Thrive* (https://www.amazon.com/Liars-Outliers-Enabling-Society-Thrive/dp/1118143302/)
- *Data and Goliath: The Hidden Battles to Collect Your Data and Control Your World* (https://www.amazon.com/Data-Goliath-Battles-Collect-Control/dp/039335217X/)

If you really want to understand computer security, why it isn't better, and its impending problems, you should read these books. You should also read Schneier's blog (https://www.schneier.com/) and subscribe to his monthly Crypto-Gram newsletter (https://www.schneier.com/crypto-gram/). There is a markedly improved difference in the quality of people who regularly read Schneier compared to those who don't. His writing style is accessible and entertaining, and he doesn't suffer the purveyors of "fake" security lightly. His past "Doghouse" takedowns on crypto-frauds are lessons in themselves. He writes regularly on the most important issues of the day.

I've interviewed Schneier many times over the years, and sometimes the interviews can be intimidating for the interviewer. Not because he's difficult (he's not) or talks above you (he doesn't), but because he often seeks to let the interviewer follow their own pre-held beliefs and suppositions to an eventual end. If you don't understand something or agree with him, he doesn't immediately discount your argument. Instead, he'll ask you question after question in an interrogative style, letting your own answers to those questions lead the way to the eventual conclusion. Schneier is always teaching, even when he's being interviewed. You realize that he's thought about the big questions and has already debated these issues with himself way more than you are likely to have done. I've tried to borrow some of that self-interrogation technique when I come up with my own new strongly held beliefs.

I asked Schneier how he first got interested in computer security. He replied, "I was always interested in math and secret codes—cryptography. My first book, *Applied Cryptography*, ended up being the book I wish I could have read. But I've always been a meta, meta, meta guy. I realized that technology wasn't the biggest problem. Humans are the biggest problem, or the interface that interacts with the human. The hardest computer security problems are not about technology, it's about how we use the technology with all the sociology, politics, and economics involved in computer security. I spend a lot of time thinking about high-risk users. We have the technology to protect them, but can we create useful solutions that don't prevent them from doing their work? Otherwise we will never convince them to use it."

I asked him what he thought about the recent insider leaks from some of the U.S. intelligence agencies. He said, "In all that data there weren't a lot of surprises, at least to those of us paying attention. What it brought was confirmation and detail, and that detail was surprising. The secrecy is surprising. I don't think the things that are being done would have been prevented if we knew more about it, because in the post-9/11 world anything they asked for would have been approved. So, sadly, it didn't end up causing a lot of change, at least right away. One minor law [preventing the wholesale collection of metadata around all US phone calls by the NSA] was passed. But it did bring government surveillance into the public arena. It did change public perceptions. People now know about it and care. It may take another decade for all the impacts to be felt, but eventually policy will change for the good because of it."

I asked Schneier what he thought the biggest problem in computer security was, and he said, "Corporate surveillance! It's the corporations, more than the governments, that want to spy on is. It's Facebook and Google spying on people against their own interests, and the FBI can demand a copy whether the corporations want to give it or not. Surveillance capitalism is the real, fundamental problem."

I asked Schneier what book he was working on. (He's always working on a book.) He replied, "I'm thinking about a possible new book about cyber security physical problems, like the Internet of Things, and how it changes things when computers actually become dangerous. It's one thing when a spreadsheet has a vulnerability and crashes or gets compromised. It's something else when it's your car. Weak computer security will kill people. It changes everything! I testified in Congress last month about this topic. I said now is the time for getting serious. Play time is over. We need to regulate. Lives are at stake! We cannot accept the same level of crap software full of bugs. But the industry isn't prepared to take it seriously, and it has to. How can the people working on better securing cars actually do that when we've never been able to stop hackers and vulnerabilities in the past? Something has to change. It will change."

Bruce Schneier has been a thought leader in the computer security world for decades and continues to be on the forefront of the most important discussions. If you're interested in computer security, let him become your unofficial mentor, too.

For More Information on Bruce Schneier

For information about Bruce Schneier, check out these resources:

- Bruce Schneier's blog: https://www.schneier.com/
- Bruce Schneier's Crypto-Gram newsletter: https://www.schneier.com /crypto-gram/
- Bruce Schneier's books: https://www.amazon.com/Bruce-Schneier/e /B000AP7EVS/

Social Engineering

4

In the computer world, social engineering can be described as tricking someone into doing something, often detrimental, to themselves or others. Social engineering is one of the most common forms of hacking because it is so often successful. It's often the most frustrating for the defender because it cannot be prevented using technology alone.

Social Engineering Methods

Social engineering can be accomplished many ways, including over a computer, using a phone call, in-person, or using traditional postal mail. There are so many ways and varieties of social engineering that any list purporting to catalog all the ways is going to missing some of the methods. When social engineering originates on the computer, it's usually done using email or over the web (although it has also been done using instant messaging and just about every other computer program type).

Phishing

A common social engineering target is to capture a user's logon credentials, using what is called *phishing*. Phishing emails or web sites attempt to trick the user into supplying their legitimate logon credentials by posing as a legitimate web site or administrator that the end-user is familiar with. The most common phishing ploy is to send an email purporting to be from a web site administrator claiming that the user's password must be verified or else their access to the site will be cut off.

Spearphishing is a type of phishing attempt that is particularly targeted against a specific person or group using non-public information that the targets would be familiar with. An example of spearphishing is a project manager being sent a document in email supposedly from a project member purporting to be related to a project they are working on, and when they open the document it executes malicious commands. Spearphishing is often involved in many of the most high-profile corporate compromises.

Trojan Horse Execution

Another just as popular social engineering ploy is used to get the unsuspecting end-user to execute a Trojan Horse program. It can be done via email, either as a file attachment or in an embedded URL. It is done on web sites just as frequently. Often a legitimate web site is compromised, and when a visiting trusting user loads the web page, the user is instructed to execute a file. The file can be a "needed" third-party add-on, a fake antivirus detector, or a "needed" patch. The legitimate web site can be directly compromised, or another independently involved element, such as a third-party banner ad service, is. Either way, the user, who often trusts the legitimate web site after years of visiting without a problem, has no reason to suspect that the trusted web site has been compromised.

Over the Phone

Scammers can also call users purporting to be either technical support, a popular vendor, or from a government agency.

One of the most popular scams is when the user is called from someone claiming to be from tech support claiming that a malware program has been detected on the user's computer. They then request that the user download an "anti-malware" program, which proceeds, not unsurprisingly, to detect many, many malware programs. They then get the user to download and execute a remote access program, which the fake tech support person then uses to log on to the victim's computer to plant more malicious software. The bogus tech support program culminates when the victim buys a fake anti-malware program using their credit card number.

Over-the-phone scammers can also purport to be from tax collection services, law enforcement, or other government agencies, looking to get paid so that the end-user will avoid stiff penalties or jail.

Purchase Scams

Another very popular scam is carried out against people buying or selling goods on web sites, such as auction sites or Craigslist-like web sites. The innocent victim is either buying or selling something.

In buying scams, the buyer quickly replies, usually offers to pay the full purchase price plus shipping and asks the seller to use their "trusted" escrow agents. They then send the victim a fake check for more than the agreed upon purchase amount, which the victim deposits into their bank account. (Unfortunately, banks readily accept these fake checks but ultimately make the victim responsible for the lost money.) The buyer asks the victim seller to return the "extra" money to their shipper or escrow agent. The seller victim is usually out at least that amount in the end.

In selling scams, the victim buyer sends the funds but never receives the goods. The average selling scam is at least a thousand dollars. The average buying scam can be tens of thousands of dollars.

In-Person

Some of the most notorious social engineering scams are those that have been accomplished in-person by the hacker themselves. In the next chapter, notorious previous blackhat, Kevin Mitnick, is profiled. Decades ago, he was one of the most brazen physical social engineers we had. Mitnick thought nothing of dressing up as a telephone repair person or service technician to enter an otherwise secure location. Physical social engineers are well known for walking into banks and installing keylogging devices on employee terminals while posing as computer repair people. As distrusting as people are by nature of strangers, they are surprisingly disarmed if that stranger happens to be a repair person, especially if that service person says something like, "I hear your computer has been acting slow lately." Who can refute that statement? The repair person obviously knows about the ongoing problem and is finally here to fix it.

Carrot or Stick

The end-user is often either threatened with a penalty for not doing something or promised a reward for doing something. The ruse begins by putting the victim under duress, as people don't weigh risk as carefully during stress events. They have to either pay a fine or go to jail. They have to run the program or risk having their computer stay infected and their bank account emptied. They have to send money or someone they care about will remain in a foreign jail. They have to change the boss's password or else get in trouble with the boss.

One of my favorite social engineering ruses when I'm pen testing is to send an email out to a company's employees purporting to be from the CEO or CFO and announcing that the employee's company is merging with their next biggest rival. I tell them to click on the attached, boobytrapped document to see if their jobs are affected by the merger. Or I send a legal-looking email to the male employees purporting to be from their ex-wife's lawyer asking for more child support. You'd be amazed how successful these two trick emails are.

Social Engineering Defenses

Defending against social engineering attacks takes a combination of training and technology.

Education

Anti–social engineering training is one of the best, most essential defenses against social engineering. The training must include examples of the most common types of social engineering and how potential victims can spot the signs of illegitimacy. At my current company, each employee is required to watch an anti–social engineering video each year and take a short test. The most successful trainings have included other very smart, trusted, and well-liked employees who share their personal experience of having been successfully tricked by a particular type of common social engineering ploy.

I think every company should have fake phishing campaigns where their employees are sent phish-looking emails asking for the credentials. Employees providing their credentials should be given additional training. There are a variety of resources, both free and commercial, for doing fake phishing campaigns, with the commercial ones obviously offering easier use and sophistication.

All computer users need to be taught about social engineering tactics. People buying and selling goods on the Internet need to be educated about purchase scams. They should only use legitimate escrow services and follow all the web site's recommendations for an untainted transaction.

Be Careful of Installing Software from Third-Party Websites

Users should be taught never to install any software program directly from a web site they are visiting unless it is the website of the legitimate vendor who created the software. If a web site says you need to install some piece of third-party software to continue to view it, and you think it is a legitimate request, leave the web site and go to the software vendor's web site to install it. Never install another vendor's software from someone else's web site. It might actually be legitimate software, but the risk is too great.

EV Digital Certificates

Web surfers should be taught to look for the "extended validation" (EV) digital certificates (`https://en.wikipedia.org/wiki/Extended_Validation_Certificate`) on many of the most popular websites. EV web sites are often highlighted in some way (usually a green address bar or highlighted green name) to confirm to the user that the web site's URL and identity have been confirmed by a trusted third party. For an EV example, go to `https://www.bankofamerica.com`.

Get Rid of Passwords

Credential phishing can't work if the employee can't give away their logon credential. Simple logon names with passwords are going away in favor of two-factor authentication (2FA), digital certificates, logon devices, out-of-band authentication, and other logon methods that cannot be phished.

Anti–Social Engineering Technologies

Most anti-malware, web filtering software, and email anti-spam solutions try to minimize social engineering done using computers. Anti-malware software will try to detect execution of malicious files. Web filtering software will try to identify malicious web sites as the visitor's browser tries to load the page. And email anti-spam solutions often filter out social engineering emails. However, technology will never be completely successful, so end-user training and other methods must be used in conjunction.

Social engineering is a very successful hacking method. Some computer security experts will tell you that you cannot do enough training to successfully make all employees aware of social engineering tactics. They are wrong. A combination of enough training and the right technologies can significantly diminish the risk of social engineering.

In the next chapter, we profile social engineering expert Kevin Mitnick. His experiences as a social engineering hacker have helped him better defend his customers for decades.

5 Profile: Kevin Mitnick

When the term "computer hacker" is thrown around, most people think of Kevin Mitnick. Back in the 1970s, 1980s, and 1990s, Kevin Mitnick was *the* hacker. Mitnick used a combination of social engineering and lower-level operating system research to pull off all sorts of outrageous stunts, although the overall harm caused by him is debatable, especially when compared to today's world of APT attacks and ransomware.

He and his exploits have been written about in several books, have been made into a movie, and have generated a peculiar subculture of eccentric hacking stories attributed to him that he never did. The government's own fear of Mitnick was so bad that he is the only U.S. prisoner not allowed to use a phone while incarcerated and kept in solitary confinement for fear that one word or sound from him could launch a nuclear missile. If you've ever seen a movie where the protagonist said one word into a phone and then a whole lot of bad cyber stuff happened, that scene germinated from the paranoia surrounding Mitnick.

I'm including Mitnick early in this book because since those early days of cyber mischief, he has dedicated his life to fighting computer crime, and he is one of the few reformed long-time blackhats that I completely trust. Today, Mitnick has written several books on computer security (https://www.amazon .com/s/ref=dp_byline_sr_book_1?ie=UTF8&text=Kevin+Mitnick&search-alias=books&field-author=Kevin+Mitnick&sort=relevancerank), **works** with several companies (including KnowBe4), has his own security consulting firm (Mitnick Security Consulting), has the busiest speaking schedule of any computer security figure I know, was on *The Colbert Report*, and has even had a cameo on the popular television show *Alias*. Mitnick's lessons to the industry have resulted in a stronger recognition of the role social engineering plays in hacking and how to defeat it. After all, if you're going to stop a criminal, it can't hurt to learn from an intelligent reformed one.

I asked Mitnick what led to his interest in hacking. He said, "I was interested in magic as a kid. I loved magic. A kid at school showed me some tricks with the phone, like how to get free long distance phone calls, how to find out someone's address with just their phone number, calling forwarding, etc. He would go into a phone booth, call someone [the phone company], act like he was someone else, and make something magical happen. It was my first experience of social engineering. It was like magic to me. I didn't know it was called phone phreaking and social engineering. I just knew that it was fun and exciting and pretty much it began to take over my life. It's all I did. I was bored with school, and because I was up all night phone phreaking, my grades began to suffer."

I asked what his parents thought about his hacking exploits. He replied, "Well, early on they didn't know anything. Or maybe they thought I was doing something questionable on a phone. But my mother must have thought, 'How much trouble can he get to on a phone besides annoying people?' But they really didn't have a clue what I was up to until my mom got an official letter from AT&T informing her that they were turning off our phone service. She was very upset. You have to remember this was in the days before cell phones. Your home phone was your only lifeline to other people. I told her to calm down and that I would fix it.

"I basically socially engineered a phone back into our house. First, I made up a new housing unit. We lived in Unit 13. I called up the phone company's Business Office department pretending to be someone else and made up Unit 13B. I waited a few days for that new unit to get into the system, then I called the Provisioning department and asked for a new phone to be installed in Unit 13B. I even went to the hardware store and got a B to add to our outside number. I called pretending to be a new customer named Jim Bond from England. I gave them a real previous phone number from England I found along with other identifying information, because I knew they wouldn't be able to verify any foreign information. Then I asked if I could pick a 'vanity number', and they said yes, and I picked a phone number ending in 007. At the end of the conversation I asked if using my nickname of Jim was okay or did I have to use my full legal name? They said I had to use my legal name and I told them it was James. So, I was registered with AT&T as James Bond with a phone number ending in 007, and my mother had her phone back. AT&T got mad about that one when my scheme was finally caught."

I realized at this point in our interview that he hadn't mentioned anything about computer hacking. He was only talking about phone misuse. I asked how he got into computer hacking. He replied, "There was a kid in high school who knew I was into phone phreaking, and he thought I would be interested in a new high-level computer science class the school was offering. I said I wasn't interested at first, but the kid said, 'You know, I hear the phone companies are getting into computers.' And that was enough for me. I had to learn about these computers.

"I had to go to the instructor of the class, Mr. Kris, and ask him if I could join it because I didn't have any of the necessary prerequisites (which at the time included advanced mathematics and physics) or grades, which had really begun to suffer from my lack of sleep due to phone phreaking. Mr. Kris wasn't sure about letting me in so I demonstrated my phone phreaking to him by telling him his unlisted phone number, and those of his kids. He said, 'That's magic!' and let me into the class.

"Our first assigned program was a Fortran program to calculate Fibonacci numbers, which I found too boring. I had actually gone to the local university, Northridge, and tried to get computing time on the computer there. They had the same computers and operating system. But I couldn't get more than five minutes of time on them. So I went to the computer lab leader and asked for more time. He said that I wasn't even a college student and shouldn't be there, but he also saw how interested I was in computers, and to encourage me he gave me his personal logon account and password to practice with. Can you believe it? Those were the type of days around computers then.

"I ended up learning about low-level operating system calls. This was stuff they were not teaching in my high school class. At the high school, we all shared a modem that used a dial-up handset and a modem coupler. The modem stayed up all the time, and people would log in and out to access the terminal and modem. I wrote a low-level program that stayed active in the background and recorded everyone's keystrokes as they typed, including their logon names and passwords.

"When the day came for Mr. Kris's students to show him how many Fibonacci numbers their class-assigned programs had calculated, I had nothing. Mr. Kris admonished me in front of the class about how he had let me into the class and taken a risk and I had nothing to show for it. Every eye in the class was on me. I said, 'Well, I've been too busy writing a program to capture your password and your password is johnco!' He said, 'How did you do it?' I explained it to him, and he congratulated me and told the whole class I was a computer whiz. He wasn't mad at all. This was perhaps a very bad first ethics lesson for me to learn."

I asked Mitnick what a parent should do if they see signs that their kid is doing malicious hacking. He offered, "Show them how to hack legally. Channel their interest into legal and ethical opportunities, like going to computer security conferences and participating in 'capture the flag' contests. The parent should challenge the kid by saying something like, 'So, do you think you're good enough to be in a capture the flag contest?' The parent can socially engineer the kid, and the kid will get the same fun and excitement but from a legal way. I just got through legally hacking a company today, and it gave me the same thrill as it did when I wasn't doing ethical and legal things. I wish they had all the legal ways to hack that they do now. I wish I could go back in time and do it differently. You know the only thing different between illegal and legal hacking? The report writing!"

I wondered how Mitnick, with experience on both sides of the fence, felt about the government's right to know something versus an individual's right to privacy. He said, "I think we all have a huge right to privacy. In fact, my latest book, *The Art of Invisibility* (https://www.amazon.com/Art-Invisibility-Worlds-Teaches-Brother/dp/0316380504/), is all about how someone can keep their privacy. I think it's very difficult to stay private against someone like the NSA or government with unlimited funds. I mean if they can't break your encryption, they can just use one of their many zero-days and break into your endpoint, or buy a zero-day. For $1.5M you can buy an Apple zero-day, for half a million you can buy an Android zero-day, and so on. If you've got the funds and resources, you're going to get the information you're after. Although in *The Art of Invisibility*, I think I have a way that will even work against them, but it's very tough to do and involves a lot of OPSEC stuff. But it can be done in a way that I think even the NSA or any government would have a tough time defeating. I understand a government's need to know in certain cases, like terrorism, but they want to see into everything and everyone. And if you are being watched, you change your behavior, and that means you have less freedom. I don't think you can have freedom without privacy."

I ended our interview by reminding Mitnick that we had briefly met once before at a security conference many years ago where he was going up to talk as the headliner after I did. As he passed me he realized he needed a USB thumb drive to get his presentation to the dedicated presenter laptop up on the stage. I had one in my pocket that I offered. He almost took it, but after reconsidering it a few seconds, he declined and said he didn't trust anyone else's USB key. A few people around us chuckled at his paranoia. After all, you couldn't get infected by a USB device—or so everyone generally believed at the time.

What no one realized was that I had discovered how to automatically launch any program off any portable media (using a trick that involved a hidden file called desktop.ini, which the Stuxnet malware program later used), and just by accident the USB key stick had a demonstration version of that exploit. I hadn't meant to intentionally infect Mitnick. It just happened to be on every USB key I had at the time, and I had innocently offered my USB key when he asked.

Mitnick's constant paranoia saved him from my zero-day. It also goes to show that it's hard to scam a professional social engineer still in their prime.

For More Information on Kevin Mitnick

For information about Kevin Mitnick, check out these resources:

- Kevin Mitnick's web site: https://mitnicksecurity.com/
- *Ghost in the Wires:* https://www.amazon.com/Ghost-Wires-Adventures-Worlds-Wanted/dp/0316037729/
- *The Art of Invisibility:* https://www.amazon.com/Art-Invisibility-Worlds-Teaches-Brother/dp/0316380504/
- *The Art of Deception:* https://www.amazon.com/Art-Deception-Controlling-Element-Security/dp/076454280X/
- *The Art of Intrusion:* https://www.amazon.com/Art-Intrusion-Exploits-Intruders-Deceivers/dp/0471782661/
- KnowBe4's Kevin Mitnick Security Awareness Training: https://www.knowbe4.com/products/kevin-mitnick-security-awareness-training/
- Kevin Mitnick's Slashdot Q&A: https://news.slashdot.org/story/11/09/12/1234252/Kevin-Mitnick-Answers

6 Software Vulnerabilities

Software vulnerabilities are susceptible weaknesses (i.e. "bugs") in software, often from exploitable flaws written by the developer or inherent in the programming language. Not every software bug is a security vulnerability. The bug must be exploitable by an attacker to become a threat or risk. Most software bugs cause an operational issue (which may not even directly manifest themselves to the operator) or even cause a fatal interruption to processing but cannot be leveraged by an attacker to gain unauthorized system access.

Exploitable software vulnerabilities are responsible for a large (if not the largest) percentage of hacking in a given time period, even though other hacking methods (such as Trojan horse programs and social engineering) are often very competitive. Some computer security experts think most computer security issues would go away if all software was bug-free, although this isn't true or possible. Still, even if not a panacea, more secure code with fewer vulnerabilities would wipe a significant category of hacking issues out and make our computing environment appreciably safer.

Number of Software Vulnerabilities

There are many sources for tracking public software vulnerabilities, although the bugs listed for each may vary significantly. On average, each year, major software developers and bug finders publicly announce 5000–6000 new software vulnerabilities. That's about 15 bugs per day, day after day. The Common Vulnerabilities and Exposures (CVE) service, located at http://cve.mitre .org, and their lists (http://cve.mitre.org/data/downloads/index.html) are considered an inclusive, trusted, independent site for reporting and tracking public vulnerabilities. Many other vendors track either their own vulnerabilities or all known vulnerabilities as well. Check out any issue of Microsoft's

Security Intelligence Report (http://www.microsoft.com/sir) to get the latest known figures and great analysis.

Of course, these are just the bugs the public gets to know about. Many vendors don't publicly announce every bug. Many don't announce bugs found by internal resources or bugs fixed in pre-production–released software. Although there is no way to confirm this, most experts think the "real" number of bugs is significantly higher than the publicly known numbers.

> **NOTE**   The number of software vulnerabilities is just one measure, and it is not the complete picture of the overall security of a program or system. The only measure that truly matters is how much damage the software vulnerabilities were responsible for. The number of software vulnerabilities might conceivably go down as the amount of damage goes up, although in general, having more secure programs is better for everyone.

Why Are Software Vulnerabilities Still a Big Problem?

These days, vendors often patch most critical exploits in a matter of hours to days. That being the case, why are software vulnerabilities still a significant problem, especially when most vendors have auto-updating mechanisms for faster patching? The answer is that a significant portion of computer devices is slowly patched, or in a significant portion of cases, never patched. And each patch has the potential of causing an unexpected operational issue, sometimes causing more frustration to the end-user than the bug itself might have caused.

The number of overall exploits is fairly overwhelming and constant. A significant portion of computer administration is spent addressing and applying patches. It's an incredible waste of time, money, and other resources that could be better spent on more productive things. Even when users and administrators have patching down to an efficient science, during the time between when the vendor releases the patch and the user or admin applies it is the opportunity for a hacker to be successful against a given system. If I'm a patient, persistent hacker against a particular target, I can just wait until a vendor announces a new patch and use it to exploit my objective.

When vendors release patches, both whitehat and blackhat resources immediately analyze the patch to locate the targeted vulnerability. They then create exploits that can take advantage of the bug. There are dozens of commercial companies, a few free services, and an unnamed number of hackers that do this every day. You can purchase and/or download vulnerability scanners that will scan each targeted device and report back on unpatched vulnerabilities. These vulnerability scanners often have thousands and thousands of exploits built in. There are many hacker web sites around the world with thousands of individual exploits that you can download to exploit a particular vulnerability. One of the most popular free tools used by blackhats and whitehats alike is Metasploit (https://www.metasploit.com/).

Defenses Against Software Vulnerabilities

The number one defense against software vulnerabilities is better trained software developers and more-secure-by-default programming languages.

Security Development Lifecycle

The process of trying to reduce the number of software vulnerabilities is now commonly known as the Security Development Lifecycle (SDL). The SDL focuses on every component in the lifecycle of a software program, from its initial creation to its patching of newly found vulnerabilities, in order to make more secure software. Although not invented at Microsoft, Microsoft Corporation has probably done more work in the area and released more free information and tools (https://www.microsoft.com/sdl) than any other single source. The fallibility of humans ensures that software code will always have exploitable bugs, but by following the SDL, we can have fewer of them (per the same number of lines of code).

> **NOTE** Dr. Daniel J. Bernstein (https://en.wikipedia.org/wiki/ Daniel_J._Bernstein) is a college professor who promotes and delivers incredibly secure code. He has created several free and widely used programs, such as dbjdns and qmail, that have a very low number of bugs. He even offers to pay bug finders money out of his own pocket. He believes in publicly embarrassing vendors by publicly announcing bugs before giving vendors a chance to analyze and patch their products.

More Secure Programming Languages

More secure programs cannot begin without more secure programming languages. Over the years, most programming languages have strived to create more secure default versions. These languages try to reduce or eliminate common causes of exploits. To this end, they have been fairly successful, and programs written in them are significantly harder to exploit than those built using more insecure languages.

Code and Program Analysis

After a program version is written, it should always be analyzed for known and recognizable bugs. This can be done using human analysis or software tools. Human analysis tends to be the least efficient, finding the least number of bugs per hour spent, but it can find significantly exploitable bugs that the tools are not coded to find. Software bug-finding tools are often classified as "static analysis" or "fuzzers." Static analyzers look at source code (or programs) checking for known software bugs in the coding itself. Fuzzers enter in unexpected data inputs looking for vulnerabilities in the runtime program. Many infamous bug hunters, including Dr. Charlie Miller, profiled in Chapter 36, relied on fuzzing for many of their discoveries.

More Secure Operating Systems

Most operating systems are not only being coded by programmers steeped in the SDL and using more secure, by default, programming languages, but are also including built-in defenses against common exploit vectors. Most of today's popular operating systems include specially designed memory defenses and protect the operating system's most critical areas. Some even include built-in anti–buffer overflow, anti-malware, and firewall software, all of which help to limit exploitable bugs or their subsequent damage.

Third-Party Protections and Vendor Add-Ons

There are thousands of programs that will defend a computer system against previously unknown software vulnerabilities, with at least some success. Some are offered as free or paid add-ons by the vendor, and others are from independent third parties. Programs that promise to detect and stop new exploits are very common, and although never perfect, they can significantly reduce the risk of new threats. One of my favorite types of defensive software is called "application control" or "whitelisting" programs. These programs won't stop the initial exploit, but they can stop or make it harder for the hacker or malware program to do further damage.

Perfect Software Won't Cure All Ills

No defense beats software that is more securely coded with less exploitable bugs from the start. However, perfect, bug-free, software is impossible and would not cure all hacking even if it was possible. Unfortunately, software vulnerabilities aren't our only problem. Trojan horse programs work by simply getting the user to run a purely malicious program. Many hackers and malware programs exploit the inherent, otherwise legitimate, capabilities of data, scripting languages, and other components to do bad things. And social engineering can accomplish what software cannot.

Still, no one argues that more secure software programs can't help. Chapters 7 and 8 cover two experts who have dedicated their lives to better perfecting software. Chapter 7 profiles Michael Howard, who popularized more secure coding practices, and Chapter 8 focuses on Gary McGraw, one of the best bug finders in existence.

7 Profile: Michael Howard

Michael Howard is infectious. He's a great educator, an energetic speaker, and after nearly 20 years is as passionate about his computer security specialty, secure code, as he was in the beginning. It's hard to be around him more than a few minutes without you wanting to help make the world more secure one line of code at a time. He first gained worldwide notice for co-authoring *Writing Secure Code* (https://www.amazon.com/Writing-Secure-Code-Michael-Howard/dp/0735615888) along with David LeBlanc and for being a significant part of the reason why Microsoft is hugely dedicated to writing more secure code. Howard, originally from New Zealand but now living in Austin, TX, has co-written several books on writing more secure code and is a frequent blogger.

> **NOTE** David LeBlanc, Howard's co-author on *Writing Secure Code*, is another forward-looking security practitioner. He is responsible for making Microsoft Office significantly more secure, and he created a more secure browser security model that ended up being used by Google, Adobe, and Microsoft.

I asked Howard how he got into computer security. He replied, "I was working on very early versions of Windows NT for Microsoft. I was doing fairly low-level stuff like access control, cryptography, and custom GINAs (graphical interfaces which used to be the way you logged into and authenticated by Microsoft Windows and other authentication providers). This really led me to start thinking about security-as-a-feature more. Around 2000 it became clear that security features do not make a product secure; rather you have to also focus on secure features, which is a different discipline."

I asked him how the SDL got started at Microsoft. He said, "Over time, various security-related practices learned by the .NET Framework, Windows,

Office, and SQL Server teams, and others evolved into the Security Development Lifecycle (SDL). SDL helped popularize the secure code and secure design movement and is now the leading force in how many companies better secure their software."

I wondered whether SDL was a small improvement over something else he read, or if SDL was something he built from the ground up without any prior reference. He replied, "Everyone builds on the work of others, but most of SDL was from doing and learning. What works stays, and what does not work or is utterly non-pragmatic is tossed. Sometimes I wonder if some of the academic models had been tried in a production environment at all, one with deadlines, performance requirements, time-to-market, economic concerns, backward compatibility requirements, and so on.

"At the time, there was a huge school of thought which believed that if you could just increase the overall quality of the code you would directly increase the security of the code as well. But I have yet to see any empirical evidence of that. You can make functional SQL code that passes all functionality tests, but it could be riddled with SQL injection vulnerabilities. If you've never been trained in what SQL injection vulnerability is, all you'll see is perfect code—it does what it's supposed to do. A secure system only does what it's supposed to do and no more—it's the 'extra functionality' that comes with the SQL injection weakness that makes it insecure."

I asked him what his role was in Microsoft adopting SDL practices. He shared, "It was the synergy of a lot of different things that I and others were involved with. It started in late 2001, when the .NET team had a "security stand down" event to look at the current security issues and potential risks. We learned a lot from it and added many new defenses. I remember that we had some t-shirts printed up for the event with the dates on it, and then a major snowstorm hit and so the event was delayed … so it was ironic that in the quest for more secure code we had the wrong date on all our t-shirts. But what came out of that event was learnings that eventually fed into the SDL. David's and my book came out and got many people to think more about code security. 2001 saw Microsoft under attack by lots of malware and hackers. The Code Red and Nimda worms hit hard. So, Bill Gates asked about the nature of software vulnerabilities and why we still had them. I got picked to be part of the team that met with Bill Gates. I handed him an early copy of our *Writing Secure Code* book, and from the meeting Bill eventually wrote his famous "Trustworthy Computing" memo (https://www.microsoft.com/mscorp/execmail/2002/07-18twc.mspx). Bill mentioned our book in the memo, which saw sales sky-rocket! I ended up working for the newly created Trustworthy Computing division at Microsoft. This started a process of additional security stand downs (also for Windows, for SQL Server, and many other Microsoft products). SDL was generated and updated out of all of this, and improved and made more efficient. It continues to be updated annually."

I asked if it was true that he and Microsoft have released more information and tools regarding secure coding than any other single entity. He said, "Unequivocally and emphatically yes! But more important, these are the tools and techniques that we use in our production environment, on millions of lines of production code every day. This is not an academic exercise. It's what one of the largest companies in the world does. And we share nearly all of it."

I asked if the world's programmers are getting better trained on computer security issues, why isn't the world seeing fewer publicly announced vulnerabilities. He said, "Well, for sure there's more software with more lines of code. But the real problem is that programmers still aren't getting trained in secure coding and have no understanding of basic security threats. Academia is still way behind in most cases. I was reviewing a university's computer security class curriculum the other day, and nearly 50% of the class focused on low-level network threats. There wasn't any training on cloud security or secure coding. Our colleges are still turning out programmers who don't know much about computer security or secure coding, which is a travesty when you consider these grads will create critical systems hooked up to the Internet. I still find very basic bugs in other people's coding. When I demo a memory corruption issue or a SQL injection vulnerability—very basic stuff, very common—it's as if I've done something magically or special. It is so hard to find an incoming programmer that actually understands basic computer security that I'll get excited if the candidate at least cares about it. If the programmer's eyes open wide when I'm discussing computer security issues, I'm pretty happy. If they are at least interested, we can teach the rest. You'd be amazed how many don't care, and a big reason for that is it still isn't taught. Or the wrong things are being taught, like focusing on network security or minutiae. Schools will teach a student how the RSA algorithm works in detail, but not spend time teaching why it should be used, what problems does it solve, and what solutions it's good for. Knowing how to use something correctly to solve real-world security problems is much more important than knowing how it works. Anyone can memorize a protocol, but we need people knowing about risks and thinking about solutions. Some teachers and colleges are doing it right, like Matt Bishop at the University of California, Davis, but it's heroic efforts by Matt and others that makes it possible. He and the other professors like him are the real heroes."

I asked since most colleges aren't adequately preparing our coders in this area, what an individual coder can do. He said, "Always learn. I put an hour every day on my calendar that says 'Learn.' And I read/code/experiment for an hour with something I don't know about—every day. I've been doing that my whole career. Second, if you aren't getting formal computer security training, make your own. Go to the CVE (http://cve.mitre.org/cve/), read about some recent bugs, really read about them in detail. Then write code that has the vulnerability and figure out what it would take to have prevented that vulnerability, at both the technical level and the process level. How did the vulnerability happen and get put in the code in the first place? And then use those lessons to keep those same types of bugs out of your own code."

I asked what most companies could do to write more secure code besides following all the current SDL advice and tools that are readily available. He replied, "Make coders understand the real threats, not just the theoretical stuff. And build the security process into the development pipeline so bad and insecure code can't even get into the pipeline. We call them Quality Gates at Microsoft. A good (non-security) example is someone who writes code that assumes that all IP addresses have four octets. That means that code will never work on a pure IPv6 environment. That code can't even be submitted to our code check-in processes because a tool that is automatically run finds the issue and the check-in is rejected. That's what we mean by Quality Gate. But for security, repeat that for SQL injection, memory-safety threats, and everything else you don't want getting into the code.

"If I had to pick a few basic security-related practices, they would be:

- "Developers need to learn to never trust input data and to validate it for correctness, preferably through the use of a well-tested and reviewed library. If you expect data that is only 20 bytes long, then restrict to 20 bytes. If you expect a number, then check that it's a number and so on.
- "Designers/architects/program managers need to learn threat modeling and verify that the correct defenses are in place for the system.
- "Finally, testers need to prove the developers wrong by building or procuring tools that build malicious and/or malformed data. The goal is to defeat the developers' checks, if they have any!

"There is more to software security than what I said, but these are, in my opinion, the fundamental security-related skills all software engineers must have."

For More Information on Michael Howard

For information about Michael Howard, check out these resources:

- **Michael Howard's books:** https://www.amazon.com/Michael-Howard/e /B001H6GDPW/ref=dp_byline_cont_book_1
- **Michael Howard's blogs:** https://blogs.msdn.microsoft.com /michael_howard/
- **Michael Howard on Twitter:** https://twitter.com/michael_howard

Profile: Gary McGraw

When I called up Gary McGraw for an interview, he told me he just got through talking to a Catholic monk who was walking near his Shenandoah River property in Virginia. Within seconds he was talking about the intricacies of computer security. These sorts of otherwise unnatural paradoxes have been with McGraw his whole life. He started programming on his first computer, an Apple II+, in 1981, at age 16. He ended up going to college for an undergraduate degree in philosophy, and along the way became a classically trained musician. He even played twice at Carnegie Hall. Today, along with being one of the world's best computer security experts, he loves to cook, garden, and mix new cocktails.

I asked McGraw how he went from being a philosophy undergraduate at University of Virginia to being interested in the field of computer security. He told me that he had gotten interested in the philosophy of the mind, which led him to taking a course called "Computers, Minds, and the Brain" at UVA being taught by Paul Humphreys. He thought the ideas that Professor Humphreys was teaching were wrong, but it started him thinking more deeply about the philosophy of the mind and AI. He ended up bringing industry luminary and American Pulitzer Prize–winner Dr. Douglas Hofstadter's ideas into play during the class, and that changed his whole career path. He had not taken a computer science class until graduate school, but he had been in love with programming since 1981 as a kid. Under Hofstadter at Indiana University, he got a dual Ph.D. in cognitive science and computer science. He even ended up writing Chapter 10 of the first book ever sold on Amazon. It was Hofstadter's book, *Fluid Concepts and Creative Analogies: Computer Models of the Fundamental Mechanisms of Thought* (https://www.amazon.com /Fluid-Concepts-Creative-Analogies-Fundamental/dp/0465024750).

After college, he joined a company of seven people that eventually became Cigital (https://www.cigital.com/). Cigital won a big DARPA grant to do computer security research, and he was hired to work on that. Cigital eventually grew to 500 employees by the time it was sold to Synopsys in 2016. Now there are 1000 people in the software security division of the larger company dedicated to improving software in a meaningful way.

My first big memory of McGraw's name and work is when he and Ed Felten took on the security of the Java programming language, wrote a book, and found dozens of security vulnerabilities. This was a bit mind-blowing at the time because Sun Microsystems had intentionally made Java a supposedly very secure programming language because they knew it would be very web-based and subject to constant hacker attack. Java came out in 1995, and Sun claimed from the start that it was a very secure programming language. It had been built by some of the big wizards of programming languages, including Guy Steele and Bill Joy. Most computer security experts wondered whether it was really going to be as secure as Sun thought or would just turn out to be another overhyped security promise. It turns out it was the latter. After some early promise, Java produced some of the most bug-ridden pieces of software known in our world, McGraw was one of the very best at finding Java vulnerabilities, and McGraw and Felten were the genesis of analyzing Java for security bugs. McGraw had met eventual frequent co-author, Ed Felten, at a conference, and that meeting led to the first of many books (https://www.amazon.com/Gary-McGraw/e/B000APFZ2S/ref=sr_tc_2_0?qid=1484584085&sr=1-2-ent). Many of McGraw's books became Amazon best sellers (one, *Exploiting Software*, even became #16 overall), which is huge for any computer book, much less a computer security book.

McGraw continued to think about software security and where someone might go to learn how to build something more secure. He wondered how the rest of us "regular" programmers were going to build secure software when the very best wizards (like Bill Joy and Guy Steele) couldn't do it properly. He wondered about what went wrong in the process and why it went wrong. He realized that all software and programs had to be designed and written from the ground up with security in mind. Around the same time, he came up with his "Trinity of Trouble," which talked about why software security remained interesting and hard. Basically, if it's networked, complex, and extensible, it is almost always going to be interesting from a security perspective and hard to secure. Java, unfortunately, had all three of these traits in spades, although its complexity was likely the toughest aspect going against it.

After he co-wrote *Building Secure Software* in 1999, he ended up visiting many companies, including Microsoft, where Michael Howard, profiled in Chapter 7, worked with Jason Garms in the very new Secure Windows Initiative. He remembers all of Microsoft's product managers being at his talk and that Microsoft was clearly ready for software security.

After several more years of practicing software security in the field (through both services and technology development), McGraw ended up co-creating his Building Security in Maturity Model (BSIMM). BSIMM is now used by well over 100 very large firms to measure, track, and understand their progress in software security.

I asked how Michael Howard's SDL and his BSIMM models differed since they both are about how to make more secure software. He said, "SDL is a particular methodology. BSIMM is a measurement tool that can be used to measure, compare, and contrast many different SDL-like methodologies. Microsoft's SDL is just one methodology, but it's very good, and they wrote it down and shared it. What Michael Howard, who I like very much, did was to institutionalize an approach for a very large organization with tens of thousands of programmers. He showed that securing software could be done on a tremendously large scale, which was very important."

As I do with every person profiled in this book, I asked McGraw what he thought was the biggest computer security problem. His answer reflected Michael Howard's, who I had previously interviewed. He said, "Even though there are a ton of great resources on how to build and design more secure systems, not enough people that build and program systems know enough about security yet. Although some colleges and commercial training companies are doing a great job, even more are doing a poor job, and that's if they are doing anything at all."

He feels that the discipline of computer security is still very sloppy. His favorite book on security and building things properly is Ross Anderson's *Security Engineering* (https://www.amazon.com/Security-Engineering-Building-Dependable-Distributed/dp/0471389226/). He said he loves that book even more than all 12 of his own books and, "I think it's the best security book on the planet."

McGraw has his monthly Silver Bullet Security Podcast (https://www.garymcgraw.com/technology/silver-bullet-podcast/) where he interviews industry luminaries and experts. He just celebrated his 10th year with his 120th podcast. In reviewing his list of interviewees, I saw that many of them are the same people profiled in this book. He clearly loves the history of computer security like I do and wants to keep learning and sharing. With our interview over, I imagined that McGraw would go back to walking with his dog along the farm's riverside trail while contemplating new types of software security design flaws. He's a Renaissance man for the ages.

For More Information on Gary McGraw

For information about Gary McGraw, check out these resources:

- Gary McGraw's books: https://www.amazon.com/Gary-McGraw/e/ B000APFZ2S/
- Gary McGraw's web site: https://www.garymcgraw.com/
- Gary McGraw's Silver Bullet Security Podcast: https://www .garymcgraw.com/technology/silver-bullet-podcast/

9 Malware

When I first started in computer security back in 1987, it was malicious programs (malware) that first caught my eye. The first computer viruses (for example Apple's Elk Cloner and Pakistani Brain) were just showing up, although Trojans and worms had been around longer. Computer viruses were so unknown and almost rare that popular media pundits declared them to be hoaxes. That was until entire companies were taken down by them, and this was before the Internet was the Internet. Back then, computer malware spread via phone dial-up bulletin boards and hand-to-hand as people copied each other's software (both legally and illegally). Malware is still one of the most popular hacking methods.

NOTE The first piece of malware I ever got "hit" by was an ansi bomb. A victim had to have a driver called ansi.sys loaded on their computer (via the config.sys) file, but this was a popular setup in the early days of IBM-PC compatibles and the Disk Operating System (DOS).

Malware Types

The traditional types of malware are virus, worm, and Trojan horse. A computer virus is a self-replicating program that when executed goes around looking for other programs (or sometimes, as with macro viruses, data) to infect. A computer worm is a replicating program that doesn't usually modify other programs or data. It simply travels around on devices and networks using its own coded instructions, often exploiting one or more software vulnerabilities. A Trojan horse program masquerades as some other legitimate program that the device or user is tricked into executing. Today's malware is often a combination of two or more of these traditional types. For example, it may initially be spread as a Trojan to gain the initial foothold and then use its own code to replicate to spread further.

Malware can be quite efficient. Thousands of different malware programs have successfully infected entire networks across the globe in hours. Hundreds of malware programs have infected a significant portion of the computers attached to the Internet in a day. The speed record still belongs to the 2003 SQL Slammer worm (https://en.wikipedia.org/wiki/SQL_Slammer), which infected most Internet-accessible, vulnerable SQL servers in around 10 minutes. The related patch had been out for five months, but back then almost no one patched in a timely manner. Today, most malware programs are Trojans and require that an end-user initiate an action (such as opening a web link or file attachment) to initiate the malware, although the involved device or user may have had no hand in (accidentally) executing the program at all. It depends on the malware scenario and how it was spread.

Number of Malware Programs

There are literally hundreds of millions of different malware programs on the planet today and an immeasurable number of new ones being made each year. Most malware programs are slight, customized variants derived from just a few thousand different base malware programs. Still, each variant must be detected by anti-malware programs, which often use a combination of digital signatures (a unique set of bytes for each malware program or family of programs) and behavioral detection. An anti-malware program must be able to quickly scan tens of millions of files against hundreds of millions of malware programs and do it without significantly slowing down the device it is installed on. It's a tough thing to do, and even if done with the maximum degree of accuracy, it can be defeated by one new malware program with a single changed byte.

NOTE Anti-malware programs are more often called antivirus programs even though they detect and remove multiple malware classes because most malware programs were computer viruses when the scanning type of program became very popular.

Mostly Criminal in Origin

One of the biggest and most disturbing trends in malware is how it is mostly used for direct criminal purposes these days. Until around 2005, most malware was written by teenagers and young adults to prove that they could write computer malware. That it functioned and replicated was enough. Sure, there were a few malware programs that did intentionally cause direct harm, but most were more bothersome than dangerous.

Now, almost all malware is created for direct criminal purposes. Most malware users are out to steal money one way or other, be it through direct financial gain, stolen identities, or stolen passwords. These days, "ransomware," which is malware that encrypts your data and asks for money to decrypt it, is very popular. Other malware steals game resources or electronic currency or makes unauthorized stock trades. Adware infiltrates your computer to force you to see advertisements (or specific advertisements) that you would otherwise not see, or covertly forces your computer to visit other targeted web sites to increase the visitor hits to generate ill-gotten advertising revenue. Some malware is used to break in and steal confidential information. Other malware may be used to cause massive distributed denial of service attacks (covered in Chapter 28, "DDoS Attacks"). Gone are the days when most malware was made by mischievous kids that printed cute little sayings on your screen, played Yankee Doodle Dandy on your speaker, or asked you to help "legalise marijuana" (such as the Stoned boot virus). Today, malware has gone professional!

Malware is often created by one person and bought and sold by others. Often, thousands of computers that are compromised by a particular malware program are collected together in what are called "bot nets." These bot nets can be rented or purchased and then instructed to attack a particular site or perform an action across multiple locations. Many times, the malware that initially breaks into a particular computer is known as the "downloader." It gets initial access and modifies the system to ensure the success of future malware or hacker ownership. Then it downloads a new malware program with new instructions. This process may be repeated up to dozens of times until the eventual program and instructions are downloaded and executed. In this way, most malware is kept up-to-date and invisible to the eyes of anti-malware products. Malware programs are even sold with 24×7 tech support and warranties against detection, and their developers are given customer satisfaction ratings by buyers.

Malware is responsible for stealing or causing hundreds of millions of dollars of damage every year. Every old computer security person who has been fighting malware for longer than a decade wishes the only problem we had was dealing with mischievous kids.

Defenses Against Malware

There are many defenses against malware exploitation, most of which are good against several other forms of hacking as well.

Fully Patched Software

A fully patched system is far more difficult for malware to exploit than one that is not. These days "exploit kits" are hosted on compromised web sites, and when a user visits, the exploit kit will look for one or more unpatched vulnerabilities before attempting to trick the user into running a Trojan horse program. If the system is unpatched, often the malicious program can be secretly executed without the user being aware of anything.

Training

A fully patched system is difficult to for malware to compromise without involving the end-user. In cases where the malware or exploit kit doesn't find an unpatched vulnerability, it will usually resort to some sort of social engineering trick. Usually it involves telling the end-user they need to run or open something in order to satisfy some beneficial outcome. Training users about common social engineering techniques is a great way to reduce the success of malware.

Anti-Malware Software

Anti-malware (frequently referred to as antivirus) software is a necessity on almost every computer system. Even the best anti-malware software can miss a malware program, and no program is 100% perfect at blocking all malware, but running a computer system without such a program is like driving with leaky brakes. You may get away with it for a while, but eventually disaster will strike. At the same time, never believe any antivirus vendor's claim of 100% detection. That is always a lie.

Application Control Programs

Application control programs (also known as "whitelisting" or blacklisting" programs) are great at stopping malware when used in whitelisting mode. In whitelisting mode, only predefined and authorized programs are allowed to run. This stops most viruses, worms, and Trojans. Application control programs can be operationally difficult to implement because by their very nature, every program and executable must be pre-approved to run. And not every malware program type or hacker can be prevented, especially those that use built-in, legitimate programs and scripting tools. That said, application control programs are an effective tool and are getting better all the time. Personally, I think for any system to be considered "very secure," it must have an active and defined whitelisting program.

Security Boundaries

Firewalls and other types of local and network security boundaries (such as VLANs, routers, and so on) are good at keeping malware away from even being able to exploit a computer device. Most operating systems come with built-in, local firewalls, but most are not configured and enabled by default. Implementing a firewall can significantly reduce malicious risk, especially if there is an unpatched vulnerability present. Firewalls are discussed in more detail in Chapter 17, "Firewalls."

Intrusion Detection

Network intrusion detection/prevention (NID/P) and host intrusion detection/prevention (HID/P) software and devices can be used to recognize and stop malware on the network or local host. Intrusion detection is covered in Chapter 14. But like traditional anti-malware programs, NIDs and HIDs are not 100% reliable and should not be trusted alone to detect and stop malware.

Malware has long been a part of computer security threats and will always remain a top threat. Back in the late 1990s, with the increasing sophistication of antivirus scanners, I was confident that malware programs would be a thing of the past by 2010. That was back when we had just hundreds of malware programs. Now, with hundreds of millions of distinct malware variants, I realize how overly hopeful (and innocent) I had been.

Chapters 10 and 11 profile Susan Bradley and Mark Russinovich, who have been successfully fighting malware for decades.

10 Profile: Susan Bradley

I met Susan Bradley over 15 years ago, when I was selected as one of Microsoft's early Most Valuable Professionals. The Microsoft MVP, as it's known, is awarded to independent community leaders who show expertise in one or more Microsoft technologies and have broad interaction with end-users, such as writing a regular blog, newsletter, or column. It was clear early on that Bradley was an MVP of MVPs. She is super smart, hard-working, and forever helping not just end-users, but MVPs. (We're end-users, too.) She was originally awarded her MVP in 2000 for Microsoft's now discontinued Small Business Server (SBS) product, but she has broad and deeply technical Windows expertise. The annual MVP (https://mvp.microsoft.com/en-us/PublicProfile/7500?fullName =Susan%20Elise%20Bradley) she has continued to get continually every year since is known as the Cloud & Datacenter Management MVP.

If you don't know what Small Business Server was, just take the majority of Microsoft's most major and complex products (including Active Directory, Exchange, SQL, Outlook, and so on), put them into one software install for small businesses, and claim it's easy. I made a lot of consulting money helping customers who quickly figured out it wasn't so easy. Bradley gave me technical support when I was stuck on a problem that I could not solve alone. We eventually met at some national computer security conferences we were both speaking at, and we bonded a bit because of our shared accounting background. We are both CPAs, although she is a partner in a CPA firm, whereas I can only spell "CPA" now. She has written contributing chapters to a few books, has her SANS Global Information Assurance Certification (GIAC) certification, and is a co-author of the *Windows Secrets* newsletter (http://windowssecrets.com/).

I asked Bradley how she got into computer security, and she said, "I started in an industry that by definition is concerned about money, privacy, and confidentiality—accounting. That foundation of ensuring that transactions we rely upon can be relied upon translates to computer security. We have to ensure what we type into the keyboard (or these days input via voice, data points, sensors, etc.) retains its same information once it gets into whatever repository it was intended to be. I got into communicating to small businesses and others because of my own needs and initial confusion, initially around patching. I had a server product that was a kitchen sink of products, and all of those products had to be patched. There wasn't an easy way to do it. Back then, people didn't even patch their products. Then the SQL Slammer worm came out [in 2003] and impacted the world. And the patch against it was out for a long time, something like six months. But patching wasn't easy. So, I learned how to patch my kitchen sink of products and figured that other business owners would appreciate what I learned and how to do it. That started me down the road of what I have done ever since."

Bradley continues to focus on small businesses, and I know from her postings and conversations that helping people avoid or recover from ransomware is something she is also very involved with. I asked her what she recommended for customers trying to avoid or recover from ransomware. She replied, "Over a few years it became clear that ransomware was a big problem not only for consumers, but small businesses. It can be difficult and overwhelming to find the right information, so a friend and fellow MVP [since 2006], Amy Babinchak, and I got together three years ago and decided to make lemonade out of the lemons of ransomware. We created the Ransomware Prevention Kit (http://www.thirdtier.net/ransomware-prevention-kit/). It contains everything you need to know. It's a bundle of good information and tools, like group policy settings and scripts, and we are now adding videos to help people. It's not free. Pricing starts out at $25.00. Originally all proceeds went to a women's scholarship fund (http://www.thirdtier.net/women-in-it-scholarship-program/). Amy's aunt loaned her the money to get her first computer certification, and Amy feels that she would not have been as successful today without that much-needed loan. So, she's trying to pay it back. The scholarship fund will reimburse women for exam fees for successfully passed IT exams. Amy's original funding goal for the scholarship was $10,000, and she got that in nine months. Today, a collected portion of the kit funds goes to the scholarship, rather than 100%. It takes a tremendous amount of time to keep it refreshed and up to date, but Amy tries her best to make sure that as the kit gets updated every buyer gets an updated copy, and that's a lot of work."

I asked Bradley what she thought the biggest problem in computer security is. She replied, "We keep going down the same rabbit holes and not getting to root causes. Take for example how we are numb over data breaches these days. Because it doesn't harm the impacted business that much, it's acceptable risk to merely meet PCI [discussed in Chapter 37, 'Policy and Strategy'] standards and do what is good enough for the checklist, but we're not stepping back and thinking how better to design the flow of the data to protect it. Part of the problem is that the technology is constantly changing. But the underlying problems aren't. Yesterday ('eons' ago), we were on mainframes. Then we got into PCs, servers, and networks—a distributed PC model. Back then people and consultants just kept throwing up servers and not really concentrating enough on how to secure them. Today, we are moving to a cloud-centric model. Everyone is cloud first! And I see some of the same underlying mistakes being made. People are moving their servers to the cloud or choosing cloud services to run some of their business but not really understanding how to best secure it. We are making some of the same mistakes again, only it's getting harder because the customer doesn't always control the security and the forensic trail is moving farther away. Sometimes it feels like we really haven't solved anything. We need to focus more on the underlying problems because the technology is always changing."

If you want to master or manage Microsoft Windows, anything Susan Bradley writes should be a must-read for you.

For More Information on Susan Bradley

For information about Susan Bradley, check out these resources:

- Susan Bradley's Microsoft MVP blog: `http://blogs.msmvps.com/bradley/`
- Susan Bradley at Windows Secrets: `http://windowssecrets.com/author/susan-bradley/`

11 Profile: Mark Russinovich

No one knows everything about Microsoft Windows. It's tens of millions of lines of code. But for more than two decades, Mark Russinovich has come close. He's the Chief Technology Officer of Microsoft Azure. C-level officers (CEOs, CIOs, and so on) of companies are rarely people that still grok technology at the deepest levels, but Russinovich does. Rarely is there a smarter person in the room or someone who knows more about a feature. He's very happy to be looking at code. I told him this during our interview, and he replied, "The details of the technology is what keeps me going!"

I've known Russinovich for nearly two decades. For a long time he ran two software companies, Winternals, a for-profit commercial company, and Sysinternals, a not-for-profit freeware company. Both the companies and their software were very popular with techies. Eventually, Microsoft acquired both companies when he went to work for them. Visit http://www.sysinternals.com to see the cool utilities he created and Microsoft still offers and updates today. Russinovich has always been a techie's techie, and he is not afraid of controversy when finding the truth during his technical investigations.

I even distinctly remember being with him at a restaurant dinner table back in 2005 (neither of us were Microsoft employees at the time) when the news of his Sony BMG rootkit scandal discovery went viral. Russinovich had discovered that when a Sony music CD was placed inside of a computer running Windows it secretly installed two pieces of software to help Sony implement Digital Rights Management (DRM). The software could not be easily uninstalled, and parts of it would install even if the user didn't accept Sony's software installation end-user license agreement (EULA) terms. It interfered with Windows' built-in CD operations, and to make matters worse, Sony's software contained vulnerabilities, which malware eventually took advantage of.

Russinovich was testing out his rootkit-finding program, Rootkitrevealer, when he stumbled across the Sony program. A rootkit modifies the operations of the underlying operating system to better hide. He likened what Sony's DRM program was doing to what would otherwise be considered a malware "rootkit" by any standard definition, which was a very remarkable claim at the time. He was calling out a huge, legitimate company for doing something that many would consider unethical. His original blog post can be found here: https://blogs.technet.microsoft.com/markrussinovich/2005/10/31 /sony-rootkits-and-digital-rights-management-gone-too-far/.

The media was all over the story, and it garnered Sony much negative publicity. At first Sony tried to claim what it was doing was normal and acceptable, but after days of public outcry, Sony was forced to admit that it did wrong and they offered an uninstall program. They eventually recalled the related CDs and offered compensation. Unfortunately, they even badly bungled both the response and the uninstaller. Class-action lawsuits followed along with government investigations. You can read more about the entire scandal here: https://en.wikipedia.org/wiki/Sony_BMG_copy_protection_root- kit_scandal. Because of Russinovich's work and the resulting public outcry, every vendor since has been warned, and secretly installing software from otherwise legitimate software has been minimized.

And that's just one of the many things Russinovich has done. He frequently teaches or presents highly technical educational sessions at conferences. Those of us who compete against him to see who can get the highest presenter scores as ranked by audience members know that coming in second place is the best we can do when he is on the conference schedule. He has written or co-written many books (https://www.amazon.com/Mark-E.-Russinovich/e /B001IGNICC/) including a best-selling cybersecurity thriller. The fact that those cyber-Armageddon stories contain things that actually can and sometimes do happen makes them as scary as any Steven King novel. He earned a Ph.D. in computer engineering from Carnegie Mellon University in 1994 and he joined Microsoft in 1996.

Russinovich is now one of the most important people in Microsoft, leading the way on many of Microsoft's biggest technology pushes. He was instrumental in speeding up and securing Microsoft's most recent operating systems, and he is now the point man in charge of Microsoft's cloud. Besides being the Microsoft Azure CTO, he is a Microsoft Technical Fellow, which is only awarded to people who have had a significant impact on Microsoft and the world in general. The irony is not lost on Russinovich because two decades ago, in 1997, Microsoft almost got him fired from the company he was working for at the time.

Russinovich, employed by Open Systems Resources, was working on software for Windows NT 3.51. In the process of learning more about Windows internals, he discovered that a single registry edit controlled whether Windows NT would function as a server versus a workstation. He clarified, "It was actually two registry entries—one called ProductType and another encoded one that was used to detect tampering with the first one. The registry entry changed 12 other system parameters, which basically turned Windows into server- or workstation-focused. And I wrote an article (http://windowsitpro .com/systems-management/inside-windows-nt-registry) on it in *Windows IT Pro* magazine." An article recapping the finding is here: http://archive .oreilly.com/pub/a/oreilly/news/differences_nt.html.

I remember the article well. I was just beginning to write professionally myself at the same level, and I was asked to be a technical editor on the article by one of the magazine's editors. Even then, before its publication, everyone understood that Microsoft was likely to be unhappy because they were selling Windows NT workstation and Windows NT server as two completely different (but similar) products, with the latter version having a significantly higher price tag.

I remember hearing that Russinovich had been fired because of the article being published. I asked him if it was true that Microsoft got him fired because of the article. He replied, "Well, they certainly were not happy, but they didn't get me fired. They did apply some pressure to Open System Resources, and that pressure did lead me to leaving OSR. I went to IBM Research from there, but I always had friends and a mostly friendly relationship with many people at Microsoft. I was still invited to present about Microsoft Windows internals and I was writing my Windows Internals books. I was eventually invited several times to work at Microsoft. They acquired me along with Winternals and Sysinternals, which were 85-employee companies at the time." The rest is history.

Today, Russinovich helps develop Microsoft's Azure technology direction, making it more feature-rich, faster, and more secure. He has been working with containers and microservices a lot lately. Containers are a virtual machine paradigm popularized by Docker (https://www.docker.com/). Containers came out of nowhere and some were worried that they might threaten the virtual machine "big boys" (such as Amazon, Google, Microsoft, and VMware). Instead, led by Russinovich, Microsoft adopted containers and Azure now runs one of the largest container shops in the world.

I asked him whether containers helped or hurt computer security. He said, "It depends on what you call a container and the container scenario. It may make computer security slightly easier in some instances. Containers are effectively stateless, which makes it harder for an attacker to get a foothold if all their hard work can be easily wiped out. But at the same, if the vulnerability that allowed them to get in once is still there, they can just get back in, or maybe the first time allowed them to access the non-stateless backend, like the SQL Server, and so a reset container isn't going to stop them. One of the downsides of containers, especially as Docker imagines them, is layers among layers of containers to create a single application or service. And if you have to patch or update the code on one Docker image, there may be dependencies that require that all the related images get rebuilt. It becomes a squared explosion of things to patch, fix, or rebuild. That's one of the bad things—more complexity."

To end our interview, I asked Russinovich what he would recommend to anyone considering a computer security career. His answer basically mimicked his own career and success. He recommended, "You need to understand, at an expert level, all the systems you are going to defend, how they interact, and everything there, including identity, policy, monitoring, and network segmentation. Step one is to become deeply familiar with the software or platform itself. Second, make sure you look for and get different viewpoints. Each viewpoint has slightly different versions of the same thing, and by searching for and understanding the different viewpoints, you can better learn what you will be trying to protect."

For More on Mark Russinovich

For information about Mark Russinovich, check out these resources:

- Mark Russinovich's Wikipedia entry: https://en.wikipedia.org/wiki/Mark_Russinovich
- Mark Russinovich's books: https://www.amazon.com/Mark-E.-Russinovich/e/B001IGNICC/
- Mark Russinovich's web site: http://www.trojanhorsethebook.com/
- Mark Russinovich on Twitter: @markrussinovich
- Mark Russinovich's Microsoft blog: https://blogs.technet.microsoft.com/markrussinovich/
- Mark Russinovich's cool Sysinternals utilities: http://www.sysinternals.com

12 Cryptography

Much of the underlying technology that makes the rest of computer security work involves cryptography. Cryptography has been around for eons, and it will be around long after we leave planet Earth for other hospitable planets. Personally, cryptography is the computer security genre that I love the most, even though after nearly three decades of being a crypto-hobbyist I don't consider myself a cryptography expert.

What Is Cryptography?

In the digital world, cryptography is the use of a series of binary 1s and 0s to encrypt or verify other digital content. Cryptography involves using mathematical formulas (called *ciphers*) along with those 1s and 0s (called *cryptographic keys*) to prevent unauthorized people from seeing private content or to prove the identify or validity of another person or some unadulterated content.

The simplest encryption example I can think of is where some plaintext (non-encrypted) content is converted to an encrypted representation by moving the alphabet of each involved character by one place (for example A becomes B, B becomes C, C becomes D, and so on, until Z becomes A). Thus, the word FROG would become GSPH. The decryptor could reverse the process to reveal the original plaintext content. In this example, the cipher (it's almost silly to call it one) is the math, which in this case is + or − (addition or subtraction), and the key is 1. As simple as this example is, hundreds of years of secret messages (and cereal box decoder rings) have used it, although they were not always successful at keeping the message secret from unintended readers.

In today's digital world, cryptographic keys are usually at least 128 bits (128 1s or 0s) long, if not longer. Depending on the cipher, a key may be longer, although if the math is resistant to cipher attacks, usually the longest key sizes are 4096 bits. If you see longer key sizes, that is usually indicative of weak math or someone who does not know cryptography very well (or is trying to sell "snake oil" to people who do not know it very well).

Why Can't Attackers Just Guess All the Possible Keys?

People new to cryptography don't understand why attackers can't simply try all the possible key 1 and 0 combinations that can result from a particular key size. Couldn't someone with a very fast computer guess all the possible combinations? In short, no. Even a modern key size of 2000 bits is resistant against "brute force guessing". Not only isn't any single computer powerful enough, but if you took every computer in the world, not only today, but for the foreseeable future, there wouldn't be enough power. (This is at least true until quantum cryptography becomes real one day.) Hence, all (pure) cryptographic breaks rely on hints in the content or weaknesses in the math. Cryptographic math is tricky (to say the least) to get right, and what might initially look like undefeatable math is often found to be full of flaws that allow significantly fast breaking. That's why encryption standards and key sizes change all the time, as old ciphers get weakened and new, more resistant, ciphers emerge.

Symmetric Versus Asymmetric Keys

If the encryption key that is used to encrypt something is the same as what is used to decrypt it later on (such as in our simple example above, the 1), then the key is called "symmetric." If the key used to encrypt something is different than what is used to decrypt it, it's called "asymmetric." Asymmetric ciphers are also known as public key encryption, where one party has the private key that only they know, but everyone else can have the "public" key, and as long as no one else knows the private key, it all works securely. However, symmetric encryption is usually faster and stronger for a stated key size.

Popular Cryptography

These days many encryption ciphers are well known and tested to become industry, if not world-wide, standards.

Popular symmetric encryption keys include Data Encryption Standard (DES), 3DES (Triple DES), and Advanced Encryption Standard (AES). The first two examples are early examples and are no longer used. The latter, AES, is considered strong and is the most popular symmetric cipher used today. Symmetric key sizes usually range from 128 bits to 256 bits, but they gain length over time. Every single bit increase, say from 128 bits to 129 bits, usually doubles the strength of the key within the same cipher.

Popular asymmetric ciphers include Diffie-Hellman (the Hellman in Diffie-Hellman is profiled in the next chapter), Rivest-Shamir-Adleman (RSA), and Elliptical Curve Cryptography (ECC). ECC is the new kid on the block and just starting to be used. Asymmetric key sizes typically range from 1024 bits to 4096 bits, although 2048 bits is considered the bare minimum for Diffie-Hellman and RSA today. ECC uses smaller key sizes, starting at 256 bits. 384 bits is considered sufficiently strong today. In general, asymmetric ciphers are used to securely transmit symmetric keys, which do the majority of the encryption, between a source and destination.

Hashes

Cryptography is also used for verifying identities and content. Both instances use cipher algorithms known as cryptographic hashes. With this approach, the plaintext content to be verified is mathematically applied to a key (again just a series of 1s and 0s) to get a unique output (called the hash result or hash). An identity or content can be hashed at any point in time and be re-hashed again, and the two hashes can be compared to confirm that the hashed content has not changed since its original hashing.

Common hashes are Secure Hash Algorithm-1 (SHA-1), SHA-2, and SHA-3. SHA-1 was found to have some cryptographic weaknesses (also shared with SHA-2), and so SHA-1 is being retired. SHA-2 is becoming the most popular hash, but cipher experts are already recommending that SHA-3 be used.

Most cryptographic solutions use symmetric, asymmetric, and hashing algorithms to produce the desired protection. Many countries, like the US, have a standards body that analyzes and approves various ciphers for government use. The officially approved ciphers often become used around the world. In the US, the National Institute for Standards and Technology (http://www.nist.gov) in conjunction with the National Security Agency (http://www.nsa.gov) have public contests in which cryptographers around the world are invited to submit their own ciphers for analysis and selection. It's conducted in a fairly public way and often even the losers agree on the final selections. Unfortunately, the NSA and NIST have also been accused, at least twice, of intentionally weakening official standards (particularly with DES and Dual_EC_DRBG [Dual Elliptic Curve Deterministic Random Bit Generator], the latter of which has a backdoor). This has created tension, and many people no longer trust what NIST and NSA declare as good cryptography.

Cryptographic Uses

Cryptography underlies much of our online digital world. Cryptography protects our passwords and biometric identities, and it is used in digital certificates. Cryptography is used every time we log on to our computer and connect to an HTTPS-protected web site. It is used to verify downloaded software, to secure email, and verify computers to each other. Encryption is used to protect hard drives and portable media against unauthorized viewing, to prevent OS boot sector corruption, and to protect wireless networks. It is used to sign programming, scripts, and documents. It allows us to have private connections over the public Internet to our companies and computers, and it is behind almost all credit card and financial transactions in the world. Good cryptography is the enemy of spies, tyrants, and authoritarian regimes. It is not hyperbole to say that without cryptography, the Internet would not be the Internet and our computers would not ever be under our control.

Cryptographic Attacks

There are a host of cryptographic attacks. The following sections will explore a few of the more prominent ones.

Math Attacks

Many attacks are simply theoretical attacks that find mathematical weaknesses. Without a mathematical weakness, a given cipher can usually withstand a brute force attack equal to the number of bits in the key minus one. Thus, a 128-bit cipher (2^{128}) like SHA-1 should be capable of withstanding 2^{127} guesses on average before it falls. Attackers have now successfully weakened SHA-1, using math to find and prove math flaws, to something like 2^{57} bits.

Although 2^{127} is considered unbreakable (at least now), 2^{57} is considered either breakable today or going to be readily breakable in the near future without a hacker needing to use a tremendous amount of computing power.

Known Ciphertext/Plaintext

Many attacks are successful because they have a hint (also known as a crib). The crib is usually in the form of a known set of bits or bytes, in either the ciphertext, plaintext content, or private key. A crib has the effect of shortening the possible number of bits in the protective cipher key.

Side Channel Attacks

Side channel attacks often attack an unforeseen implementation artifact to be able to more easily determine the secret keys. A common example is when a computer's CPU changes its sound or magnetic frequency wave when processing a 0 versus a 1. Thus, someone with a very sensitive listening device might be able to determine what 0s and 1s a computer is processing when accessing a private key. Another related example is an attacker being able to determine which keyboard keys you are typing simply because they record the sound of you typing.

Insecure Implementations

The vast majority of successful attacks against cryptography in the real world do not attack the cipher's math or keys. Instead, attackers find implementation flaws that are the equivalent of placing a locked door's key under the door mat. Even strong math cannot save a weak implementation.

. There many other types of cryptographic attacks, although those listed above are the most common methods. The only defense against cryptographic attacks is good, proven math, secure implementations, and invisible or easy-to-understand end-user interfaces. Nothing else matters.

Chapter 3 profiled Bruce Schneier, who is considered the father of modern computer cryptography. Chapter 13 covers one of the most famous cryptographic co-founders in the world, Martin Hellman, and Chapter 15 focuses on Dr. Dorothy E. Denning, who wrote one of the first books on computer cryptography.

13 Profile: Martin Hellman

One of the things I've learned when talking to the best people in a particular field is that they tend to be good at multiple things. They aren't just good at the thing for which they are known. They usually have intense hobbies they are obsessed with and are trying to "hack" a lot of problems, many of which have nothing to do with why they are famous. Martin Hellman, one of the original creators of public key cryptography, is a great example. While still being one of the world's best cryptographers and thinking about how to solve the latest cryptography problems, he's also a guy who likes to soar gliders, improve marriages, and stop nuclear wars … not necessarily in that order.

Hellman is famous for being the co-inventor of public key cryptography in 1976, along with his colleagues Whitfield Diffie and Ralph Merkle. The November 1976 paper that publicly announced everything to the world was called "New Directions in Cryptography" (https://ee.stanford .edu/~hellman/publications/24.pdf). The resulting cipher algorithm became known as *Diffie-Hellman Key Exchange*, but Hellman prefers to call it *Diffie-Hellman-Merkle*, and did so during our interview. About a year after "New Directions in Cryptography," building upon Diffie and Hellman's previous work, Ron Rivest, Adi Shamir, and Leonard Adleman, all of MIT, created the *RSA* algorithm, and with their subsequent company's marketing efforts, public key cryptography took the world by storm, forever encasing all their names for posterity.

I've been telling the story of how Hellman and his colleagues invented public key cryptography for a long time, without ever really being sure if my version was accurate. It's an incredible tale of three people, none of whom had formal cryptography training, discouraged by nearly everyone they met along the way other than themselves. In my version of the story, before corrections, I told how Diffie had given an informal, brownbag talk at IBM about public cryptography and persuaded no one. On their way out the door, one of the last people told Diffie about another "crazy guy" named Hellman with similar ideas. Diffie dropped what he was doing, drove across the country, and met with Hellman, who was at first put off by a stranger who had driven across the country to meet him, but quickly realized they had similar ideas, and they formed a partnership that made history.

I asked Hellman how close my story was to being the truth as opposed to a myth. He replied, "When I first met Whit, I was entranced, not 'offput.' Here's what happened: I had worked at IBM years before Diffie showed up, but had left to go to MIT and then Stanford. I came back in 1974 and gave a talk about the problems with current cryptography. At the time at IBM, they weren't very interested. Although I didn't know it at the time, they had just invented what became the symmetric DES cipher and couldn't break it. IBM's management felt they had solved all the cryptographic problems and it was time they moved on. Whit, unknown to me, came to IBM a few months later in 1974 and gave a similar talk with a similar outcome, with one exception. Alan Konheim, who headed the Math Department, told him to contact me when he returned to the [San Francisco] Bay Area. Whit was already going around the country talking to cryptographers, including David Kahn, the author of the popular crypto book, *The Codebreakers* (https://www.amazon.com/Codebreakers-Comprehensive-History-Communication-Internet/dp/0684831309). When Whit got back to the Bay Area, he called me and we set up a meeting. Far from being offput by him, what was supposed to be a 30- to 60-minute meeting turned into hours, and I even invited him and his wife home with me to continue our conversation and meet my family. We talked until 11 PM that night. That was the fall of 1974. Prior to meeting Whit, all my other colleagues were discouraging me from working in cryptography. They told me that NSA had a huge budget and a several-decades head start. How could I hope to discover something they didn't already know? And, they continued, if I did anything good, they would classify it. Both arguments were valid, but given the awards we've won, it was very wise to do something that seemed foolish. While I might have persevered in spite of all that discouragement, meeting Whit gave me a real boost. Plus, we worked really well together for the next few years, including on public key cryptography."

I asked Hellman who invented what out of the partnership. We know that Merkle, working in isolation as a student at Berkeley, independently came up with half of the idea for public key encryption—exchanging a key over an insecure channel with no prearrangement. But what did Hellman do as opposed to Diffie? He replied, "I don't like to split up work effort or success. We were working on it together, talking, and sharing. But Diffie definitely first stated the idea of a public key cryptosystem. We had already come up with the idea of a 'trapdoor' cryptosystem, where a cipher has a built-in weakness (i.e. the trapdoor) that only people given some information about the trapdoor can utilize. Diffie went further and conceptualized about what it would take to make that happen, public key cryptography, and specifically about how to do it with what is now called a public key cryptosystem, which can do both public key exchange and digital signatures. He did that in 1975. Later on, we learned that Merkle had, independent of us, also thought of public key exchange, but we didn't know it at the time. I came up with the mathematical implementation of that idea in 1976—what is now often called Diffie-Hellman Key Exchange—and because it was closer to Merkle's idea than ours, I've argued it should be called Diffie-Hellman-Merkle Key Exchange. I'm right now sitting at the same desk where I came up with the algorithm back then, in the wee hours of the night in May 1976."

I asked how RSA came about. He said, "I had given a talk at MIT and Ron Rivest and I had been corresponding with each other. Shortly before what became known as the RSA system came out publicly, he sent me a draft. When I saw it, my first reaction was, 'We missed it!' They had figured out how to use large prime numbers to make factoring work as a public key cryptosystem. Diffie-Hellman-Merkle used large prime numbers, but not factoring. A paper I'd written with my student Steve Pohlig a few years earlier included RSA as a variant, but we hadn't yet thought of public key cryptography, so we missed that."

I asked Hellman how he felt with RSA taking off and making millions for its creators, with his team's own contribution hardly making any money for its inventors. He said, "People over the years ask me how I felt about it, with RSA coming so soon after our discovery, their paper credited Diffie and me with inventing public key cryptography, but their company (RSA Data Security) refused to pay royalties. My feelings have changed over time. Initially, I felt like RSA hadn't adequately highlighted the connection between their work and mine with Steve Pohlig. But over time I came to see it differently. RSA did such a brilliant job of marketing public key crypto that they created an entirely new industry. I got recognition and opportunities that might have never come my way if RSA had never happened. I see it quite differently now and I'm thankful. I'm good friends with Ron Rivest to this day. In fact, I tried to call him about something just before this interview."

I wondered how much Hellman is still into cryptography these days. I asked him if he thought quantum cryptography would ever happen. He said, "Are you referring to quantum cryptography or quantum computing, because those are two very different things. Quantum crypto is the ability to securely transmit keys or information using quantum properties. In contrast, quantum-based computers could break all the currently used public key systems. I'm not sure when it will happen or even 'if.' It seems like nuclear fusion, 20 years off for the last 50 years. But it may happen one day. And I have some possible solutions. We need to encrypt and sign things with two methods so that if one method is broken, the other still protects. For example, we've got public key cryptography and key distribution centers [as are used in PGP applications]. People should encrypt their keys with both, so that if quantum computing breaks public key crypto, the KDC portion still holds. Or sign a document using traditional public key signatures and also use Merkle tree signatures (https://en.wikipedia.org/wiki/Merkle_signature_scheme). If you're serious about cryptography and you're worried that what you are using may be broken in the future, then run a dual backup system. The NSA has a phrase for this: 'belts and suspenders.' If you use both, you'll never be caught with your pants down even if one fails." I guess that answered my question.

The last bit of our conversation focused on nuclear deterrence and improving your marriage. Hellman and his wife wrote a great book (https://www.amazon.com/New-Map-Relationships-Creating-Planet/dp/0997492309/) that figures into both areas. He had sent me a copy to review before our interview, and to be honest, I was sort of cringing at the idea of one of my cryptography heroes trying to get me off subject. Then I read it. It's great. I bought a copy for each of my married children. Hellman somehow intertwines a lot of his cryptography history and frustrations into a book about improving relationships and avoiding nuclear devastation. In 2015 Hellman and Diffie won the ACM's A.M. Turing Award (http://amturing.acm.org/award_winners/hellman_4055781.cfm), which is basically seen as computer science's version of the Nobel Prize. Hellman and his wife are using their $500,000 prize portion to reduce the risk of a disaster involving nuclear weapons—a threat that is gaining new interest since the 2016 election. Bravo!

For More Information on
Martin Hellman

For information about Martin Hellman, check out these resources:

- *A New Map for Relationships: Creating True Love at Home and Peace on the Planet*: https://www.amazon.com/New-Map-Relationships-Creating-Planet/dp/0997492309/
- Martin Hellman's Stanford bio: http://www-ee.stanford.edu/~hellman/
- Martin Hellman's work on cryptography: http://www-ee.stanford.edu/~hellman/crypto.html

14 Intrusion Detection/ APTs

Intrusion detection is the art of detecting unauthorized activity. In the computer world, it means detecting unauthorized connections, logons, and resource accesses, or attempts at the same. Intrusion detection is part of the reason why nearly every computer device has an event-logging system. The two have been forever linked since James P. Anderson's groundbreaking 1980 paper called "Computer Security Threat Monitoring and Surveillance" (http:// csrc.nist.gov/publications/history/ande80.pdf).

While computer systems have been good at generating lots of events, humans and their evaluating alert systems haven't been so good at making sense of them. To most computer users, event log files are full of thousands of events that muddy up any chance for true maliciousness to be detected.

The best report on the gap between badness entering a system and being detected is captured in Verizon's annual "Data Breach Investigations Report" (http://www.verizonenterprise.com/verizon-insights-lab/dbir/). The 2016 report (http://www.verizonenterprise.com/verizon-insights-lab /dbir/2016/) showed the following disturbing long-term trends:

- The average time from an initial compromise by a hacker to the exfiltration of private data or logon credentials is usually measured in minutes to a few days.
- Most attackers (70% to 80%) are in the system for long periods of time (months) before discovery.
- Discovery of a breach by internal resources only happens about 10% of the time.

This is despite the evidence that most breaches are in the event logs and would have likely been detected if only the logs were looked at or managed correctly. To be clear, I'm talking about computer system event logs and also the log files of computer security defense devices (e.g. firewalls, intrusion detection systems, and so on).

Traits of a Good Security Event Message

Unfortunately, most computer security defenses generate thousands, if not billions, of event log messages that do not indicate maliciousness. Or if they do indicate actual maliciousness, they document an event that has very, very low risk to an environment (like when a firewall logs a blocked packet). The end result is that most security event logs are very "noisy," meaning full of more useless information than useful. With that in mind, a good computer security event message should have these traits:

- Low noise
- Low false positives and low false negatives, meaning that an occurrence likely indicates true maliciousness
- Readily understood description of event
- As much surrounding detail as can be captured and useful to investigators
- Generation of the event always triggers an incident response investigation

These traits are the Holy Grail of intrusion detection.

Advanced Persistent Threats (APTs)

Advanced persistent threats (APTs) attacks are conducted by professional, criminal groups and have been responsible for compromising a large majority of businesses, military systems, and other entities over the last decade. In fact, most security experts believe that all Internet-connected entities have been successfully compromised by APTs, or at the very least, could easily, at will, be compromised by an APT. APTs are run by full-time, professional hackers who are different from traditional hackers in the following ways:

- They intend to remain permanently engaged after the initial compromise.
- They do not "run" when discovered.

- They have dozens to hundreds of compromises and exploits they can use, including zero-days.
- They always get total ownership of environment.
- Their objective is often stealing victim's intellectual property (IP) over the long-term.
- Their origination is often a "safe harbor" country that will never prosecute them for their activities. (Indeed, they are often state-sponsored and celebrated.)

The reason why APTs are covered in this chapter is that they are more difficult to detect using traditional intrusion detection—not impossible, just difficult without preparing and adjusting traditional intrusion detection methods. Some of the newer methods covered in this chapter are becoming quite accurate at detecting and preventing APTs.

Types of Intrusion Detection

There are two basic types of intrusion detection: behavior-based and signature-based. Many intrusion detection systems are a combination of both methods.

Behavior-Based

Also known as anomaly detection, behavior-based intrusion detection looks for behaviors that indicate maliciousness. For example, a file trying copy itself into another file (for example computer virus), a program trying to perfidiously redirect a browser away from its user-intended URL (for example adware, a MitM attack, and so on), an unexpected connection to a honeypot, or a person copying all the contents of an authentication database (for example credential theft). The basic idea behind behavior detection is that there too many bad things to individually identify, so look for their malicious behavior instead. It makes great sense. For example, there are tens of millions of computer viruses, most of which could be detected by looking for a single behavior of writing itself to a new host file. Dr. Dorothy E. Denning (profiled in Chapter 15) is a big proponent of intrusion detection systems (IDSs) and wrote her landmark paper on anomaly detection (https://users.ece.cmu.edu/~adrian/731-sp04/readings/denning-ids.pdf). in 1986.

Signature-Based

Signature-based intrusion detection systems take the opposite approach. They believe that malicious behaviors change too often or that legitimate programs can create too many false-positive indications to be reliable. Antivirus scanners are the perfect example of signature-based programs. They contain millions of unique bytes (signatures), which if detected will indicate maliciousness.

Intrusion Detection Tools and Services

In a general sense, any computer defense hardware or software that looks for and indicates maliciousness is an intrusion detection program. This includes firewalls, honeypots, anti-malware programs, and general event log management systems. Some experts only like to include solutions with "intrusion detection" in their name.

Intrusion Detection/Prevention Systems

Intrusion detection systems (IDSs) are purposefully built to detect maliciousness, usually using a combination of behavior- and signature-based methods. Intrusion prevention systems (IPSs) detect and prevent maliciousness. Many IDSs come with IPS preventive mitigations, so the term IDS can easily mean IPS as well. Few hold to the strict definition. Some defenders are hesitant to activate automatic preventative mitigations even if they are available because of the frequent false positives many IDSs/IPSs have. Other times, for lower risk IPS systems like anti-malware solutions, defenders want the automatic prevention enabled.

An IDS/IPS is further classified as being a host-based IDS/IPS (HIDS/HIPS) or a network-based IDS/IPS (NIDS/NIPS), depending on whether the defense protects an individual host system or analyzes packets running across the network for maliciousness.

The first widely popular HIDS I remember was Tripwire (https://en.wikipedia.org/wiki/Tripwire_(company)), back in 1992. It was co-founded by a Purdue University student, Gene Kim, and his professor, Dr. Eugene Spafford. It's not coincidental that Purdue University is also where Dr. Dorothy Denning went and taught.

The first super popular NIDS I remember was open-source Snort (https://www.snort.org/). I was lucky enough to get taught how to use it by its inventor,

Martin Roesch, at a SAN Institute class back in the early 1990s. It is now also a very popular commercial product, with both the open-source and commercial versions developed by Sourcefire.

Event Log Management Systems

Behind every successful intrusion detection or event log solution is a system that detects and collects events from one or more "sensors." In any enterprise with more than a few computer devices, it becomes essential to collect and analyze these events as a whole to get the best benefit. Event log management systems are responsible for collecting these events, analyzing them, and generating alerts. How well and accurately these systems do their job determines the effectiveness or ineffectiveness of the overall system. There are a lot of components and considerations to any event log management system. NIST's Special Publication 800-92, "Guide to Computer Security Log Management" (http://csrc.nist.gov/publications/nistpubs/800-92/SP800-92.pdf), is considered the definitive guide on effective event log management. Good event log management is hard and resource-intensive. Accordingly, there are many commercial vendors willing to do all the hard work for you. These are known as Security Information and Event Management (SEIM) companies or services.

Detecting Advanced Persistent Threats (APTs)

Professional APT hackers are very skilled at infiltrating a company with a minimum of maliciously detected activity. For many years it was considered difficult, if not impossible, to detect them. But the field of intrusion detection eventually rose up to the challenge, and now there are several products, services, and companies that are very good at detecting APTs and APT-like activities.

Operating system vendors are building in features and services that are significantly better at detecting these sorts of online criminals. Examples of this are Microsoft's Advanced Persistent Threat (https://www.microsoft.com /en-us/cloud-platform/advanced-threat-analytics) and Advanced Threat Protection (https://www.microsoft.com/en-us/WindowsForBusiness/ windows-atp) services.

Many companies now routinely follow dozens of different APT groups, readily detecting where they go and what they are doing. Many companies offer services that can quickly detect APTs in your environment and alert you to their presence. Probably the biggest difference between traditional intrusion detection and the newer forms is the ability of the data to be collated across many, many companies distributed across the Internet. Some of the names in this space are CrowdStrike (https://www.crowdstrike.com), AlienVault (https://www.alienvault.com), and long-time anti-malware player TrendMicro (http://www.trendmicro.com).

It's clear that it's starting to get harder for malicious hackers to hide. The next chapter, Chapter 15, profiles early intrusion detection pioneer, Dr. Dorothy E. Denning. Chapter 16 profiles Michael Dubinsky, a product manager of one of the more advanced intrusion detection services available today.

15 Profile: Dr. Dorothy E. Denning

Over the decades, I've come to believe that one of my few special talents in the world of computer security is detecting malicious hackers and their activities. I'm able to see a potential hacker threat and then figure out how that threat could be detected better and earlier to generate alerts. I still think I can do it better than anyone in the world, but for a while I felt like I had some original thinking on intrusion/anomaly detection. I even sort of got a big head about it. Then I found out about Dr. Dorothy E. Denning's seminal IEEE paper on real-time intrusion detection expert systems (https://users.ece.cmu.edu/~adrian/731-sp04/readings/denning-ids.pdf). It covered everything I thought I was doing original thinking on, except Dr. Denning wrote her paper in 1986, long before my own "discovery."

It was the first of many times when I would discover that my "original" thinking was not original at all. We all stand on the shoulders of giants, and Dr. Denning certainly belongs in the category of security giants. She was an early pioneer in computer security back when few people were working in the area. She told me, "There wasn't a computer security field to get into when I first started. There were no books, no journals you could read, and no conferences you could attend that were devoted to security. All we had to read were doctoral theses and a few papers published in more broadly focused conferences and journals like the *Communications of the ACM*. But I was lucky to be at Purdue University, one of the few universities starting to do work in computer security, along with MIT and a few others."

When she first started college, Dr. Denning enjoyed math and saw herself as being a high school mathematics teacher. While at the University of Michigan getting her B.A. in Mathematics, she ended up working for the Director of Radio Astronomy, who encouraged her to learn programming to solve some problems. In her senior year, she took one of the few computer science classes available anywhere. Later on, at the University of Rochester, she created a command language translator to make running programs on an IBM mainframe easier, and she developed and taught courses in programming languages and compilers. Her love of teaching led her to pursue a PhD at Purdue, where she took a course on operating systems from her eventual husband, Peter Denning. The course included principles of computer security at the OS level. This began her lifelong pursuit of improving information security. She even taught one of the first computer security courses that existed in the country.

NOTE Dr. Denning's translator took commands in Rochester's Easy Control Language and translated them into IBM's Job Control Language, which users found difficult to use.

Dr. Denning earned her PhD in 1975 creating the Lattice security model, which can be summarized as an information classification structure that forms a lattice so that information can only flow in one direction through the lattice, and only from lower to higher or equal classifications. The concept of one-way information flow still drives much of the "original" computer security thinking being developed today. Two of the recent projects I've been working with at Microsoft, secure admin workstations (https://msdn.microsoft.com/en-us/library/mt186538.aspx) and "red forest" Enhanced Security Admin Environment (https://technet.microsoft.com/windows-server-docs/security/securing-privileged-access/securing-privileged-access-reference-material), are underlain by a strict information flow that follows the same rules.

Dr. Denning's work expanded the Lattice mathematical model into information protection. She told me, "I spent a lot of time thinking about data classification and protection, and when I came up with a model and math to go with it, I thought it was original. I shared my theorems and proofs with my husband and he informed me it was called *Lattice Theory* and told me the name of the expert [Garrett Birkhoff] who wrote the book on it. Up until then I thought I had invented new math theory." Dr. Denning's story gave me a little solace about my own "discovery."

Dr. Denning published her paper "A Lattice Model of Secure Information Flow" (http://faculty.nps.edu/dedennin/publications/lattice76.pdf) in 1976. It moved Lattice Theory into the information protection field. Her paper is full of simple explanations and math formulas, although it doesn't necessarily go into how a Lattice model would be directly implemented in an operating system. Even though she never implemented it herself, her thesis and a later paper (`http://faculty.nps.edu/dedennin/publications/CertificationProgramsSecureInfoFlow.pdf`) described how a compiler could be modified to check the flows of programs, which others used to implement her model.

One of the larger themes across Dr. Denning's work was protecting sensitive information even as it was processed by software processes. She said, "I think one of the examples cited is when you send your tax return to a tax preparation software or service for processing. They should be able to process your return without having sensitive information get into the hands of people that shouldn't have it."

I asked her how she thought people's sensitive information was being handled today. She said, "Well, it's not being done well. Information is stolen all the time and accessed by people who should not access it. Right now, many companies aren't doing enough to protect information."

In 1982, Dr. Denning wrote an influential textbook, *Cryptography and Data Security* (`https://www.amazon.com/Cryptography-Security-Dorothy-Elizabeth-Robling/dp/0201101505`). The original reason she wrote the book is because she couldn't find the book she needed to teach a course on the subject. It was the first of several books and more than 170 articles and whitepapers that she would write over her career. In 1983 she started at SRI International, a non-profit research institute established by Stanford University trustees, and began to work on intrusion detection for the Navy, which eventually culminated in the intrusion detection whitepaper I referenced at the beginning of the chapter.

She moved to Digital Equipment Corporation (DEC), which was a pretty hot computer company at the time and where thousands of computer patents emanated from. It was during her time at DEC that she ended up interviewing a bunch of computer hackers to understand their motivations and psyches. Of course, more learnings and papers were the result. Simultaneously interviewing hackers and working to prevent their illegal activities created a bit of controversy at the time. Although she doesn't necessarily seek controversy, it's clear she doesn't avoid it when seeking solutions. It's another theme that occasionally pops up in her work as she pushes boundaries and provokes conversations. In another past interview, Dr. Denning lamented that she was sometimes disappointed when the emotion of others about a particular issue prevented a much-needed public discussion.

She left DEC in 1991 to go back to academia at Georgetown University, where she taught information warfare and cyberwarfare as the director of the

Georgetown Institute of Information Assurance. Then she went to the Naval Postgraduate School in 2002 as a professor in the Department of Defense Analysis where she remains today. While at Georgetown, she wrote her last book in 1999, *Information Warfare and Security* (https://www.amazon.com /Information-Warfare-Security-Dorothy-Denning/dp/0201433036/). She said she didn't write another book after that since she was finding it too difficult to keep up with the field and didn't want to write something that would be obsolete even before it was published.

Over her career she won many of the awards that any computer scientist would be proud of, including the Ada Lovelace Award (http://awc-hq.org /ada-lovelace-awards.html) and the National Information Systems Security Award (https://www.acsac.org/ncss-winners.html). In1995 she was named a Fellow of the Association for Computing Machinery (http://awards.acm .org/award_winners/denning_1239516.cfm), and in 2012 she was inducted into the inaugural class of the National Cyber Security Hall of Fame (http:// www.cybersecurityhalloffame.com).

As Dr. Denning officially retired at the end of 2016, I asked her if she would still be working on computer security issues. Could she actually not work after all these years of working? She said, "I'm still going to keep my office, except I'll be a Professor Emeritus, which means I can do what I want to do without having too much direct responsibility. I'm still actively working on several things. I'm getting ready to write something right now. But I also like to go on hikes without any noise. It clears the mind." I think any professional would love to have the career, longevity, and impact on this world that Dr. Denning has had.

For More Information on Dr. Dorothy E. Denning

For information about Dr. Dorothy E. Denning, check out these resources:

- Gary McGraw's Silver Bullet Security Podcast interviewing Dr. Dorothy E. Denning: https://www.cigital.com/podcasts/show-011/
- The University of Minnesota's Charles Babbage Institute's transcripts of an interview with Dr. Denning from 2012: http://conservancy.umn .edu/bitstream/handle/11299/156519/oh424ded.pdf

16 Profile: Michael Dubinsky

I'm a long-time, big curmudgeon about almost all computer security products. It's hard to be anything else after seeing malware and exploitation seemingly get easier over two decades, especially with almost every new security product failing to meet its initial hype. I get paid to review computer security products for a living, and I often get pitched as many as twenty new products a day. If I see one product a year that seems like it might actually do what it says it can do and might have a significant impact on reducing risk, I get ecstatic. I often go years without seeing a capable, interesting product. My criticism often applies to my employer's products as well.

With that said, I've truly been blown away by Microsoft's new Advanced Threat Analytics (ATA) product. I would love it no matter who makes it. ATA uses truly advanced event and network traffic analytics to recognize active threats, including those that many security experts thought would be difficult to detect, like pass-the-hash (https://en.wikipedia.org/wiki/Pass_the_hash) or golden ticket (http://www.infoworld.com/article/2608877/security/fear-the-golden-ticket-attack-.html) attacks. After watching it in action and seeing it mature over time, it's so good that I want to quit what I do for a living and solely work to promote ATA. That's not hyperbole. I would change jobs if they offered the opportunity. It's that good.

Microsoft's ATA came from an acquisition of a product from an Israeli startup company called Aorato in November 2014. Thousands of computer security startups get formed each year. If you've ever worked for a startup company, you know that it involves long hours, few weekends off, and a flurry of hard, exciting work, surrounded by like-minded colleagues. I've known plenty of people who burned out working for startups that never took off. They risked it all for a low-salary, high-hour, high-risk payoff that never came. My twin brother, Richard A. Grimes, often worked for early Internet startups, and he once told me, "If another startup company offers to pay me in future stock, I'm going to tell them that you can't buy groceries or pay the electricity bill with future stock."

Israeli Michael Dubinsky was lucky. Within half of a year of his joining Aorato, it was acquired by Microsoft. Dubinsky now works for Microsoft as a Product Manager Lead for the ATA product. He still works long hours, but he's got the comfort of a much larger corporate parent behind his efforts.

Because of what it means to be Israel and Israeli, the small country has been an incredible hotbed of computer security defense products. Israeli-based companies are always creating new and advanced computer defenses. A few years ago, I was hired to teach honeypot technology to members of the Israel Defense Forces (IDF), which every Israeli must serve in for a few years. I've spent my professional career using and teaching honeypots, and I had even written a book about them. But when I showed up, it was the young men and women of the IDF who schooled me. They knew nearly everything I knew and had already used all the cool honeypot products I was going to demonstrate to them. They just needed me to help make their honeypots even more attractive and realistic.

I've since learned that my experience is common to foreigners who visit the country to teach computer security defense. The Israelis grow up thinking about defenses in a way that most other countries don't have to contemplate. There were several missiles fired at Tel Aviv during the week I was visiting. I asked the class of about 20 people how many people had seen a missile fired in their direction, which if not stopped, would have likely landed near them. Nearly every hand in the class went up. Living that way changes your priorities and perspective. It also helps make great computer security products.

I asked Dubinsky if he had lived his whole life in Israel. He said, "I was born in Latvia, which is in the northern Europe, in the Baltic region. It was a part of the U.S.S.R. after World War II, until it declared its independence in 1990. I moved with my parents to Israel about the same time in 1990. I grew up just south of Tel Aviv after that."

I asked Dubinsky how he got into computer security. He said, "I was interested in computers as a kid, and one of my neighbors was a software engineer, and he helped a whole lot. I started messing around with computers, programming BASIC and Pascal, and disassembling stuff. Then I started finding remote access Trojans (RATs) like SubSeven (https://en.wikipedia.org/wiki/Sub7). They were really interesting, and I started to use them to prank friends. Using social engineering or phishing, I could get my friends to install them, and then I would do pranks on them, like making the CD-ROM tray eject without them doing it. Then I progressed, with friends, to deciding to steal someone else's Internet credentials. These were the days of dial-up modems and expensive Internet use. I used my same hacker skills that I had used to prank friends to steal someone else's Internet logon credentials. I was successful, but I also got caught. My parents were very upset, and they took my computer away. Later on when I began working for the Israeli Army, I worked on the computer defense side. I was especially interested in authentication and how to ensure strong authentication."

I asked how he got involved with Aorato. He replied, "I joined in 2014 as the thirteenth person in the two-year old company. I started right away working out engineering problems and figuring out how to build new detections and land successful PoCs. There were always two main work streams going on. One side had to figure how to detect something, and the other how to make the product detect it and improve the product. I was only with Aorato six months before Microsoft bought them out. Microsoft has given us 100% backing and trust. We are still working hard with great people and delivering a great product that is successful."

I asked Dubinsky what he thinks the biggest problem in computer security is. He said, "Education. Eventually most people will click on anything. No matter how much technology you build in, some people will still click on anything. Education is the key to preventing attacks."

For More Information on Michael Dubinsky

For information about Michael Dubinsky, check out this resource:

- Michael Dubinsky on Twitter: https://twitter.com/michaeldubinsky

17 Firewalls

Firewalls are a great example of technology being a victim of its own success. Firewalls have worked so well at defending computers for three decades that the threats they were created to prevent have almost stopped even being tried. The bad guys are giving up! At least on those types of threats. Some experts have even argued whether firewalls are even necessary anymore, but most believe that firewalls, like anti-malware scanners, are an essential item in anyone's computer security base configuration.

What Is a Firewall?

In a nutshell, a firewall is a software or hardware component designed to prevent unauthorized access between two or more security boundaries. It is traditionally accomplished by a protocol name or port number and usually at the network level using packet filtering. Many firewalls can also allow or deny traffic based on user names, device names, group membership, and information found in the upper levels of the application traffic. They often offer additional and advanced features such as high-level packet analysis, intrusion detection/prevention, malware detection, and VPN services. Most firewalls come with detailed log files. Turning on any firewall will usually result in a log file full of entries.

The Early History of Firewalls

The beginning of what security experts would later identify as being an early application-level firewall was created in 1987 by AT&T Bell Labs admins Dave Presotto and Howard Trickey on a VAX computer running BSD with two network interfaces to protect internal users and computers. Their software allowed internal users to access the Internet, but it did not allow any undefined inbound connections. They used a custom circuit-level gateway that predated the eventually very popular SOCKS proxy by about seven years. It was later taken over by William Cheswick in early 1988.

NOTE   The word "firewall" was used in the 1983 movie *Hackers*, but it wasn't clearly defined.

The first mention of a firewall in technical documentation is in a 1987 presentation called "The Packet Filter: An Efficient Mechanism for User-level Network Code" by Jeffery C. Mogul (he is an ACM Fellow and now works at Google [https://research.google.com/pubs/JeffreyMogul.html]), Richard F. Rashid, and Michael J. Accetta, at an ACM Symposium on Operating Systems Principles.

Cheswick's firewall-protected network was tested by the infamous November 1988 Morris Internet worm hit (https://en.wikipedia.org/wiki/Morris _worm). Assisted by a little luck due to previous service changes, the firewall and the computers it protected remained unaffected, while hundreds of other networks and thousands of other computers did not. It was one of the first times a firewall proved its value in overall computer security in a real-world scenario. The luck part bothered Cheswick, who updated the firewall's original configuration by adding another security boundary between the internal and external interface. He eventually renamed it proxyd, which was the first time the word "proxy" was used in that sort of context.

Cheswick described firewalls in a 1990 USENIX proceeding, and in 1994 with Steven Bellovin wrote the seminal book on firewalls, *Firewalls and Internet Security: Repelling the Wily Hacker*. Cheswick recalls the book's surprising popularity this way: "Checkpoint's Firewall Zone 1 (which was eventually renamed the Checkpoint Firewall) first appeared at the Spring 1994 Las Vegas Interop, which was within a week or so of the publication of our firewalls book. Our publisher estimated that our book would sell 8–12,000 copies. The first printing of 10,000 copies sold out in a week, and they rushed the second printing of 20,000 out so fast they didn't let us fix bugs. We sold about 100,000 copies total, in about a dozen languages. It came at just the right time."

Brian Reed and other Digital Equipment Corporation (DEC) people were doing similar work on firewalls, interfacing DEC's corporate DECnet with the Internet. However, their firewall was a bit more focused on blocking outgoing access, as DEC had previously lost important software by unauthorized data exfiltration.

Marcus Ranum wrote the first major commercial firewall product for DEC in 1990 and another version called Screening External Access Link (SEAL) along with Geoff Mulligan in 1991. At the same time, Jeffery Mogul released screend, one of the first firewalls (`https://www.researchgate.net/ publication/2443301_Using_screend_to_Implement_IPTCP_Security_ Policies`). Other commercial firewalls from many different vendors followed, including TIS Gauntlet, Checkpoint, and DuPont's Raptor Eagle. Ranum made the open-source Firewall Toolkit in 1993 as part of a project for DARPA (the funder of the early version of the Internet) and the U.S. White House.

All of this activity culminated in firewalls now being an essential component of any popular operating system. Microsoft Windows created one called the Windows Firewall, first released with Windows XP in 2001. By the second service pack in August 2004, it was turned on by default. This change is directly related to a huge drop in Windows-based malware that could have otherwise been successful. Today, many devices, including your Internet router, wireless router, and cable/satellite entertainment box, contain user-configurable firewalls.

Firewall Rules

All firewalls have rules (or policies). The most common default firewall rule is this: Allow anything to go out by default, but deny any undefined inbound connections that were not previously created by an outbound connection. Very secure firewalls also restrict any previously undefined outbound traffic. Unfortunately, when very strict rules are implemented, it often causes too much operational interruption or management, and so most implementers go with the most common default rule.

Where Are Firewalls?

Firewalls can be placed at the network level or directly on computer hosts.

Network-Based

Traditionally, most firewalls are located as network devices between two or more network segments. The only thing that has changed is that the number of managed segments has increased to the point that some firewalls can manage dozens of segments at once. Today's newly emerging software-defined networks (SDNs) contain some packet-forwarding components that can directly trace their origins back to traditional firewalls.

Host-Based

Many people believe that even a firewall-protected network cannot be trusted. Even Cheswick infamously said that inside a network firewall's perimeter is a "soft, chewy center." Cheswick was stating that we must make sure all our hosts are securely configured and hardened to help defend against things that get past the network firewall perimeter.

Host-based firewalls help with that process. They normally still work at the network and packet level, but they often have additional capabilities because they are integrated with the host and its operating system. For example, the Windows Firewall can be easily configured on a per-service basis and by user and group. Windows comes built-in with nearly 100 firewall rules that are enabled by the operating system even if you disable the user-controllable software application.

Many computer security boundary purists believe that every host should only be able to communicate with other explicitly defined hosts, following essentially very secure, strict firewall rules that define exactly what traffic is and isn't allowed into and between all hosts. This sort of ultra-granular control is considered to be the Holy Grail of firewalls. Unfortunately, the complexity and management of such firewalls makes them unlikely to be widely scaled beyond some small, super-secure scenarios.

Advanced Firewalls

Advanced firewalls have been around for decades and usually refer to features that a traditional packet-filtering–only firewall doesn't typically offer. A traditional firewall may be able to block by protocol (by name or number), but an advanced firewall can often block by almost any detailed, individual component of the protocol (sometimes called "deep-packet inspection"). Or it can aggregate multiple packets to identify specific attacks. A traditional firewall may drop a particular number of packets, but only an advanced firewall can say you're under a distributed denial-of-service attack. Application-level firewalls can look at the application layers of the network and detect maliciousness or prevent it from reaching the host. For example, an advanced firewall could drop a buffer overflow sequence from reaching a web server. Advanced firewalls are so common that most firewalls are advanced to some degree.

What Firewalls Protect Against

Firewalls prevent malicious attacks originating from unauthorized network traffic. Traditionally, remote buffer overflow attacks against vulnerable services were the number one threat that firewalls prevented. But over time, services became more robust (often because their underlying operating systems became more secure by default), and firewalls made it harder for attackers to be successful using these types of attacks. Accordingly, few of the attacks today, due to the way they are implemented, would be prevented by a firewall. For example, if an end-user can be tricked into running a Trojan horse program arriving in email, there's isn't much a firewall can do to prevent the subsequent maliciousness. Still, because firewalls are readily available (often free and implemented by default) and can stop certain types of attacks, most people believe every network and computing device should have one activated. You can choose to implement a firewall or not to implement one. Either way, that choice essentially points to the firewall's great success.

Chapter 18 will profile one of the early main firewall creators, William Cheswick.

18 Profile: William Cheswick

As discussed in the previous chapter, William Cheswick is one of the original creators of the modern-day firewall. He took over the management of the first documented firewall, invented the circuit-level firewall, and if you say the word "proxy" in your computer security life, you have him to thank. Cheswick has more than a dozen patents and co-wrote the first definitive book on firewalls, *Firewalls and Internet Security: Repelling the Wily Hacker* (https://www.amazon.com/Firewalls-Internet-Security-Repelling-Hacker/dp/020163466X) with Steven Bellovin in 1994. I was into firewalls before reading that book, but his book taught me much of what I know about firewalls today, and a dog-eared version of it was on my office bookshelf for nearly two decades.

His infamous "An Evening with Berferd in which a Cracker Is Lured, Endured, and Studied" whitepaper (http://www.cheswick.com/ches/papers/berferd.pdf) introduced many of us to honeypots. Thanks to Cheswick, the term "jail" is now a direct command word in FreeBSD, and a "chroot jail" is one of the easiest and most popular ways to isolate particular subsystems in Unix and Linux. Few individuals have had as much broad impact on computer security boundaries as he has. He is also one of the optimistic experts I've met in the computer security field while also realizing that a lot of things still need to be fixed.

I asked Cheswick how he came to join the AT&T Bell Labs hotbed of computer security talent. He said, "In 1968 I was a chemistry guy, but I saw the first early computers, and I figured they would be becoming more popular in the future, and so I got interested in them. And eventually more into them than chemistry. Eventually I ended up at SET, a consulting firm, as a contracted techie. We would do techie work for other companies. Over my nine years there, I had met some of the people at Bell Labs. I loved the people and the place. I could have been a janitor there and been happy. So in fall of

1987, I interviewed there. The people interviewing me were giants—gods in the field, people like Dennis Ritchie [creator of the C programming language] and Ken Thompson [co-creator of Unix along with Ritchie]. I would have been completely happy just from the day of interviews, but for some reason they liked me and I became a member of their team. In one of my first days, I walked up to Dave Presotto [creator of the first firewall] and volunteered to be postmaster and take over the firewall. And he said yes."

I asked the creator of the circuit-level firewall to explain what a circuit-level firewall is. He replied, "It literally re-creates the traffic, bit-by-bit, between the two (or more) legs of the firewall. Every packet is reconstructed and is changed to make it appear as if every outgoing packet originated from the firewall. To everyone outside the firewall, the firewall looks like the originator of all the traffic. Before that, anyone outside would see the packets as coming from the original computers they originated from." Today, every firewall does that by default.

I asked Cheswick how he met his future co-author Steven Bellovin. He said, "Steven already worked at Bell Labs before I had arrived. Dave Presotto taught me in a TCP/IP class that Steven also attended. We became friends and were always talking about firewalls and other threats. We eventually created a 'packet telescope' (an early packet sniffer). We had gotten a big Class A network for AT&T, and it had so many IP addresses that we couldn't even handle them. Subnetting on such a big network didn't work very well at the time. So I announced the '12 network' to the Internet to see what would happen. Pretty soon, we had 25 MBs of data coming in every day. Much of it ended up being 'death traffic' from other compromised computers. We learned a lot. Steven talked about it in his paper, 'There Be Dragons' (https://academiccommons.columbia.edu/catalog/ac:126916). We eventually made the first DNS proxy because of what we learned. And from there our book. Our book came out at the right time, because there were not any books on firewalls before that and firewalls were very popular. We sold a lot of copies and made some good money."

I asked him about all his patents. I've worked on a few myself and they are tough to get. He said, "I would have a lot more patents if I knew what we were doing was patentable. Early on everything seemed 'obvious' ('obvious' is a legal term that means 'isn't patentable') or so I thought. What we were doing seemed obvious—common sense—to me and the 12 other guys that we talked to about it. I even had patent lawyers come around and ask if what

I was working on at the time was patentable. I said no, because it was obvious. Looking back, if I had just shut up I would have a lot more seminal patents. Years later someone else gets the patent for something you were thinking of and doing long before. I even have a few patents and copyrights that are often ignored, like for my Internet maps (http://cheswick.com/ches/map/) I did. It was truly revolutionary work for the time. We even started a company, Lumeta, around mapping. Now I see my Internet maps all over the place, almost always uncredited. I was at a recent conference and the speaker put up one of my Internet maps, uncredited of course, and about half the audience around me looked at me because they knew it was one of my maps. Another example is DNS proxies. I have the patent for that, but there are plenty of DNS proxies out there, and they aren't paying attention to my patent."

I asked him what bothers him the most about computer security. He said, "It's constantly the same ol' stuff that is working. Almost nothing is new. Maybe Stuxnet, but the old stuff keeps on working. We've known at least since 1979 that passwords don't work, so why are we still doing it? I'm currently working on some new password and authentication ideas. Another example was the recent DYN DDoS attacks (http://dyn.com/blog/dyn-analysis-summary-of-friday-october-21-attack/). It was accomplished because of all these root passwords cooked into the firmware of IoT devices. I would give a student a failing grade for putting in hardcoded passwords. They aren't even trying."

Still, Cheswick thinks computer security will greatly improve. He said, "I give lots of talks around the world and one of my go-to stump speeches is called 'Internet Security: I Think We're Going to Win.' Here's an example of that presentation: https://cacr.iu.edu/events/2016/bill-cheswick-comp-sec-we-can-win.php. We are at the Model T stage of computer security. We are not really trying, but we will. Right now, we have market failure, but the market will resolve it. We will have significantly better Internet security in the future. A lot of people don't believe me when I say this, but we will. Other industries had the same problems early on but grew and improved. The Internet will do the same thing."

I asked him what one of the major improvements will be. He replied, "I'm still amazed that we are allowed to run arbitrary software on your computer. Even with an antivirus checker, it's like running a background check on the hobos in your bathroom. Operating systems should only allow trusted and checked code to run, and this is happening. Operating systems are starting to lead the way on this already."

I asked him why he thought it was taking so long to get better computer security. He said, "There are a lot of issues, but one of the main ones are all the legacy support issues. It's like having a city. All cities have legacy support issues from past development that they just can't ignore."

I asked Cheswick what he was thinking about lately. He said, "One of the biggest problems is how do you measure security in software? There's been a lot of attempts. What does an accurate system of metrics even look like? One simple example is to measure the number of total network services on your network, with each one being a potential attack vector, and reducing the number means less risk. But that's far too simplistic. Another simple measure would be to measure the number of daemons running with setuid root [which means the program is intentionally elevated to run as the most privileged security account context]. Again, less would certainly be better. But again, that's too simplistic. Another way to measure the security of let's say an operating system or software program is how expensive is a zero-day exploit to buy on the open market. *Forbes* magazine wrote an article in 2012 on this (http://www .forbes.com/sites/andygreenberg/2012/03/23/shopping-for-zero-days-an-price-list-for-hackers-secret-software-exploits/#43f3035e6033). The cost of the exploit would be a factor of how difficult it was to break into a program or operating system and the desirability to break into that system. For example, maybe a full exploit of an OS costs $500,000, but breaking into a frequently broken-into program only costs $50,000. The larger cost tells you that vendor is doing a better job at security.

"Everyone wants to get—even a general I spoke to recently—a better measurement of whether they are doing better or worse in securing their environment. They want a number. They want to be able to show that they had a 27 last year, but this year they have a 63 and are doing demonstrably better now. The more realistic measurement is to define all the possible measurements and give them weights and then combine all those measurements into a larger metric. That's what any leader, including the general, wants. I'm thinking about that issue a lot these days. It is getting harder and harder to break into the new software these days. Even the complaints by the FBI not being able to break into something is a good sign. It is getting better."

For More Information on William Cheswick

For information about William Cheswick, check out these resources:

- William Cheswick's web site: `http://www.cheswick.com/ches/index.html`
- *Firewalls and Internet Security: Repelling the Wily Hacker* (co-authored with Steven Bellovin): `https://www.amazon.com/Firewalls-Internet-Security-Repelling-Hacker/dp/020163466X`
- "An Evening with Berferd in which a Cracker Is Lured, Endured, and Studied" whitepaper: `http://www.cheswick.com/ches/papers/berferd.pdf`

19 Honeypots

I have been intrigued by computer security honeypots ever since I read Clifford Stoll's 1989 book *The Cuckoo's Egg* (https://www.amazon.com/Cuckoos-Egg-Tracking-Computer-Espionage/dp/1416507787/), with his identification and capture of a foreign spy. Since then I've run up to eight different honeypots at a time tracking malware and hacker behavior. I'm frequently involved in professional honeypot projects, and I even wrote a book on them called *Honeypots for Windows* (https://www.amazon.com/Honeypots-Windows-Books-Professionals/dp/1590593359/). I believe that all companies should include one or more honeypots in their defenses.

What Is a Honeypot?

A "honeypot" is any system set up for the expressed purpose of being a "fake" system to detect unauthorized activity. A honeypot can be a computer system, a device, a network router, a wireless access point, a printer—anything the honeypot administrator wishes to deploy. A "honeynet" is a collection of honeypots. A honeypot can be created by deploying a real but otherwise unused system or by deploying specialized honeypot software that emulates systems.

The emulation can be anywhere along the Open Systems Interconnection (OSI) model layers—Physical, Data-Link, Network, Transport, Session, Presentation, or Application—or any combination of these layers. There are many open-source and commercial honeypot options, each offering various features and realism. The buyer must beware though. There are some honeypot products that have been around for longer than a decade, but the vast majority of honeypot offerings come and go in a few years, free or commercial, so be aware of longevity issues.

Interaction

How well a honeypot system emulates or works at a particular layer determines its "interaction." A "low-interaction" honeypot only mimics very simplistic port connections and logs them. The connecting user may or may not be offered a logon screen, but usually a successful logon isn't allowed. A "medium-interaction" honeypot allows the user to log on and tries to offer up a moderate but realistic experience. If it is emulating a web site, often it tries to emulate a decent but fairly static web site. If it does FTP emulation, the FTP site allows logons, has files that can be downloaded, and allows multiple FTP commands to be used. "High-interaction" honeypots mimic a real production system to the point that a hacker interacting with it should not be able to tell the difference between it and a real production asset. If it is emulating a web site, the web site is broad and realistic-looking with frequently updated content.

Lower emulation is far easier to maintain, but sometimes the goal of the honeypot requires higher interaction. Of course, a real system offers the best emulation but can be more difficult to configure and manage over the long-term.

Why Use a Honeypot?

There are many reasons to have a honeypot, including:

- As an early warning system to detect malware and hackers
- To determine the intent of a hacker
- For hacker and malware research
- To practice forensic analysis

A honeypot, when appropriately fine-tuned, is incredibly low-noise and high-value, especially when analyzing logs or generating alerts. For example, firewall logs are always full of tens of thousands of dropped packet events every day, most of which have nothing to do with maliciousness. And even if there was a malicious probe, good luck in deciphering which one of those packets among the multitude is the one you are supposed to generate an alert on and respond to.

A honeypot is a fake system, and by design, no one (or thing) should be attempting to connect to it. You have to spend a little time filtering out the normal broadcast traffic and legitimate connection attempts (for example from your antivirus updating programs, patch management and other system management tools, and so on). But once that is done (which usually takes anywhere from two hours to two days), any other connection attempt is, by definition, malicious.

A honeypot is absolutely the best way to catch an intruder who has bypassed all other defenses. It sits there waiting for any unexpected connection attempt. I've met and tracked a lot of hackers and pen testers in my decades of experience, and one fact that is true is that they search and move around a network once they have gained initial access. Few hackers know which systems are or aren't honeypots, and when they move around and simply "touch" the honeypot, you've got them.

Case in point: One of the most common attack worries is the advanced persistent threats (APTs), covered in Chapter 14. They move laterally and horizontally with ease, usually without detection. But place one or more honeypots as fake web servers, database servers, and application servers, and you'll be hard pressed not to detect an APT.

Sure, you've got hackers who will simply go from their first internal compromise to a specific asset or set of assets, but that is rarely the case. Usually, even after compromising an intended primary target, they will look around. And when they look around and touch a honeypot, boom, you've got them. Or at least you know about them. I'm a big fan of placing low- to medium-interaction honeypots around the internal environment to give early warning of a successful compromise.

Catching My Own Russian Spy

I've deployed dozens of honeypot systems over the years, but one of my favorite stories is when I was deploying a honeynet at a defense contractor. The contractor was concerned about external hacking, but our honeypots quickly turned up an unauthorized insider attack.

We tracked it back to a Russian data entry person in the payroll department. We already had a camera installed in the department so we could see everything that she was doing. She had inserted an unauthorized wireless card in her PC to "bridge" two air-gapped networks, and she was exfiltrating large amounts of private data to another external partner. After two days of watching and determining her intent (she was definitely going after top secret projects), we walked into the room to confront her along with corporate security. She immediately broke into tears and was such a good actress that had we not been already watching her for days I would have believed her. She was an uber hacker, but the payroll department had thought she was so computer illiterate that they had sent her to keyboarding school to learn how to type better.

She was just one of many Russian employees that had been hired as part of a temp agency contract. In the end, all were found to be spying and dealt with accordingly.

Honeypot Resources to Explore

The Honeynet Project (http://www.honeynet.org) is the single best place for honeypot information and forensics. Its Honeywall CD-ROM image (http://www.honeynet.org/project/HoneywallCDROM) is a great, free, all-in-one honeynet software for users not scared of a little Linux configuration. It is menu-driven, full of functionality, and easier to get up and running than a brand-new Honeyd install.

Honeyd (http://www.honeyd.org) is a flexible, free, open-source, feature-rich honeypot software program, but it requires solid Linux and network skills to deploy and operate. It performs excellent, broad emulation of over 100 operating systems, and it can be easily linked with other products and scripts. On the downside, it hasn't been updated in years. I think it's a good first-time honeypot for those who want to see everything that is possible.

My favorite honeypot software is Kfsensor (www.keyfocus.net). It's a commercial product that only works on Windows computers, but the maintainer is constantly updating and improving the product. Kfsensor has its flaws, but it's feature-rich and fairly easy to set up. It has hundreds of options and customizations, and it allows logging and alerting to a variety of databases and logs. Free trial versions are available.

There are many (more than a hundred) honeypot products out in the world. A few new ones appear on the Internet every year. If you're interested in honeypots, give some of them a try. There is no doubt that every corporate entity should be running a honeynet of honeypots if they are interested in the earliest warning possible of a successful hacker or malware infiltration.

Chapter 20 profiles Lance Spitzner, who has probably done more honeypot research than anyone.

20 Profile: Lance Spitzner

"Nothing makes me more frustrated than when a security geek says 'you can't patch stupid'"—Lance Spitzner

In the late 1980s, I read a book by Clifford Stoll called *The Cuckoo's Egg* (https://www.amazon.com/Cuckoos-Egg-Tracking-Computer-Espionage/dp/B0051CSCG6/). It's the story of how a $0.75 error leads an American astronomer into discovering an international spy ring. Stoll's chief investigative tool was a honeypot. The book really piqued my interest into computer security and fighting hackers.

Ten years went by before I ran into another huge honeypot advocate, Lance Spitzner. Today, most consider Spitzner to be the father of modern-day computer honeypots. He wrote and published so much information on them in the 2000s, including a book (https://www.amazon.com/Honeypots-Tracking-Hackers-Lance-Spitzner/dp/0321108957), that even today, a decade later, no one has written more. Spitzner's fresh take on the subject led to my own multi-decade interest in honeypots, including my own book on them (https://www.amazon.com/Honeypots-Windows-Books-Professionals/dp/1590593359).

Spitzner's contribution to the field was to update the whole idea of honeypots and take the honeypot from being treated as a toy to instead being considered a much-needed discipline, helping develop the field of cyber intelligence. His main interest was in getting know how and why hackers compromised organizations, something he called "Know Your Enemy." He also created definitions to describe the different styles and classes of honeypots and helped figure out, by actually deploying them, what worked and didn't work. Spitzner is a doer, and he has learned and taught by doing.

He is also a great study in how someone who didn't major in computers can make a great career in computer security. He went to college and became a history major. He joined the ROTC (Reserve Officer Training Corps) to help pay for his studies, and after graduating he joined the Army as an M1A1 Abrams tank officer for four years.

Spitzner thoroughly believes that you don't need to be a computer major to make a career in computer security. He said, "You don't need to be in or start out in computers to have a good computer security career. Twenty to thirty years ago, it was easier to do it because there wasn't a standard career path like there is now. Now I'm concerned that the field is being overly populated by highly technical computer security majors. We need more "soft skills" in our profession, not just people who understand bits and bytes. Many of the biggest problems we need to solve today aren't technological anymore."

There must be something about tank soldiers and computer security, because I've known a handful of them through the years who are excellent at their jobs. I asked Spitzner about it. He said, "In the military you are constantly trained to know your enemy. I was trained not only in my tank's operations, but the operations of the enemy's tanks and how they would attack our forces. I was surprised that in the computer security world how little anyone really knew about the enemy, because I was coming from a place where we knew everything about the bad guy. It was 1997 or 1998, and no one really cared about computer security yet."

I asked him to explain further about how he got into computer security full-time after his time in a tank. He replied, "While I was in my MBA program in grad school after the Army, I got sucked into the computer security world. It was a natural fit after being in a tank. I started an internship with a Unix consulting company. We got sent some firewalls to deploy, and since I was the new guy, they dumped them on me. I loved it. I got to learn about firewalls, get trained in them, and stop bad guys. It was great. After that, I spent four years working for Sun Microsystems' security team securing customers around the world."

I asked him how he turned his love of firewalls into a love of honeypots. He replied, "I read three things about honeypots. First, I read a paper by Dr. Fred Cohen, considered the father of computer virus defenses (https://en.wikipedia.org/wiki/Fred_Cohen). Second, I read Clifford Stoll's *The Cuckoo's Egg*. And third, I read a whitepaper by Bill Cheswick ["An Evening with Berferd in Which a Cracker Is Lured, Endured, and Studied" (http://www.cheswick.com/ches/papers/berferd.pdf)]." Bill Cheswick [profiled in Chapter 18] was one of the first firewall computer scientists and an early honeypot user. Clifford Stoll's honeypot experiences were from 1986. Bill Cheswick's was from 1991. For a long time, these two sources were all that most of us knew of honeypots."

Spitzner continued, "For a long time, there were not any good honeypots out there. I had little coding skills, so I couldn't write my own honeypot software. So, I decided to deploy honeypots using real computers. I simply put a firewall, which I did know well, in front of real systems. Everything else I wrote about was from lessons I learned from doing that."

Spitzner's most productive honeypot years were when he worked full-time from 2004 to 2009 for the Honeynet Project (http://www.honeynet .org). The Honeynet Project was sponsored by the U.S. National Intelligence Council (https://www.dni.gov/index.php/about/organization/national-intelligence-council-who-we-are). The National Intelligence Council (NIC) was established in 1979 as a strategic analysis center. It has built a team from some of the best minds in academia, government, and the private sector. The NIC has long provided expertise and collaboration on intelligence issues and has spearheaded several significant and important projects.

Anyone interested in honeypots knew that the majority of the most current and up-to-date information and tools were located on the NIC's site, and they still are. It is still active to this day. If you're interested in honeypots, you should spend a lot of time at the Honeynet Project web site. It was during his time working for the Honeynet Project that Spitzner wrote most of his public information about honeypots and helped anyone who asked questions (including me).

Sadly, Spitzner eventually left the Honeynet Project and no longer focuses on honeypots. I asked him why and he said, "Because of my work in the Honeynet Project, I got to know the enemy very well. Since we have become so good at using technology to defend technology, I saw cyber attackers quickly adapt and target the human element. Today, hackers are progressively leveraging social engineering. When's the last time you saw a big worm? Conficker. [Conficker peaked in 2009.] There's a reason why we haven't seen any big worms anymore. The default technology got much better, and now the attackers go after the weakest link, the human. I saw this move and formed my own company around security awareness. SANS Institute (http://www.sans.org) eventually acquired my company in 2010, and now it's known as SANS Securing the Human (https://securingthehuman.sans.org/). We have over 1000 customers. We help them create high-impact security awareness programs. I work with our customers, hands-on in the field like always, and I also teach classes and present at conferences."

In closing, I asked Spitzner what concerned him the most about computer security today. He replied, "Well, it has to do with the human component. There's still an overemphasis on the technology side and a lack of focus on the human. It's why I'm in the field. I like and believe in what I do. The bad guys have gotten so good at what they do that there is nothing to detect, no infected attachment, no malware, no rootkit. They just identify a target in accounts payable with a phishing email or a fake invoice, and they get through. Then they use legitimate tools like PowerShell to move around the network and do bad things. Antivirus and technology is not going to detect it. Ironically, the biggest blocker to human security is often other computer security professionals. There is such a focus on continuing to invest in more technology that many security professionals feel something can only be security-related if its bits and bytes. Nothing makes me more frustrated than when a security geek says 'you can't patch stupid,' meaning that you can't fix the human. As a result, little if anything is done to secure the human element, and yet we blame them for being the weakest link. It's so crazy."

For More Information on Lance Spitzner

For information about Lance Spitzner, check out these resources:

- *Honeypots: Tracking Hackers*: https://www.amazon.com/Honeypots-Tracking-Hackers-Lance-Spitzner/dp/0321108957
- Lance Spitzner on Twitter: https://twitter.com/lspitzner
- Lance Spitzner's SANS classes: https://www.sans.org/instructors/lance-spitzner
- "Know Your Enemy" whitepaper: http://old.honeynet.org/papers/enemy/
- "Know Your Enemy" series of whitepapers: http://www.honeynet.org/papers

21

Password Hacking

acking passwords has always been a popular activity for cyber attackers, although the newer methods have evolved from simple password guessing. The Hollywood notion of the hacker is someone who sits in front of a logon screen and simply guesses the correct password out of thin air. Although this does happen, it is fairly rare. Real password hacking usually involves a lot more guesses or no guessing at all.

Authentication Components

To understand passwords, you really have to understand authentication systems in general. The user (or device), also known as the security principal or subject, must submit something (such as a text label, a certificate, and so on) that uniquely identifies them and their logon to the authentication system service. For most traditional password scenarios, this is a label known as a username.

The subject must then be able to prove ownership of the label, which is usually done by submitting another bit of information tied to the label that only the subject and the authentication system knows and agrees upon. This is what the password is. When the user submits the correct password associated with the username, that proves the subject controls the username, and the system allows them access (in other words, they are authenticated) and may track them while they are accessing the system (which is called accounting or auditing). Most operating systems also ensure that the subject is supposed to access the objects they are trying to access (a process called access control). Thus, you might hear the entire authentication process known as the four As (authentication, access, auditing, and accounting). They are related but usually evaluated separately.

Passwords

A password can be any acceptable set of characters that the authentication system accepts. For example, on a Microsoft Windows system, the local Security Accounts Management (SAM) database or the networked Active Directory authentication system (NTDS) can accept thousands of different characters, many of which require special keystroke combinations (for example Alt+0128) to create.

Authentication Databases

Passwords are stored in a local and/or networked database known as the authentication database. The authentication database is usually protected or encrypted, and it is rarely directly accessible by non-privileged users. Passwords are also often stored in local and/or remote memory (if networked) while the user or device is active.

Password Hashes

Most typed passwords are converted into some other intermediary form for security reasons. In most traditional operating systems, passwords get converted into a cryptographic hash. The hash can be used in the authentication sequence itself or simply stored for later authentication purposes. Common password hashes on Windows systems are LANManager (LM), NTLANManager (NT), and PBKDF2 for local password cache storage. Linux systems often use MD5, Blowfish (created by Bruce Schneier, profiled in Chapter 3), SHA-256, or SHA-512. The best hashes create and use a random value (called the "salt") during the creation and storage of the password hash. This makes it harder for a hacker obtaining the password hash to convert it back to its plaintext original value.

Authentication Challenges

Secure network authentication scenarios do not pass the password or the password hash across a network link. Instead, an authentication challenge is performed. Usually the remote server, which already knows the client's password or password hash, creates a random value and performs a cryptographic operation that only the legitimate client, with the same legitimate password or hash, can also correctly perform. The server sends the random value to the client, and the client uses the password (or intermediate representation) to perform the expected calculations and sends the result back to the server. The server compares the result sent by the client to its own internally expected result for the client, and if the two agree, the client is successfully authenticated. This way if an intruder captures the packets used in network authentication, they will not immediately have the password or the password hash, although it is often possible with cryptographic analysis to sometimes work back to one or the other over time.

Authentication Factors

Because passwords can easily be stolen (and sometimes guessed), authentication systems are increasingly asking for additional "factors" for a subject to prove ownership of a logon label. There are three basic types of factors: something you know (such as a password, PIN, passphrase, or screen pattern), something you have (such as a security token, cell phone, or smart card), or something you are (such as a biometric identity, like a finger print, retina print, or hand geometry).

In general, the more factors required to authenticate, the better. The idea is that it is harder for an attacker to steal two or more factors than it is to steal just one factor. Using two factors is known as two-factor authentication (or 2FA), and using more is known as multi-factor authentication (or MFA). Using two or more of the same factor is not as strong as using different types of factors.

Hacking Passwords

There are many ways to hack passwords, including the methods described in the following sections.

Password Guessing

Just like in the movies, hackers can simply guess a person's password. If the password is simple and the hacker knows something about the person, they can try guessing a password based on the person's interests. It's well known that users often create passwords named after themselves, loved ones, or their favorite hobbies. The hacker can manually try to guess a person's password at a logon screen or use one of the many hacker tools for automating password guessing. If the automated password guesser blindly tries every possible password combination, it is known as a "brute force" guessing attack. If it uses a predefined set of possible password values, which is often a dictionary of words, then the password guessing tool is known as a "dictionary" password guessing attack. Most password guessers use a tool that begins with a dictionary set of words that then supplements the plaintext words with different combinations of numbers and special characters to guess at more complex passwords.

NOTE Once in my life I literally randomly guessed a password for a user I knew nothing about and had it work on my first try. The password I guessed was "rosebud," because I had just finished watching the famous Orson Wells movie, *Citizen Kane*, where trying to guess that previously unknown word is the plot of the whole movie. But that was the one time in my career that this happened.

Phishing

The hacker can also use a realistic-looking, but fraudulent, online request (via web site or email) to trick the user into revealing their password. This is known as "phishing." If the phishing attempt uses what was previously private or internal information, it's known as "spearphishing." Hackers can also use a phone or show up in person to attempt to trick users out of their passwords. It works far more often than you would think.

Keylogging

If the hacker already has elevated access to the victim's computer, they can install a program called a "keylogger," which captures typed keystrokes. Keyloggers are great for capturing passwords, and they don't care if the password is long or complex.

Hash Cracking

If the hacker can access the victim's authentication database, they can access the stored password, or more likely, password hashes. Strong hashes are cryptographically resistant to converting back to their original plaintext forms. Weaker hashes, unsalted hashes, and even strong hashes of short passwords are subject to "hash cracking." A hash cracker tries (either using brute force or dictionary methods) to input every possible password, converts it to a hash, and then compares the newly created hash to the stolen hash. If they match, then the hacker now has the plaintext password. "Rainbow tables" are related to traditional hash crackers, only their hash table stores an intermediate form used for password or hash comparison that significantly speeds up the cracking. There are many free password guessing and cracking programs available on the Internet. If you're interested in trying a password hash cracker, the open source John the Ripper (http://www.openwall.com/john/) is a great one to learn with.

Credential Reuse

If the hacker already has elevated access, they can steal the user's password hash or other credential representation from computer memory or the stored authentication database, and then replay it to other computers that accept authentication using the stolen credentials. This type of attack, and in particular one known as "Pass-the-Hash" (or PtH), has become quite popular over the last decade. In a traditional PtH scenario, the attacker first breaks into one or more regular end-user computers, locates the local elevated account hashes, and then uses that access to eventually access the computer's or network's storage of all credentials, which essentially compromises the whole IT environment. PtH attacks have happened to nearly every company and entity connected to the Internet over the last decade.

Hacking Password Reset Portals

Many times, the quickest way to hack a password is to hack the password's related reset portal. Many authentication systems, especially the big, online systems, allow the end-user to answer a series of predefined questions to reset their password. Hackers have found that it is far easier to guess or research the answer to a particular victim's reset questions (such as "What is your mother's maiden name?" "What is the first elementary school you went to?" "What was your first car?" "What is your favorite color?" and so on) than it is to guess at their password. Many big celebrity hacks have occurred using this method.

Password Defenses

There are just as many ways to defend against password hacks as there are ways to attack them.

Complexity and Length

Long and complex passwords make it significantly harder for password guessing and cracking tools to be successful. Longer is better than complexity (unless you can get true strong entropic complexity). Today most password experts recommend 12-character or longer passwords, and that's just for regular users. Privileged user accounts should be 16 characters or more. The length of the recommended minimum password size increases over time. However, this has no effect on credential reuse attacks, like PtH attacks.

Frequent Changes with No Repeating

Enforcing a maximum number of days that a particular password can be used (usually 90 days or less) with no repeating is a common password defense recommendation/requirement. The thinking is that it usually takes a password guesser a long period of time to guess or crack a long and complex password, but it can eventually be done with enough time and computing power. Enforcing periodic changes in the password reduces the risk that the hacker will be successful before the new password is used.

NOTE Some recent password papers are questioning whether the traditional password defenses of long and complex, frequently changed, and nonrepeating passwords really does reduce risk. Although those defenses might seem on the surface to be good things, the data is showing otherwise. Check out Microsoft Research's "Password Guidance" whitepaper by Robyn Hicock (https://www.microsoft.com/en-us/research/publication/password-guidance/) and password papers by Dr. Cormac Herley, profiled in the next chapter, which question traditional password recommendations.

Not Sharing Passwords Between Systems

This is one of the best defenses, but very hard (if not impossible) to enforce. Users should never use the same password between any system that has a different authentication database. Re-using credentials between different systems increases the risk that the hacker will compromise one of the systems, capture your shared logon credentials, and then use it to attack another.

Account Lockout

This is a frequent password-guessing defense. For systems where hackers try to guess against active logon screens (for example interactively), the authentication system should lock out or freeze the account after a set number of incorrect password guessing attempts. The lockout can be temporary or require that the end user call the help desk to get it reactivated or to reset it at a password reset portal. This defensive measure defeats many password-guessing hackers and tools, but has its own risks, as the lockout feature can be used by the hacker to create a widespread, denial-of-service, lockout attack.

Strong Password Hashes

Authentication systems should always use strong hashes and prevent the use of weak, vulnerable hashes. Most operating systems default to strong hashes, but some allow weak hashes to still be used for backward compatibility purposes. In Microsoft Windows, LM hashes are considered weak and shouldn't be used. In Linux, MD5 and SHA-1 hashes are considered weak.

Don't Use Passwords

These days the conventional wisdom is that password requirements are getting so long and complex that most users might be better off not using a password at all. Instead, users should use 2FA, biometrics, security tokens, digital certificates, and anything other than a simple logon name and password combination. This has been the recommendation for decades, but it is now becoming fairly common in both company networks on popular online systems. If your web site allows you to use something better than a password, use it.

> **NOTE**   The work of the FIDO Alliance (https://fidoalliance.org/) to get rid of passwords across the Internet is gaining momentum unlike many of the previous attempts to do the same thing. Check it out.

Credential Theft Defenses

Because credential theft attacks such as PtH attacks have become so popular lately, many operating systems come with built-in anti–credential theft attack defenses. Most of these focus on making sure the passwords or password hashes aren't available in memory to easily steal, or they don't share the password or hash across network connections.

Reset Portal Defenses

Password reset portals are often the weakest link in an authentication system. Portals should always allow users to make up their own unique and hard-to-guess/research questions and answers. If they don't, users should give hard-to-guess "non-answers" to the questions and securely save the answers for later on use. For example, if the question is "What was your mother's maiden name?," the answer could be "giraffedogfish." You are essentially turning the password reset question answer into another alternate password.

Chapter 22 covers Dr. Cormac Herley, whose research into passwords challenges conventionally held beliefs.

22 Profile: Dr. Cormac Herley

Dr. Cormac Herley is an unintentional disruptor. He says things that challenge long-standing dogma, which not everyone wants to hear, especially if they've invested millions of dollars and decades of resources into doing the exact opposite for years. Dr. Herley uses data mining to seek the truth. He's even well aware that some of his contrarian views, backed by data, may take a decade or longer before people will even listen.

One example is his research into computer passwords. The conventional wisdom is that passwords need to be long, complex, and frequently changed. Dr. Herley's research (https://www.microsoft.com/en-us/research/wp-content/uploads/2016/09/pushingOnString.pdf) showed that the globally accepted security reasoning, supported by nearly every computer security expert in existence and a requirement on every computer security guideline ever produced, is probably wrong at the very least and is likely exacerbating the problem. Dr. Herley's research showed that long and complex passwords don't mitigate most password hacking these days and often result in higher risk due to end-user issues (such as writing passwords down or reusing on different sites).

He's even been bold enough to say that "most [computer] security advice is a waste of time" (https://www.microsoft.com/en-us/research/wp-content/uploads/2016/02/SoLongAndNoThanks.pdf). And he does it with data and evidence. Dr. Herley is my kind of guy.

Dr. Herley got his PhD from Columbia University, an MSEE from Georgia Tech, and a BE from University College Cork, Ireland. He is currently a Principal Researcher at Microsoft Research's Redmond Machine Learning Department. Although he's only been in the computer security world for 10 years, he has written a ton of research papers and been quoted and interviewed in the mainstream media (including *The New York Times*, *The Wall Street Journal*, Bloomberg, and NPR).

I asked Dr. Herley how he got into computer security. He replied, "Serendipity, I think. My background is in audio and video signal processing and digital photography. That field is very data-centric. You have to collect a lot of data, analyze it, get statistics, and figure out the truth. It really prepared me well for computer security, although I was surprised that almost none of that was going on. I guess I got into computer security when someone sent me a new proposed anti-phishing defense based on logo analysis, which involved some of the things I specialized in, to review. I saw many flaws. It wasn't robust enough. I eventually got into passwords and computer security. I saw lots of declarative statements about passwords, but not any evidence that any of things being recommended actually worked. It struck me as strange, coming from my background, that no one was doing what I expected was already done, which is collecting data, making experiments using two different groups [including a control group], and looking at the results. Instead, people were making declarative statements, which even after decades of use didn't have the data to support them. Even though data can be scarce in computer security, data is my ground truth. That's the way we answer questions. Anything else is an intermediate halfway measure or worse.

"We have some framework for protecting high-value assets, which is to do absolutely everything we can, but what about regular business assets? Clearly, we have to make priorities. We can't do everything. It would be ridiculously difficult to do everything, but tell me which ones I can neglect. Rank the list, or give me some way of ranking the list. You can answer the hard questions with data, because the alternative is going in circles."

There are a lot of people in the computer security world who are either ignoring Dr. Herley's work or bothered by it. I asked him about that, and he said, "I didn't come into the computer security world to intentionally, deliberately antagonize anyone. But because I've only recently come into the security world, I didn't have the long-standing cultural biases that many others get. I had a different background, driven by data and the need to see supporting data. When I didn't see good data, it allowed me to ask fundamental questions about things which the culture had already long accepted. I wanted to get the data, test, and do the empirical analysis . . . do things with math. It's not only a desirable way of doing things, but necessary. You might have a model of how you think 2 billion users will behave, but 2 billion users will respond the way they are going to respond regardless of your model. You can hope that it happens the same way, but you have to measure what happens to see if there is any resemblance to what you said would happen in your model. And if your model is wrong, change it."

Dr. Herley's password research has really turned the computer security industry's dogma on its ear. I wondered how he felt about the likelihood of his research and password proposals possibly taking a decade or longer before they become commonly accepted. He said, "Well, NIST [www.nist.org] had a call for comments on their password recommendations, I wrote back, and they are trying to get the battleship turned around. I can totally see why it's frustrating to computer security people and organizations. They've been told something was true by everyone for 30 years, and now just a few people are saying that's wrong. There are a thousand other people saying the reverse, and even if the few are better backed up by data, I can see how it would be frustrating, especially for CSOs and CIOs. I've had the ability and luxury to sit down and do the research, collect data, and consider alternatives. But CSOs and CIOs don't have the luxury of time to research just one issue. They are seeing a bunch of contradictory messages and trying to determine which ones they need to pay attention to. They just have to do their best and use their wisdom as to what happens."

I asked Dr. Herley what he thought was the biggest problem in computer security. He replied, "We know how to perfectly protect high-value assets like nuclear launch missile codes. Compromising the asset is not allowed and so we do everything that's possible to protect them. Everything less critical than the top priority creates a decision of what to do and what not to do. We're not very good at reasoning what is enough with everything else below the highest criticalities. We don't have really good tools and data to make the cases about what must be done. The net effect is that people do the best they can, muddling through, essentially randomly making the decisions they've been told they have to make. It's easier with the high-value assets. We can more easily articulate the risk, quantify it, and create a policy. When you don't have a high-value asset to protect, we end up doing the things we can more easily articulate and quantify than the stuff that would be more beneficial if we tried to quantify it. For example, I'm not sure choosing a super-strong password is in my top ten list of things I think people should be doing, but it certainly gets a huge share of attention and resources." And that hurts us all in the end.

For More Information on Dr. Cormac Herley

For information about Dr. Cormac Herley, check out these resources:

- Dr. Cormac Herley's web site: http://cormac.herley.org/
- Dr. Cormac Herley on Twitter: https://twitter.com/cormacherley
- Dr. Cormac Herley's Microsoft profile: https://www.microsoft.com/en-us/research/people/cormac/
- Dr. Cormac Herley's Google Scholar citations: https://scholar.google.com/citations?user=1FwhEVYAAAAJ&hl=en&oi=ao

23 Wireless Hacking

Today's computing world works on wireless networking. It's a rarity that anyone plugs in a network cable to their desktop or laptop computer, and no one does that for their cell phones and other computing devices, even though the wired world is faster and more secure. It is a wireless world—a world that hackers are constantly attacking.

The Wireless World

The wireless world is big and broad. The wireless networking that we have on our home network access points is the 802.11 Wi-Fi standard, but the term "wireless" encompasses a huge swath of the electromagnetic spectrum, which includes X-rays, light, radio, and other forms of wireless energy. The identification and allocation of a portion of the wireless spectrum is determined by the number of waves per second (i.e. frequency) and distance of the wavelength. 802.11 is the wireless networking standard among the 900 MHz and 2.4, 3.6, 5.0, 5.8, and 60 GHz frequencies. The computers in our lives use many different wireless technologies, including magnetism, light, satellite, terrestrial radio, Bluetooth, Near Field Communications (NFC), RFID, and microwave. Much of the wireless spectrum is controlled by laws and regulatory bodies, which is good because without them much of the spectrum would be unusable and unsafe.

Types of Wireless Hacking

Each part of the wireless spectrum and the various communication standards for it determine the types of hacking that are likely to be performed on them, although the sheer number of attacks on the Wi-Fi spectrum is a good representation of what can happen in them all. In general, most wireless hacking is done to either conduct eavesdropping, capture information, unauthorizedly share the wireless communication's broadcast spectrum, cause denial of service, control the service, or attack attached clients.

Attacking the Access Point

Every wireless technology has one or more access points (APs) to allow transmitting and/or receiving, and these are often connected to terrestrial or other types of communication systems. Hackers can directly attack the AP to compromise the wireless communications. They can crack the AP's admin password, change its operations, conduct eavesdropping, or trick the victim into connecting to a rogue AP.

Denial of Service

The simplest form of wireless hacking is crudely interrupting or overpowering the legitimate communication's signal, otherwise known as "jamming" or "flooding." If I can stop you from communicating over your intended wireless channel and deny you service, it becomes useless. Or a hacker can even take over the channel. If flooding is done correctly, the AP may accidentally reconnect to another, illegitimate resource.

Guessing a Wireless Channel Password

Some wireless technologies require a password (or other authentication proofs) for a client to join the wireless spectrum provided by the participating AP. Rarely do APs lock out devices after a set number of incorrect guesses. So wirelessly cracking devices can guess away until they uncover the correct password.

Session Hijacking

Many attack types have the ultimate goal of taking over the victim's legitimate communication session. This is often done by flooding the wireless network, causing a disruption, and then either tricking the client into allowing the hacker's client to take over, modifying the session in an unauthorized way, or tricking the client into connecting to a rogue AP. These types of attacks have become very popular, especially by hackers trying to steal HTML web site "cookies" over shared wireless networks found in public locations (such as coffee shops, airports, and so on).

Stealing Information

Stealing information is more of an outcome of wireless hacking, but I'm treating it here as its own hacking method because oftentimes the entire hacking session is done to steal information. Such is the case with RFID hacking. Millions of credit cards are RFID-enabled to allow the holder to make purchase transactions without having to insert the card physically into a credit card device. Hackers with RFID scanners can obtain credit card information by simply using a device to surreptitiously energize the RFID transmitter. RFID is also being used on other devices and documents, like cell phones and passports.

NOTE Electromagnet eavesdropping has been used against devices that do not intentionally communicate wirelessly. All electronic devices emit an electromagnetic field, which can be read, sometimes from far away, with the right sensitive listening device.

Physically Locating a User

Many hackers, often law enforcement types, use the traits and weaknesses of a particular wireless technology to locate participating clients and their devices. Law enforcement is particularly fond of using "stingray" devices, which create fake APs, to physically locate intended targets by their cell phone location. Read https://en.wikipedia.org/wiki/Stingray_phone_tracker to learn more about these fascinating devices and their questionable legality.

Some Wireless Hacking Tools

There are dozens, if not hundreds, of hacking tools that can be used to perform wireless hacking. Any general-purpose protocol capturing program, like Wireshark (http://www.wireshark.com/) or Ethereal (https://sourceforge .net/projects/ethereal/), can be used, but most wireless hackers use a program specialized in it. These tools are great ways to learn about wireless technologies and hacking.

Aircrack-Ng

The most popular 802.11 wireless cracking tool is Aircrack-ng. Released in 2005 as an open-source wireless auditing tool, this frequently updated tool has become both an attacker and defender tool of choice. It's creator, Thomas d'Otreppe de Bouvette, is profiled in the next chapter.

Kismet

Kismet (`https://www.kismetwireless.net/`) has become another of the go-to 802.11 hacking tools. It can help someone break into a wireless network or alert you if someone else is trying to do the same to you.

Fern Wi-Fi Hacker

Fern Wi-Fi Hacker (`https://github.com/savio-code/fern-wifi-cracker`) helps hackers with many of the hacking methods I mention above.

Firesheep

Walk into a coffee shop and fire up Firesheep (`http://codebutler.com/firesheep`). It will look for and steal any HTML cookies it can find on the shared wireless media. Stealing HTML cookies was possible way before Firesheep came into being, but Firesheep made it as easy as starting a browser. Firesheep was the tool that started many places seriously thinking about wireless (and web site) security.

Wireless Hacking Defenses

There are as many defenses as there are attacks.

Frequency Hopping

One of the biggest early problems with any wireless technology is that anyone could jam it. Famous Hollywood actress Hedy Lamarr (and her composer partner, George Antheil) created and patented the "frequency hopping spread spectrum" wireless technology during World War II. Frequency hopping works as a defense because the legitimate signal is sent over different frequencies (very quickly) that only the sender and receiver have agreed upon (or computed) ahead of time. Anyone wishing to disrupt the signal would need to jam a wide set of the spectrum. Without this defense, most of what we use as wireless today would not be possible. Read about Lamarr's discovery today. My favorite book dedicated to the subject is *Hedy's Folly* by Richard Rhodes.

Predefined Client Identification

Many wireless technologies have defenses that only allow predefined clients to connect. In the 802.11 spectrum, many APs allow only devices with predefined MAC addresses to connect. An AP can also only accept digital certificates from predefined, trusted, digital-certificate certification authorities or look at the device's unique hardware address. Any identification parameter can be used.

Strong Protocols

No defense beats a strong protocol. 802.11 started off with Wired Equivalent Privacy (WEP), which was later found to be very vulnerable, irreparably so. It was replaced with Wi-Fi Protected Access (WPA), which has proven to be remarkably resistant to attack ever since. WPA can be used with passwords, digital certificates, or other enterprise authentication methods. There have been a few successful attacks against various versions of WPA, but far fewer than most experts would have predicted, and most can be remediated by moving to a different WPA method.

Long Passwords

If the wireless AP requires a password to join, make sure that the password is very long (30 characters or longer). The same thing applies to making sure the AP's admin password has been changed from the default and is long and complex, as well.

Patching Access Points

Access points often have vulnerabilities, so applying the vendor's patches in a timely manner is a must.

Electromagnetic Shielding

For remote wireless attacks, like those against RFID-enabled credit cards, putting anti-electromagnetic shielding around the physical transmitter (or the whole device) can prevent eavesdropping. EM shielding is also known as EMI shielding, RF shielding, or Faraday cages. Some electronic devices, such as some cell phones, contain shielding, but most people concerned about EM eavesdropping buy third-party shielding cases. Shielded cable, like that used in normal cable television cabling, is also shielded by default to prevent unintentional signal interruption.

There are far too many ways to commit wireless hacking and ways to defend against those hacking methods than can fit in a short chapter, although I've hopefully summarized some of the major ways.

Chapter 24 profiles Thomas d'Otreppe de Bouvette, the creator of the Wi-Fi security-auditing suite Aircrack-ng.

24 Profile: Thomas d'Otreppe de Bouvette

The previous chapter covered wireless hacking, and no one in the wireless hacking computing community is more respected than Belgium-born Thomas d'Otreppe de Bouvette, the creator of Aircrack-ng (http://aircrack-ng.org/). Composed of 16 different programs, Aircrack-ng is the most popular, free, Wi-Fi security-auditing tool suite. D'Otreppe de Bouvette first released Aircrack-ng in February 2006. Today, every Linux hacking distro includes it by default, and if you want to do wireless hacking or auditing, you probably either use Aircrack-ng or used it before you paid for some commercial product that does similar things. Aircrack-ng is so popular that it shows up in TV shows and movies (http://aircrack-ng.org/movies.html) that are trying to realistically portray their actor as an uber-cool wireless hacker. D'Otreppe de Bouvette has also created and released a wireless intrusion detection program called OpenWIPS-ng (http://www.openwips-ng.org/).

I asked d'Otreppe de Bouvette how he got into computer security. He replied, "I got into computers and programming very early, between six and eight years old. I was immediately interested in programming, and I created a tiny game even back then. As any kid, I first played the games on a computer and then got bored with them. That's when I decided to look through the books that came with the computer and found out I could program it. My native language being French and manuals being in English, it was not easy to figure out how to get into the "programming" mode that offered some kind of BASIC language. On top of that, you couldn't save your code, so I was forced to write it down on paper. To this day, I still remember what the game is and how to beat it.

"I then got into computer security through the program Aircrack, which was originally created by Christophe Devine. I was contributing to it, very small patches to fix issues here and there, and talking to the developer, when all of a sudden in December 2005 he stopped being involved in the project. He was the only one developing it, and back then, it was only seen/perceived as a tool to crack your neighbor's WEP key. All of a sudden he disappeared from IRC and never connected back. Then rumors of what happened to him started to spread in the IRC channel, I guess spread by friends of his . . . enough for me to start downloading all the resources, releases, and other stuff before the server was shut down completely a few days later. There were a lot of rumors at the time about what happened to him, but later I met him a few times and learned that he was just too busy with his real job, and it was either spend time developing Aircrack for free or keep his job. But at the time we didn't know what happened.

"After three months of waiting, I decided to start making my own version. That was in December 2005. I've never made a profit off of it, but I love the project and the people I've met and the travel. And even though I've never made a profit for Aircrack-ng, I got a job because of it. I've always liked the challenge of hacking my own network. And I'm starting my own business now. My parents were even against me doing Aircrack, telling me I would get in trouble (as I was starting), and I'm actually glad I didn't listen to them since that's one of the best things that's happened to me: I had the chance to meet a lot of awesome people, and most of my friends now are people I've met directly or indirectly thanks to the project."

I asked d'Otreppe de Bouvette if he thinks wireless security has improved over the years. He said, "Yes, definitely. When I first started out, most of wireless hacking was cracking weak WEP keys. Now WEP is discouraged or isn't even a choice. Now wireless security uses WPA and WPA2 and the encryption is pretty strong. Now to break into a wireless network, you have to find a flaw, either in the embedded wireless chip (see https://www.youtube.com/ watch?v=4WEQpiyfb50 to see an example of what I'm talking about) or the human flaw. You can have the best encryption in the world, but if the vendor or the owner only uses an eight-character Wi-Fi password, then we'll be able to break it.

"Here's another example: At the last apartment I rented, they used the MAC address of the access point as a key and told me I just need to flip [the AP over] to know the key. Well, this can be found easily if you have a network card capable of monitor mode, and I could most likely decrypt the other tenants' traffic if I wanted to try. To top it off, they wouldn't allow us to change it.

"The thing is that some vendors sell devices with a pre-generated passphrase, which is usually some kind of hash based on the MAC address mixed in various ways. Here is an example to illustrate it: A cable modem from [a popular vendor] came with WPA (or WPA2) with the passphrase set to [the vendor's four-character name] followed by the last four hexadecimal values of the MAC address. Which means, you only have to go through 10,000 combinations to find the right key if you don't know what you're doing (which is gonna take a minute or two at [longest])."

I asked what the biggest problem in computer security is. He said, "There are a lot of big problems in computer security, but the common denominators of all of those problems are the users themselves. They want convenience and security (as in privacy, data encryption). However, security and convenience are pretty much enemies. You can't have both at the same time. The more convenience, the less security you have. And obviously, more security will be a lot less convenient."

For More Information on Thomas d'Otreppe de Bouvette

For information about Thomas d'Otreppe de Bouvette, check out these resources:

- Video of Thomas d'Otreppe de Bouvette's and Rick Farina's DEF CON presentation on wireless hacking: `https://www.youtube.com/watch?v=XqPPqqV_884`
- PDF of Thomas d'Otreppe de Bouvette's and Rick Farina's slideshow from their DEF CON presentation on wireless hacking: `https://def-con.org/images/defcon-16/dc16-presentations/defcon-16-de_bouvette-farina.pdf`

25 Penetration Testing

This chapter covers the requirements that make a hacker a legal, professional penetration tester, plus other hints that can help any pen tester's career. In addition, I cover the most sought-after certifications.

My Penetration Testing Highlights

There is no doubt that penetration testing was one of the more enjoyable periods of my career. Hacking is fun. It's hard to pick the best projects I participated in, but the following sections examine some of the most memorable ones.

Hacked Every Cable Box in the Country

We had been hired to see if we could break into a new cable box that the largest cable company in the world was planning to release. I used a port scanner to enumerate all the network ports, which found about a dozen open ports. I then used Nikto, a web server scanner tool, to scan all the ports hoping that one of the ports might have a web interface. One did. Nikto identified one of the ports as an obscure web server software program that I never heard of and said it had a particular vulnerability. But when I tried to exploit the vulnerability, it was not exploitable. But I knew the web server software was old, which meant it was likely full of old bugs that newer web servers had long ago patched. The first thing I tried was something known as a directory traversal attack (essentially I typed in http://..//..//..//), and it worked. I was now the admin and had complete control of the cable box.

We reported the vulnerability to the customer, and the next day every senior executive in the company was flying in for a presentation I had to give. It turns out that this particular vulnerability was present on every cable box, millions of them, that the company had in the country, and they were all connected to the Internet.

Simultaneously Hacked a Major Television Network and Pornography

For the same company as in the previous cable box story, we were hired to see if we could steal pornography, which was one of the cable company's top revenue generators, and also to see if we could steal major feature movies for the same reason. We were stuck in one of the company's computer rooms with two cable boxes and two televisions that were running 24×7, one showing pornography and the other showing major feature movies. As you might imagine, watching pornography for days upon end quickly became monotonous. But that didn't stop dozens of people from stopping by to "check up" on us each day. For the record, we were able to steal both pornography and major feature movies and prove that we could steal customers' credit card numbers.

We even used a cross-site scripting exploit to take over the entire cable company—from a single cable box. We had found that the cable box was running a web server and contained firewall logs. The firewall logs contained a cross-site scripting error. We "attacked" the cable box in such a way that we knew that we were injecting additional hacking attacks (in this case, one that would retrieve admin passwords). Then we called the cable company and asked one of the techs to check our firewall logs because we were wondering if we were under a "hacker attack." When the company's help desk technician checked out the cable box log, the technician's admin password popped up on our screens. It turns out that admin password was the same admin password used across the entire enterprise.

Hacked a Major Credit Card Company

As part of a certification test, my company was hired to see how much we could hack a "test" web site. There was a contest to see how much we could hack the web site—how many vulnerabilities we could find and take advantage of. We were competing against dozens of other companies, and whoever found the most vulnerabilities would win the contest, get the certification, and get hired to "certify" potentially tens of thousands of other web sites. One of the members on my team was able to not only thoroughly hack the web site, but our team ended up being able to completely own the customer's production environment. We won the contest.

Created a Camera Virus

One day an idea came to mind about how I could get my "malware" code to automatically execute from a digital camera media card. I tried out my trick and it worked. I showed a co-worker, and he realized that it would work from any removable media card. We tested my code some more and it worked. It worked across digital cameras, music players, and cell phones. My employer at the time, a penetration testing company, was delighted. We decided that I would present my findings at an upcoming Blackhat conference. I also reported my findings to the involved vendor. They verified the issue and asked if they could have several months to create a patch to fix the problem.

It was a dilemma. If I waited, the content would not be as exciting at Blackhat. It would be old, patched news. If I didn't wait, I left the vendor and their customers exposed until the vendor could hurriedly create a fix. I remember being very torn between both outcomes. Ultimately, I decided I was a good-guy hacker and my primary concern was more about making sure the computing world was safer and less about my own ego and fame. I gave the vendor more time. A few months later, another event publicly exposed the same vulnerability, but the vendor was ready for it by then and released an immediate patch. My contribution to its discovery got buried in the news, but my "camera virus" never did become a huge threat, which means we all won.

How to Be a Pen Tester

Penetration testing (pen testing) is all the legal hacking and fun you could ever want. It requires more than just the ability to hack into computers and devices, although that is a given starting point.

Hacker Methodology

In order to be a successful pen tester you'll need to follow the same Hacking Methodology steps that were covered in Chapter 2:

1. Information Gathering
2. Penetration
3. Optional: Guarantee Future Easier Access
4. Internal Reconnaissance
5. Optional: Horizontal or Vertical Movement

6. Intended Action Execution
7. Optional: Covering Tracks

I won't cover the steps again in this chapter, but suffice to say that pen testers are hackers, and they will usually follow the same steps. But being a legal pen tester requires more than testing.

Get Documented Permission First

The single most important thing that separates an illegal hacker from a legal pen tester is having permission to attack/test the assets you are investigating. You must have prior, documented, signed permission from the company or person who owns the assets or has the legal authority from the owner.

Looking for and finding a vulnerability in someone's web site and then asking them for a job is not ethical. Many new pen testers looking for their first professional job try this tactic. They often think they are being helpful and that maybe the company they are contacting will find their discovery to be incredibly helpful and offer them a job. Instead, they are usually seen as unethical, threatening, and possibly illegal, regardless of their true, original intent. If you truly accidentally come across a vulnerability while surfing the web or messing with a device, confidentially report it to the owner/vendor, and follow up with the owner if they have questions. You may even get work out of it, but don't directly request a job or money.

Get a Signed Contract

Penetration testers always get a signed contract. The contract should include the names of the contracting parties, the scope of the engagement (which targets, dates of the project, what will be done, and so on), a non-disclosure agreement (NDA) to protect both parties, what tools and techniques will be used, and an indemnity disclaimer warning of possible operational interruption despite better efforts otherwise. If you don't have any contract templates to use, contact a lawyer and/or look around on the Internet for pen testing contract examples.

Reporting

The height of professionalism is a well-written, detailed report. It should include a short executive summary at the beginning followed by more detailed descriptions of the project, scope, what was done, and the findings. Include the detailed findings as separate attachments. Many consultants think the longer the report, the better. Personally, I think shorter reports with sufficient detail to back up the findings are read and appreciated by customers. But always have the more extensive details ready to deliver and talk about.

Certifications

Get certified. Certifications don't mean that you are smarter or dumber than someone else who doesn't have certifications, but they can absolutely get you the job over someone else who doesn't have them. Certifications are easy-to-see statements of someone's bare minimum knowledge and expertise. The following sections discuss certifications that I'm familiar with and recommend.

CISSP

There is no doubt that the International Information Systems Security Certifications Consortium's (ISC)² (https://www.isc2.org/) Certified Information Systems Security Professional (CISSP) certification (https://www.isc2.org/cissp/default.aspx) is the most coveted and accepted computer security certification of them all. It's a general computer security knowledge exam that covers eight different "Common Body of Knowledge (CBK) domains." The certification test consists of 250 multiple-choice test questions that must be answered in under six hours. Candidates must already have four to five years of professional experience in two or more of the CBK domains, and they must be endorsed by another previous CISSP holder. The initial exam cost is $599.

SANS Institute

I'm a huge, huge fan of anything the SysAdmin, Networking, and Security (SANS) Institute (http://www.sans.org) does, whether it be training, research, education, books, or certifications. I profile the co-founder, Stephen Northcutt, in Chapter 42. If you're interested in being a respected technical expert, this is your cert. They even offer two master-level accredited degrees, under the brand of the SANS Technology Institute. SANS has a host of certifications, ranging from very niche-specific security topics (such as malware analyzing, firewalls, host security, and security controls) to their hugely respected Global Information Assurance Certification (GIAC) Security Expert (http://www.giac.org/certifications/get-certified/roadmap) designation. GIAC certifications are classified in the following subject areas:

- Cyber Defense & ICS
- Penetration Testing
- Digital Forensics & Incident Response
- Developer
- Management & Leadership
- Security Expert

Some of the their most popular GIAC exams are GIAC Information Security Professional (http://www.giac.org/certification/gisp), **GIAC Certified Incident Handler** (http://www.giac.org/certification/gcih), and GIAC Reverse Engineering Malware (http://www.giac.org/certification/grem), but their courses cross the gamut, including ones for Windows, web servers, penetration testing, Unix security, wireless networking, programming, leadership, and program management. GIAC testing is meant to be taken after attending SANS training, which usually last a week. If a GIAC test is taken in conjunction with the official training, then the GIAC test is $659. But you can challenge (not take the official training) any test for $1149.

If you are interested in Unix and Linux certification, SANS also offers a GIAC Certified Unix Security Administrator (GCUX) certification (http://www.giac.org/certification/certified-unix-security-administrator-gcux).

Certified Ethical Hacker (CEH)

The EC-Council's Certified Ethical Hacker (CEH) (https://www.eccouncil.org/programs/certified-ethical-hacker-ceh/) certification is well-respected and essentially teaches you how to be a whitehat hacker (or professional penetration tester). CEH introduced me to some interesting hacking tools that I still use to this day. The exam is a maximum of four hours for 125 multiple-choice questions. The Application Eligibility fee is $100.

EC-Council has a bunch of other useful exams, including Computer Hacking Forensic Investigator (https://cert.eccouncil.org/computer-hacking-forensic-investigator.html), Licensed Penetration Tester (https://cert.eccouncil.org/licensed-penetration-tester.html), Certified Incident Handler (https://cert.eccouncil.org/ec-council-certified-incident-handler.html), and Certified Disaster Recovery Professional (https://cert

`.eccouncil.org/ec-council-disaster-recovery-professional.html`). They even have an exam for a Chief Information Security Officer (`https://cert.eccouncil.org/certified-chief-information-security-officer.html`).

CompTIA Security+

The Computing Technology Industry Association (CompTIA) (`https://certification.comptia.org/`) offers entry-level, but comprehensive exams in IT infrastructure support (A+) (`https://certification.comptia.org/certifications/a`), Networking (Network+) (`https://certification.comptia.org/certifications/network`), and Security (Security+) (`https://certification.comptia.org/certifications/security`). Because a CompTIA exam is often the first exam many people new to the computer industry take, it unfortunately got the reputation for being too basic of a certification and easy. This is not true. The exams are very comprehensive and you must study hard to be assured of passing. CompTIA Security+ certification covers network security, cryptography, identity management, compliance, operation security, threats, and host security, among other topics. You get 90 minutes to take a maximum of 90 questions, and the price is $311.

ISACA

Information Systems Audit and Control Association (ISACA) (`https://www.isaca.org`) offers a range of professional-respected exams on auditing, management, and compliance. Certifications include Certified Information Systems Auditor (CISA) (`http://www.isaca.org/Certification/CISA-Certified-Information-Systems-Auditor/Pages/default.aspx`), Certified Information Security Manager (CISM) (`http://www.isaca.org/Certification/CISM-Certified-Information-Security-Manager/Pages/default.aspx`), Certified in the Governance of Enterprise IT (CGEIT) (`http://www.isaca.org/Certification/CGEIT-Certified-in-the-Governance-of-Enterprise-IT/Pages/default.aspx`), and Certified in Risk and Information Systems Control (CRISC) (`http://www.isaca.org/Certification/CRISC-Certified-in-Risk-and-Information-Systems-Control/Pages/default.aspx`). If you're an accountant or auditor, these exams can attest to your skills as they relate to computers and computer security.

Vendor-Specific Certifications

Many vendors, like Microsoft, Cisco, and RedHat, offer computer security-specific exams.

Years ago, Microsoft had several security-specific specialist exams, like MCSE: Security. But as security became a general concern for all platforms and technologies, Microsoft started to bake all the security questions and testing into all their exams. That trend is being somewhat reversed by the announcement by Microsoft of their new (in development) Securing Windows Server 2016 exam (https://www.microsoft.com/en-us/learning/exam-70-744.aspx). The exam goes far beyond just technically securing Windows Server 2016. It covers red/green forest design, Just-in-Time Administration, Just-Enough Administration, and Microsoft's latest security technologies like Advanced Threat Analytics (ATA). Microsoft security techs may want to take Microsoft's Security Fundamentals test first (https://www.microsoft.com/en-us/learning/exam-98-367.aspx) for $127.

Cisco's certification exams have always had the reputation for industry respect and toughness to pass. Cisco's Cisco Certified Internetwork Expert (CCIE) certification (http://www.cisco.com/c/en/us/training-events/training-certifications/certifications/expert/ccie-program.html) is known as the hardest to pass in the industry. According to Cisco, fewer than 3% of Cisco exam students will ever obtain it, even after paying thousands of dollars, creating home labs, and spending an average of 18 months studying for it. Cisco's Certified Network Associate (CCNA) Security certification (http://www.cisco.com/c/en/us/training-events/training-certifications/certifications/associate/ccna-security.html) is easier to obtain and still very well respected. You must first hold any other valid Cisco certification to take the CCNA Security. After you have your CCNA Security (or any passed CCIE certification), you can take the Cisco Certified Network Professional (CCNP) Security exam (http://www.cisco.com/c/en/us/training-events/training-certifications/certifications/professional/ccnp-security.html). But the CCIE Security exam (http://www.cisco.com/c/en/us/training-events/training-certifications/certifications/expert/ccie-security.html) is the mack daddy Cisco security exam. It consists of both a two-hour written exam (which must be passed first) and then an eight-hour lab portion. All Cisco certification exams are hard, but if you get your CCIE Security certification, you'll be able to earn a very good living almost anywhere in the world.

Red Hat has dozens of certification exams (https://www.redhat.com/en/services/all-certifications-exams), and like other major vendors, it offers at least one security specialty exam. RedHat's security exam is called Red Hat Certificate of Expertise in Server Hardening (https://www.redhat.com/en/services/certification/rhcoe-server-hardening). Besides normal Linux server hardening information, successful candidates have to be prepared to handle Common Vulnerabilities and Exposure (CVE) and Red Hat Security Advisory (RHSA) reports. The price is $600.

The Linux Professional Institute (LPI) (https://www.lpi.org/) offers a vendor-neutral Linux security exam (https://www.lpi.org/study-resources /lpic-3-303-exam-objectives/). The LPIC-3 Exam 303 security exam covers a host of security topics, and candidates must have successfully passed four prior lower-level LPI exams. LPI Level 3 exams, which LPIC-3 303 is, cost $188 to take.

As mentioned earlier in this chapter, SANS also offers a GIAC Certified Unix Security Administrator (GCUX) certification (http://www.giac.org /certification/certified-unix-security-administrator-gcux).

Apple doesn't appear to a have a security-specific exam, but the normal OS exams, such as Apple El Capitan (http://training.apple.com/pdf /elcapitan101.pdf) and Mac Integration Basics (http://training.apple.com /pdf/mac_integration_basics_1010.pdf), have some security components.

Every certification I've studied for and taken has improved my skills. Getting certified can only help your knowledge, career, and ability to get work.

Be Ethical

Be ethical and professional. Never conduct unauthorized actions or seek to improve your own position over the commitment and needs of the customer. If you're wondering if something is ethical, it probably isn't. Chapter 50 covers the Hacker Code of Ethics.

Minimize Potential Operational Interruption

Try your best to never cause a customer operational interruption. Many penetration testing tools have "safety modes" that remove the higher risk tests. Always start out by thoroughly testing your tools and methodologies before initiating them more widely. I've only caused widespread operational interruption once, and it still haunts me. It occurred because I did not do enough appropriate testing before the wide-scale deployment.

If you follow all the steps provided in this chapter, you should be a successful penetration tester routinely invited back for more projects.

Chapter 26 covers Aaron Higbee, one of the best penetration testers I've ever known, and Chapter 27 profiles Benild Joseph, a penetration testing specialist, cyber security expert, and renowned ethical hacker.

26 Profile: Aaron Higbee

Riding in Aaron Higbee's car is an experience only familiar to car tech geeks and ingrained engineers. He has enough externally connected computer equipment and gauges hooked to his car's CPU brain and engine to easily qualify it as a car in a *Back to the Future* prequel. Those of us who have known him for a few years are not surprised. Higbee rarely does anything halfway. He's either all in and fully enmeshed or not interested. It's obvious that the "play hard or go home" motto plays a big part in his life.

I first worked with Higbee on a penetration engagement where we were on a team hired to break into one of the world's largest cable television providers. I covered this particular engagement in the last chapter on penetration testing, but I left out one part of the story. We had successfully compromised not only the cable television company's intended target, the set-top cable box, but the entire cable company. And that was just day one! Higbee was bored with nothing really left to explore on our week-long contact, so he began to hack the hardware we had been given by the vendor. He started manipulating the customer's onsite controlling hardware, switching wires, manipulating motherboard jumpers, and installing cross-over electrical cables. He kept trying different configuration hacks, and at one point he literally set the unit on fire. Smoke poured out of the unit as we all hurried to unplug the electricity and stop the small fire. We had to wait a few minutes as the smoke cleared to see whether the computer room's fire detectors would release toxic halon gas and force us to evacuate.

After the smoke cleared and we all shared a collective chuckle of relief, I was surprised to see Higbee go back and continue his hardware hack. None of the cajoling from the rest of the team could get him to stop. Eventually, he accidentally created a bigger fire within the hardware unit, one we could not put out as easily. The whole time that we were running away to escape the now-guaranteed fire suppressant release, he was chuckling and, unbeknownst to me, filming everything with his cell phone. Within a few minutes, his film was up on the Internet. This story is definitely not included as something that should be duplicated by other penetration teams. It wasn't smart to do anything that had even the remotest possibility of causing a fire. But this anecdote does give you a sense of what it was like to work with Higbee. Most of his friends and co-workers have similar stories.

Along with being a fun guy to hang out with, Higbee is one of the best, most dedicated penetration testers you'll ever meet. He had grown up in a fairly religious household with strict rules. I think that sort of strict upbringing led to his passion for life and ability to make everyone want to laugh, including himself. Today, he is a lot more professional, but he still brings his same youthful exuberance and experience to fighting hackers and spammers.

Later we both left that company. I went to work for Microsoft, and Higbee co-founded his own incredibly successful company called PhishMe (https:// phishme.com/). PhishMe focuses on security awareness training for end-users against phishing attacks. Specifically, PhishMe makes it easy to send "fake" but realistic phishing attacks against your employees to see which ones can successfully be tricked out of sensitive information. There were previous ways to do this before PhishMe, but PhishMe is one of the companies that made it incredibly easy to do. It has expanded over the years, now with 350 employees and $12M in revenue and growing. Although I'm doing well financially, let's just say that Higbee is doing better.

I asked him how he got into computer security. He replied, "I got into computers in the BBS [bulletin board system] era, and some of the BBSs I wanted to call were long-distance calls, which were expensive then. So I started to learn about phone phreaking to make free long-distance phone calls and through that started to learn about hacking. I got my first computer security job at EarthLink . . . I was literally the abuse@earthlink.net email address guy. Whatever came into that email address is what I handled. I was fighting spam, credit card fraud, legal compliance, etc., whatever came into it. I liked it so much I quit college. My parents told me I was making a big mistake. They thought the Internet was a passing fad like CB [citizens' band] radio."

I applauded Higbee and PhishMe's core focus on anti-phishing. Many of his competitors have spread out into doing much more, but PhishMe has stayed focused. And that singular focus seems to be paying huge dividends for PhishMe and its customers. He stated, "Some people don't understand what PhishMe does. They think it's a waste of time and that instead of trying to help people deal with email and the phishing problem as it is today, we should be trying to fix email itself . . . that we should try to make computing perfectly safe for people by default.

"That's a great idea. But it's also pie-in-the-sky. I mean I saw my first phishing email in 1997 at EarthLink. If you would have told me that it would still be a problem . . . the huge problem that it is today . . . and that I would have still been making a living fighting it, I would have never believed you. The overall problem is that the email protocol is broken and it doesn't look like it's going to be fixed any time soon. Ten years from now it will still be broken. Many people have tried to bolt things onto it over the years to make it better, but none of the additions have really ever taken hold. And I don't understand it because we have fixed other protocols and gotten rid of a few, like Telnet. No one uses Telnet anymore. We use SSH instead. But for some reason the broken email protocol continues to live on despite all of its huge problems, and if it does, I want to help companies be safer with it."

I shared that I'm surprised more companies don't do more anti-phishing testing and training because it's probably the number one or number two best thing they can do to diminish computer security risk. He said, "Part of the problem is some of the people conducting phishing tests go in guns ablazing and end up causing political issues. That's a big part of what we do. We don't just do a surprise PhishMe test. We tell them to communicate with all employees and management and let them know that we're going to be conducting phishing tests over the next year. Less surprises and more about education. Part of what we do is coach customers how to solve the political problems so that everyone wins."

Probably the best part of my interview with Higbee is that he seems just as joyful and happy as he did when I worked with him over 10 years ago. He said creating and running a business has been incredibly stressful, but it has also been fulfilling and he still has fun. Apparently, so too do his employees. PhishMe was just voted one of the best places to work by the *Washington Business Journal*, and they just had their annual meeting in Cancun.

Man, why couldn't I have thought of an anti-phishing company 10 years ago?

For More Information on Aaron Higbee

For information about Aaron Higbee, check out these resources:

- Aaron Higbee on Twitter: https://twitter.com/higbee
- Aaron Higbee LinkedIn profile: https://www.linkedin.com/in/aaron-higbee-6098781
- Aaron Higbee's PhishMe blog: https://phishme.com/author/aaronh/

27 Profile: Benild Joseph

At 25 years old, Benild Joseph, from the Bangalore region of India, is one of the youngest people profiled in this book. But in his short career of only 8 years (as of our interview), he has built quite a track record for himself, and he diligently works to improve the computer security of his home country and region. He specializes in web application security and has discovered critical vulnerabilities in many popular web sites including Facebook, AT&T, Sony Music, BlackBerry, and Deutsche Telekom. Suffice it to say that he has distinguished himself. At present, he is the Chief Executive Officer for "Th3 art of h@ckin9," part of the International IT Security Project (an initiative with support of the government of India) as well as acting as a board member of the Information Systems Security Association (ISSA) of India. He is listed as a "Top 10 Ethical Hackers in India" by Microsoft Social Forum and was named as one of "India's 8 Most Famous Ethical Hackers" by *Silicon India* magazine. He frequently writes and teaches.

India is a wonderful emerging country with many bright people, but at the same time it has only over the past ten or so years come strongly into the Internet age. Much of its population is very poor. With this in mind, I asked Joseph how he got into computer security. He said, "I was always interested in hacking, and initially I wasn't interested in computer security at all. It wasn't something really known or talked about in India at the time. I was just mostly interested in hacking my friend's email ID. I decided to think about taking an ethical hacking class to learn more about hacking. I remember even telling the instructor that I wasn't there to learn about ethical hacking or computer security, but just to hack my friend's email. I was pretty sure that getting the certification was just a big waste of my time. But he saw something in me and taught me the first things I knew about ethical hacking and computer security.

He became my mentor. Even as I learned more and more about ethical hacking, he told me I had a long way to go to be a security pro. He challenged me and I kept learning."

He now frequently works on behalf of cybercrime agencies and the Indian government, including projects for the Cyber Crime Investigation Bureau (CCIB), International Cyber Threat Task Force (ICTTF) and Cyber Security Forum Initiative (CSFI). He is the co-author of *CCI*, a book written for law enforcement agencies in India. He specializes in Web Application Penetration testing and Digital Forensic Investigation. Not bad for a guy who just wanted to hack his friend's email. He continued, "Now I've worked for many companies and projects. My roles keep changing. I'm currently working for the Indian government on a cybersurveillance project trying to stop cybercriminals. I also spend a lot of time thinking about cyberwarfare, which is happening a lot against India. Not only against the government and businesses, but also its citizens."

I asked him what the biggest problem his country faced in computer security was. He answered, "India is in the top ten of IT but not in computer security. Ten years ago, you didn't even hear about it. It wasn't taught. There were no jobs being advertised for computer security professionals. My country wasn't doing economically well for a long time. In the beginning if someone needed to use a computer, they had to go to an Internet shop to use one. Now they may have one at home or in their hand as a mobile phone. So, computers and computer security problems are new. We have lots of doctors, lawyers, engineers, and lots of other professionals, but not a lot of computer security people. That's changing. The government and businesses realized we needed better computer security and computer security professionals. Today, many universities are offering master's programs in computer security. The government realizes how important it is and is starting many programs. I spend a lot of my time traveling around India and other parts of the world teaching computer security. India is a different place now, and I'm helping to improve it."

We can only hope that India and all the other countries of the world have plenty of Benild Josephs.

For More Information on Benild Joseph

For information about Benild Joseph, check out these resources:

- Benild Joseph's LinkedIn profile: `https://www.linkedin.com/in/benild`
- Benild Joseph's Google+ site: `https://plus.google.com/107600097183424443393`
- Benild Joseph YouTube video about Kaizen and Hacker5 projects: `http://www.youtube.com/watch?v=BH_BNXfjOpQ`

28 DDoS Attacks

Y ou can think you have the best computer security only to have your false sense of security taken away by matters beyond your control. Welcome to distributed denial of service (DDoS) attacks. What originally started as a single hacker overwhelming a server by sending way more traffic than it could handle has turned into an escalating war of multiple layers and dependencies, sent by groups and professional-looking service providers. Today's massive DDoS attacks often involve Internet-connected home devices and send hundreds and hundreds of gigabits of malicious traffic per second. DDoS attacks are committed for many reasons, including revenge, exhortation, embarrassment, political purposes, and even gaming advantages.

Types of DDoS Attacks

There are many types of denial of service attacks. The following sections will explore some of the more prominent ones.

Denial of Service

A denial of service (DoS) attack is when a single host attempts to flood a victim with overwhelming traffic to prevent or decrease wanted, legitimate transactions. The simplest and earliest of these were "ping floods," where as many ICMP Echo (ping) packets were sent to a host as possible. These were replaced by TCP packet floods, which because of the resulting three-packet handshake could generate more traffic. TCP floods were replaced by UDP floods because the source IP address's connectionless state allows it to be spoofed, making UDP floods harder to trace and stop.

These simple types of attacks have given way to massive DDoS attacks where multiple hosts (sometimes hundreds of thousands) are focused on a single target. A DoS attack may be able to cause tens of megabits per second of malicious traffic, whereas even the lowest DDoS attack starts in the hundreds of megabits per second. DDoS attacks don't even make the news unless they are above 600 gigabits of attack traffic per second. Each year a new record is made. The first terabit (1000 gigabits) attack may be confirmed by the time this book is published or soon after.

Direct Attacks

A direct DOS attack is one in which all the maliciously created traffic is being generated by the single host sending it. The attacker may (randomly) change the originating IP address in an attempt to hide, but in direct attacks, there is only one sender crafting the traffic that then heads directly to the target without any intermediate hosts used. Direct attacks are not very common anymore because they are easy to detect, attribute, and mitigate.

Reflection Attacks

Reflection attacks are when the attack uses one or more intermediate hosts to generate DDoS attacks. Most of the time there are DDoS "bot" malware programs waiting for commands to be instructed to attack a particular host. Typically, hundreds to tens of thousands of hosts are used against the intended target. The originating "command-and-control" (C&C) server sends the instructions for the bots to follow. Thus a few packets from the C&C server can end up being millions of packets per second.

Amplification

Amplified DDoS attacks use "noisy" protocols, which respond with more than one packet when receiving a single packet (thus the amplification), against the intended targets. For example, the DDoS attacker may send a single malformed request to a web server with the origination IP address being falsified as belonging to the victim. The intermediate web server gets the malformed request and sends back to the originating IP address (the target victim) with multiple responses or attempts at error correction. Another popular DDoS amplification attack abuses DNS servers by requesting larger amounts of legitimate DNS information to which the DNS server sends back multiple, if not dozens of, packets to the intended victim. You can read more about DNS amplification attacks at `https://technet.microsoft.com/en-us/security/hh972393.aspx`. The bigger the amplification, the happier the DDoS attacker. When amplification is coordinated with tens to hundreds of thousands of bots, huge DDoS attacks can be accomplished.

Every Layer in the OSI Model

DoS/DDoS attacks can be accomplished along every layer of the OSI model (Physical, Data-Link, Network, Session, Transport, Presentation, and Application). A physical attack can be accomplished by physically destroying a central service dependency, such as a router, DNS server, or network line. All the other attack types abuse one or more protocols at the different layers.

Escalating Attacks

Today's most successful DDoS hackers attack targets with a wide, varying array of attacks along the OSI model. They may start with a simple flood at a lower layer protocol and increase the traffic over time with brief pauses in between. Maybe they start out with simple reflection and then move on to amplification methods. Then they switch attack layers, moving up through the OSI model, and add even more traffic. The attacker often uses the application layer, faking traffic that initially looks like legitimate customers but taking up what very little bandwidth remains.

So just as the victim thinks they have the DDoS under control, it changes and morphs. Starting out slowly, this way the victim keeps thinking they've understood the scope of the attack and how to defeat it, and then it changes. This confuses the victim and the defenders and makes it take longer to set up a successful mitigating defense. And each time the victim thinks they have found the solution, the attack changes again, back and forth, back and forth, and on goes the struggle until the attacker doesn't have any new types of attacks.

Upstream and Downsteam Attacks

Victim sites that have been targeted in the past often implement anti-DDoS techniques and services, and these techniques are often successful. DDoS attackers will then move upstream or downstream of the victim and target a dependency. Sending hundreds of gigabits of malicious traffic per second will make almost any provider scream uncle. The provider has to decide if hurting all their customers is worth keeping the one victim online. Most of the time the victim gets dropped or told to move. If the victim is lucky, they get time to make the move before a complete shutdown and can come up with another service willing to assume the malicious onslaught. Other times the victim is simply shut down for days, if not longer, until the massive DDoS is mitigated. In a few cases each year, the victim never recovers and permanently drops off the Internet.

You can read more details about DDoS attacks at https://www.incapsula .com/ddos/ddos-attacks/, https://javapipe.com/ddos-types/, and https://en.wikipedia.org/wiki/Denial-of-service_attack.

DDoS Tools and Providers

There are many tools and service providers to help anyone accomplish a DDoS attack.

Tools

There are dozens and dozens of tools and scripts available on the Internet to help anyone perform a DoS or DDoS attack. Just type "DDoS tool" into your Internet browser, and you'll quickly find them all over the web. Most tout themselves, often duplicitously, as legitimate testers, "booters," or "stressers." Some examples are: Low Orbit Ion Cannon (https://sourceforge.net/ projects/loic0/), DLR (https://sourceforge.net/projects/dlr/), and Hulk (https://packetstormsecurity.com/files/112856/HULK-Http-Unbearable-Load-King.html). Hackers should only use these tools against sites that have given them permission to do so. Many a budding hacker learned the hard way, through being arrested, that it's very hard to hide once the right people are looking for you.

DDoS as a Service

There are even dozens of services available on the Internet from which you can rent or launch DDoS services. Many are available for under $100. As with DDoS tools, most claim to be testing services (which just happen not to check to ensure that the user has the permission to use them against a particular site). Sadly, even services that claim to be anti-DDoS services have been caught being part of DDoS services. Some of these dual-faced services are being investigated and some have been shut down, but others continue to thrive. Investigative reporter Brian Krebs has written several excellent stories on this issue, including this one: https://krebsonsecurity.com/2016/10 /spreading-the-ddos-disease-and-selling-the-cure/.

DDoS Defenses

There are many defenses that you can use to fight DDoS attacks.

Training

All the human resources involved in putting up your sites and services should be educated about DDoS attacks and how to prevent them. Education is the first step toward detection and prevention.

Stress Testing

Stress test your own sites, potentially using some of the same "testing" tools that hackers would use. Think like a hacker and attack all the links and dependencies needed to provide your site or service. Find out what it takes to "knock yourself off the Internet" and determine what the weak links are. Once you've found them, engineer out the easy ones and determine the cost/ benefit relationship to the rest.

Appropriate Network Configuration

Make sure your sites and services are protected by firewalls and routers that are capable of detecting and stopping DDoS attacks. Make sure all the involved hosts have been configured to withstand DDoS attacks with a minimum of disruption. Build in as much redundancy as possible. Alternately, many companies have "peering agreements" with other vendors and even competitors, to be able to move or borrow resources if under DDoS attack. Some of these involve free resources or a minimal cost-recovery fee structure.

Engineer Out Potential Weak Points

When building services, think about all the potential points for DoS attacks. For example, Microsoft realized that a large number of Remote Desktop Protocol (RDP) connections could be made to Microsoft Windows by unauthenticated connections, effectively using up all available resources. Microsoft changed RDP so that an authenticated session had to be first made before Windows began allocating more resources, and they limited the number of connection attempts that could be made at one time from all sources. These two new RDP features make it very hard to cause a DoS attack using RDP.

Anti-DDoS Services

There are many premium anti-DDoS services, including Imperva (https://www.incapsula.com/) and Prolexic/Akamai (http://www.prolexic.com/). Most protect customers using a multi-layered combination of huge, redundant bandwidth and security defenses specifically dedicated to mitigating DDoS attacks. The downside is that these services are fairly costly and many companies cannot afford the expense against an attack that may never come. If you ever decide to use an anti-DDoS service, do your research to make sure the provider isn't one of those that causes DDoS attacks as well as solving them.

Just as there are many DDoS attackers in this world, there are many DDoS defenders. When thought about and planned for, DDoS attacks can be less damaging than without planning and defense.

Chapter 29 profiles Brian Krebs, computer security reporter and investigator, and the man most singled out by DDoS attackers.

29 Profile: Brian Krebs

Brian Krebs opened his front door in the middle of preparing for a small dinner party only to be greeted by a S.W.A.T. team, complete with black tactical gear, assault rifles, and shotguns pointed at him. After they screamed at him not to move and frisked and handcuffed him, Krebs realized this was yet another day in his battle against hackers as the world's premier Internet crime reporter and investigator. He has been diligently fighting spammers, skimmers, and hackers of all varieties for more than a decade. He has been part of several investigations and raids that have resulted in those same hackers losing millions of dollars and being arrested. In retaliation, hackers have sent all sorts of illegal contraband, including drugs and forged currency, along with multiple death threats to him and his family. A great recap of the SWAT incident can be found here: http://arstechnica.com/security/2013/03/security-reporter-tells-ars-about-hacked-911-call-that-sent-swat-team-to-his-house/.

The police were sent so many times to his house after an anonymous "good samaritan" called in a tip that the local law enforcement agencies eventually had both physical and electronic notices not to overreact to the latest called-in tip. Ultimately, Krebs got tired of all the harassment and decided to move "off the grid" for a while. He figured his family deserved the rest from constant threats as much as he did. But the hackers didn't win. Krebs continues his daily investigations to bring down hackers who cause others harm.

It wasn't always this way. For many years, Krebs was simply a beat reporter for paper-driven *The Washington Post*. His investigations into computer crime got so involved and detailed that the newspaper and he parted ways. He immediately created his own blog, Krebs on Security (https://krebsonsecurity.com/), and continued his investigations with even more zeal and focus. His blog is routinely one of the most popular on the Internet, he has produced an awesomely readable best-selling book, *Spam Nation* (https://www.amazon

.com/Spam-Nation-Organized-Cybercrime-Epidemic/dp/1492603236/), and Hollywood has even considered making a movie about his life.

His investigative reporting is first class. When Krebs learned that the world's best spam companies were located in Russia, he learned to read, write, and speak Russian and then travelled there to interview the rich and powerful Russians behind those firms. When I spoke to him after that visit, I told him that I could not believe that he was risking his life to cover a story. He told me that he obviously didn't feel that way, but several other friends had said as much as well. Krebs's public research was depriving these criminals of tens of millions of dollars, and now he was visiting them in their homeland where he had very few rights. Many of us expected to read about Krebs's untimely demise while "visiting" Russia. Instead, he came back with enough facts to write a book (*Spam Nation*), and some of the people he interviewed went to jail.

Most computer security journalists simply repeat well-known facts they've learned by reading public press releases. Krebs investigates and learns new facts. As he said in his blog when defending NOT covering a recent popular hacking storyline, "I've avoided covering these stories mainly because I don't have any original reporting to add to them and because I generally avoid chasing the story of the day—preferring instead to focus on producing original journalism on cybercrime and computer security."

Although Krebs investigates many types of hacking, his main focuses include financial crime, spammers, skimmers, and denial-of-service providers. Krebs is great at following the money and data trails. He has identified the people behind many of the world's biggest hacker organizations and attacks by name and picture. Often after Krebs identifies someone, they are arrested and charged with crimes. It's like the world's law enforcement agencies read his blog and wait for Krebs to reveal the perpetrator's real identity so they can go get a warrant. I'm sure it isn't exactly happening that way, but it seems like it. One of the best measures of Krebs's overall success is a phenomenon his followers have dubbed the "Krebs Cycle." Krebs often knows about many of the world's biggest hacks and data breaches for days before the victim vendor does. The Krebs Cycle is the length of time between when Krebs tells the world of the latest hack and when the vendor publicly acknowledges the same.

Krebs isn't afraid to point fingers at organizations that we would otherwise think are the "good guys." He's lambasted credit card companies and banks for helping to perpetrate financial crime. He's called out online tax preparers for making it easier for criminals to file false tax returns. He's made it transparently clear that big pharmacy companies are allowing otherwise illegal drug sales of their products because they don't want to admit that their unadulterated drugs (and not counterfeits) are being sold for less. He has proven that some of the firms that claim to protect us from hackers are themselves likely to be either conducting hacking activities or protecting hackers. He's called out Internet service providers and bullet-proof hosting services for catering to hackers as a business model. Krebs follows the money wherever it may go.

For this reason, Krebs's web site is constantly being DDoS attacked (covered in the previous chapter). His website has suffered what were at the time some of the largest attacks sent across the web. DDoS attackers often include personal taunts to Krebs inside their malicious traffic and require that new members to their activities prove themselves by attacking Krebs's sites as a requirement to join. And often Krebs finds out who the main perpetrators are, and they go to jail.

Krebs is able to pull off what so many other people and law enforcement agencies can't seem to do—identify the hacker. It's not unusual for his blog to go silent for a week or more, but when he pops up and writes, he's telling the name of some hacker. He often finds out their identity by following digital breadcrumbs that eventually link the hacker's secret identity to their public online identity. You end up seeing this very malicious and unethical hacker on vacation with their family, hugging their wife and kids, and you know those wonderful, money-fed vacation days are getting ready to come to an end. Many of his outed hackers have become international fugitives, while others seem to enjoy the benefits of corrupt local officials. Either way, they all hate Krebs while the rest of the world loves him. I think Brian Krebs is truly an American hero!

Besides identifying specific hackers and other questionable, dubious businesses, Krebs's writings allow readers to see the big business of computer hacking. It isn't some teenager sitting in their bedroom eating cereal and downing colas. It's big business with payrolls, HR departments, CEOs, and sometimes publicly traded stock. And sometimes even the legitimate business brands we all love and trust are in on the take. The world of hacking is as complex as life itself. Krebs's investigative reporting is responsible for my personal awakening on that point. It's a difficult pill to swallow, but we're all better for having taken it.

For More Information on Brian Krebs

For information about Brian Krebs, check out these resources:

- Brian Krebs on Twitter: https://twitter.com/briankrebs
- Brian Krebs's LinkedIn profile: https://www.linkedin.com/in/bkrebs

30   Secure OS

 One of the most popular computer security jokes with multiple punchlines is, "If you want a secure computer, then:

■ Lock it in a closet without a network card.
■ Get rid of the keyboard.
■ Get rid of the end-user."

Today's popular computer operating systems (OSs) are more secure than ever. They come with fairly secure defaults, require passwords, automatically patch themselves, encrypt data by default, and come with a myriad of other features. This doesn't mean they all have the same commitment to security or the same record of success. Still, the overall success of "secure-by-default" has reached a level where most hackers and malware have resorted to social engineering or exploiting a vulnerability that has an available patch that the end-user has not applied.

This did not happen by accident. It took years, if not decades, of experience and security analysis for operating system vendors to figure out an acceptable line between too secure and too insecure. End-users just want their operating systems to work for their intended actions without too much hindrance. If the end-user gets too bothered, they will either try to work around the security feature, disable it, or choose an entirely different operating system. Many security commentators diminish any operating system that doesn't choose the strongest possible security solution for every decision, without giving rationale consideration to the ability of the vendor to sell the operating system or appeal to end-users. With that said, there are very secure operating systems out there to choose among.

How to Secure an Operating System

There are three basic ways to secure an operating system: Build it to be secure and have secure defaults, improve its security using security configuration tools, or follow secure guidelines. Of course, most of today's operating systems use all those methods to ensure a secure operating system.

Secure-Built OS

The best, and some say only, way to have a secure operating system is to build it to be secure from the start. Not only should it be securely designed, but it should have the appropriate security features with secure defaults. Study after study shows that most end-users accept the default security settings, so if the default is set wrong, it undermines security.

Common Criteria

The internationally accepted standard for evaluating and ranking the security of an operating system is known as Common Criteria for Information Technology Security Evaluation, although it's often just called the Common Criteria. Vendors submit their operating systems or applications for Common Criteria evaluation, hoping to get certified as having a specific Evaluation Assurance Level, which ranges in increasing difficulty and security from EAL1 through EAL7. Although it would seem natural to assume that all operating system vendors that care about security would want the highest (EAL7) rating, that isn't the reality.

The levels EAL5 and above are not only very, very difficult to obtain, but generally require an operating system that isn't all that functional in the real world. Want to connect to the Internet and download a program? Well, you're probably not doing that with an EAL5 or higher system. EAL5 and higher systems are usually earned by very specific security applications (like smartcards, hardware storage modules, and so on) or government-related high-risk operating systems, like missile systems. The majority of the operating systems we know and love today, including specific versions of Microsoft Windows, Linux, Solaris, AIX, and BSD, are rated at EAL4 or EAL4+. (The plus sign indicates that it has achieved some classes above its clearly rated EAL.)

There is an effort underway to move away from EAL ratings to something known as Protection Profiles (PP). More information can be found at https://blogs.ca.com/2011/03/11/common-criteria-reforms-sink-or-

swim-how-should-industry-handle-the-revolution-brewing-with-common-
criteria/.

NOTE As far as I know, Apple iOS has never been submitted for or passed a traditional EAL certification process.

Meeting a higher level Common Criteria EAL rating or PP doesn't mean a hacker can't successful hack a rated system, but it does mean that it's probably harder to do, all other things considered equal. It also doesn't mean that an unrated operating system isn't secure or wouldn't meet the same certification if it was submitted for the certification process.

Federal Information Processing Standards

The United States has another popular standard under the banner of Federal Information Processing Standards (FIPS) for which operating systems, or parts of operating systems, can be submitted for security evaluation and certification. Although FIPS (https://www.nist.gov/topics/federal-information-standards-fips) only officially applies to government-related computer systems, it is a respected standard around the world. FIPS certifications are usually known by a specific number, such as 199-3 or 140-2. FIPS 140-2 applies to cryptographic routines, and submitted products can be certified as FIPS 140-2, Level 1 to 4, with 4 being the strongest security.

Because of customer demand, most operating system and application vendors that obtain a Common Criteria or FIPS certification will usually advertise the fact. Some customer scenarios require a particular evaluation or rating before they can consider purchasing it.

A Tale of Two Secure Operating Systems

In the world of general-purpose, popular operating systems, there are two operating systems (both are open-source) that intend to be more secure than average: OpenBSD and Qubes OS.

OpenBSD (www.openbsd.org) was created by Theo de Raadt as a new fork from NetBSD in 1995. De Raadt almost always falls on the security side of things when there is a security versus usability question. Many of the security features that are optional in other operating systems are enabled by default in OpenBSD. It's developers frequently audit their code looking for security bugs. OpenBSD is specifically respected for having the least number of bugs found by outside parties of any popular operating system.

Qubes (https://www.qubes-os.org/) was created by the Warsaw, Poland-based Invisible Things Lab and its founder and CEO, Joanna Rutkowska (profiled in the next chapter) in 2012. Qubes uses an isolated Xen hypervisor to allow an additional operating system and components to run in additional, highly isolated virtual machine environments. Even the network functionality runs in its own domain. Each domain can be classified according to its security needs and can run different additional operating systems. Perhaps it's said tongue-in-cheek, but it's described as "a reasonably secure operating system" by its own founders. Others consider it the most secure popular operating system available, and it is particularly loved by many privacy and security experts.

Not that this is required for developing and leading a more secure OS, but both de Raadt and Rutkowska are known by some for their intelligence and occasional social abrasiveness. They are not afraid of hurting others' feelings when standing their ground or stating an opinion, especially when confronting long-held but mistaken dogma. Neither suffers fools lightly so to speak. They bring this seriousness and intelligence to the products they develop. You don't need OpenBSD or Qubes to ensure a relatively secure OS, but using them will generally make it easier to obtain an above-average security profile.

Secure Guidelines

Most popular operating systems come with relatively secure defaults and settings, but they aren't always set to their recommended best security settings. For example, Windows 10 comes with a minimum password length setting of just 6 characters, even though Microsoft and most of the security world recommends a minimum of 12 characters, if not 16 characters. The problem is that popular operating systems need to appeal to a wide range of people and security scenarios. Seemingly harmless-looking security settings like minimum password length, if enabled at their "recommended" settings, could cause operational issues in a large number of environments and could even potentially lead to worse security. So most operating system vendors set many of their OS's individual features at one setting even though they recommend something stronger.

These guidelines can be downloaded from the vendors and often third-party security organizations. For example, Microsoft's recommendations can be downloaded from https://blogs.technet.microsoft.com/secguide/2016/07/28/security-compliance-manager-4-0-now-available-for-download/

and Apple's can be downloaded from https://support.apple.com/en-gb /HT202739. The Center for Internet Security's benchmarks (https:// benchmarks.cisecurity.org/downloads/) are among the most popular third-party guidelines.

Secure Configuration Tools

OS vendors and third parties offer tools and programs to assist with the secure configuration of various operating systems and applications. Microsoft has its Security Compliance Manager (link shown in the previous section). Many Linux distributions start with a GUI-based configuration screen that asks a couple of general security questions during installation to help you configure the OS. The Center for Internet Security also offers commercial configuration tools for members. There are, no exaggeration, hundreds of security configuration tools to choose from. All of them have the goal of helping the end-user or administrator to apply and manage their security settings more easily.

Security Consortiums

The computer security world is full of trusted industry security consortiums that attempt to make computing more secure. Two groups that have had a big recent impact are the Trusted Computing Group and the FIDO Alliance.

Trusted Computing Group

My favorite industry consortium is the Trusted Computing Group (https:// trustedcomputinggroup.org/), which works to think of and standardize more secure hardware and software. It is responsible for many of the most widely accepted, secure-by-default security standards, such as the Trusted Platform Module chip and OPAL self-encrypting hard drives. If you want to learn what it will take to have truly secure devices and operating systems, read everything the Trusted Computing Group publishes.

FIDO Alliance

The FIDO (Fast IDentity Online) Alliance (https://fidoalliance.org/) focuses on replacing simple logon password authentication with stronger alternatives. Formed in 2012, FIDO is focused on stronger authentication through browsers and security devices when accessing web sites, web services, and cloud offerings. Currently, all FIDO authentication methods use public/private key cryptography behind the screens, which makes them highly resistant to traditional credential phishing and man-in-the-middle attacks. At this time, FIDO has two authentication specification experiences: Universal Authentication Framework (UAF), which is a "passwordless" method, and Universal Second Factor (U2F), which is a two-factor authentication (2FA) method. The latter method can involve a password, which can be non-complex because the additional factor assures the overall strength. FIDO authentication must be supported by your device or browser, along with the authenticating site or service. FIDO-based authentication is just starting to become popular, but it should be very popular within one to two years.

No operating system has perfect security or can prevent a dedicated adversary from exploiting it. But many operating systems can be relatively secure either out of the box or by following recommended security guidelines.

Chapters 31 and 32 profile Joanna Rutkowska and Aaron Margosis, two of today's leading minds on secure operating systems.

31 Profile: Joanna Rutkowska

Polish citizen Joanna Rutkowska came on the world's computer security scene in a dramatic way. She announced in 2006 (http://theinvisiblethings.blogspot.com/2006/06/introducing-blue-pill.html) the ultimate rootkit malware program. A rootkit is a malware program that modifies the operating system in order to better hide from the operating system and any program using it. Rutkowska had discovered a method whereby a malicious program could hide in such a way that it could not be easily discovered by any known method, even if you knew about the malicious program and that it was on the operating system. She called her idea the "blue pill."

The blue pill allegory comes from the famous movie *The Matrix* (http://www.imdb.com/title/tt0133093/). In the movie, the protagonist, Neo, is offered two different pills, one red and one blue, to take after discovering that what he thought was the real world is revealed to be a cyber-illusion. If he takes the red pill, he will be able to stay in the real world. But if he takes the blue pill, he will go back to the illusory, more comfortable world he knew. Every movie goer knows he decided on the red pill and started to fight the movie's antagonists to save the world!

Rutkowska named her discovery the blue pill because her rootkit method utilizes the built-in virtualization features of today's CPUs to execute itself as a virtualization hypervisor with the unaware operating system running off of it. The subjugated operating system thinks it is running unencumbered with itself completely in control, when in fact it is completely under the control and potential misdirection of the hypervisor parent.

Rutkowska described her discovery like this: "The idea behind Blue Pill is simple: Your operating system swallows the Blue Pill, and it awakes inside the Matrix controlled by the ultra-thin Blue Pill hypervisor. This all happens on-the-fly (i.e. without restarting the system), and there is no performance penalty, and all the devices, like graphics card, are fully accessible to the operating system, which is now executing inside virtual machine."

Her announcement was quite revolutionary for the time. Hypervisors and virtualization were just starting to become more popular. Most people, including most security experts, didn't understand the technology all that well, much less all of the security implications and needed controls. And here was Rutkowska stating that all this new technology could be used to bypass any detection method. It created a sort of existential crisis in the security world. For a while there were concerns that malware writers would start producing blue pill malware programs and the anti-malware would have a tough time responding.

I wrote an *InfoWorld* column at the time trying to allay people's overwrought fears. While I agreed with what Rutkowska had proposed, I felt its additional complexity would probably hamper its use by malware developers. I stated that as long as the simple stuff malware writers were doing was working well, they were unlikely to move to newer, harder-to-invoke methods, and if they did use them, I felt that the anti-malware world and operating systems vendors would respond adequately. In the decade since, my conclusion (not to worry too much about blue pill threats) was proven correct. Still, Rutkowska established that she was not only smart and thought outside the box, but she was challenging whether the traditional methods used by the computer security world could deliver reliable, safe systems.

Since her blue pill release in 2006, Rutkowska become a very popular conference speaker, and she has continued to ask good questions and to provide good security solutions. She continues to publish her ideas and solutions on her Invisible Things Lab website (http://invisiblethingslab.com/) and blog (https://blog.invisiblethings.org/), although these days other projects are also demanding more of her attention. More recently, she has devoted much of her time to the Qubes project (mentioned in the previous chapter).

Rutkowska has always been exploring the real and artificial security boundaries in operating systems. She found an unacceptable security vulnerability in nearly every default Linux distribution that allowed one program to access any other program within the same operating system if they used the same desktop (http://theinvisiblethings.blogspot.com/2011/04/linux-security-circus-on-gui-isolation.html). It's a common type of vulnerability that is shared with most operating systems. While many operating system vendors and security experts feel it's an acceptable risk because you have to be running on the same desktop on the same OS for it to begin to be a problem,

Rutkowska strongly feels it isn't acceptable if you really care about security. Especially because doing something as simple as browsing the web can end up allowing your entire operating system and critical, trusted, applications to be completely compromised.

For these and other reasons, in 2010, she developed the Qubes OS (`http://qubes-os.org/`). Qubes is a hypervisor-enabled desktop system with a focus on security isolation. It can run other operating systems, each within its own virtual machine instance, and the Qubes administration back-end and network run in their own isolated virtual machines as well. Qubes is a security-oriented back-end, which makes creating, managing, and operating all the virtual instances easier. Each virtual instance can appear co-mingled in a GUI desktop, although they are completely separated by hypervisor-enforced security boundaries. Like any piece of software, it has its own vulnerabilities and is impacted by other vulnerabilities beyond its control (like those within the hypervisor program, Xen). Even though Rutkowska calls Qubes only "a reasonably secure" operating system, it is probably the most security-focused general-purpose OS you can download and use for free.

Along the way, Rutkowska continues to explore other security problems like rogue PDF files and USB vulnerabilities. She is a strong advocate for real computer security, and she continues to challenge the rest of the world to be better.

For More Information on Joanna Rutkowska

For more information about Joanna Rutkowska, check out these resources:

- Joanna Rutkowska on Twitter: `https://twitter.com/rootkovska`
- Invisible Things Lab web site: `http://invisiblethingslab.com/`
- Invisible Things Lab blog: `https://blog.invisiblethings.org/`
- Qubes Project web site: `http://qubes-os.org/`

32 Profile: Aaron Margosis

One of the sad facts of the computer security world is that even though everyone acts as if having safe and reliable computing is THE most important base feature to have in a computer, that really isn't true. Users are far more interested in having the latest, cool, gee-whiz feature, computer security be damned! Vendors and developers that spend too much time on security end up getting beaten to market by their competitors. Designers who make their devices and applications too secure end up being out of a job. You can architect security into a product as long as it doesn't bother the customer, and that's a difficult thing to do.

Hence, most people don't run the most secure operating system on the planet. The vast majority run a popular, well-supported, fairly secure operating system, but it's not the most secure one. If end-users really cared about security the most out of all their considerations, more would be running Qubes (https://www.qubes-os.org/), created by Joanna Rutkowska who was profiled in the previous chapter, or OpenBSD (https://www.freebsd.org/). They are the most secure, general-purpose operating systems, and they are free, yet most of the world does not run them. This isn't necessarily a bad thing, as we make similar trust decisions in our lives all the time. Security is rarely the first or only consideration in a decision we make. The majority of the world, at least right now, runs Microsoft Windows, Apple iOS, and Android operating systems.

Fortunately, most of today's operating systems are fairly secure. In most cases, if you follow the operating system vendor's best practice recommendations, quickly apply security patches, and don't get socially engineered into doing anything against your best interests, you won't be exploited. A big part of staying safe is following the OS vendor's recommendations. If you've ever wondered how those recommendations were chosen, it is based on the vendor's accumulated experiences and lessons learned from history, plus a few dedicated people who explore each recommended setting and try to determine the best cost/benefit balance for the majority of the vendor's customers. Aaron Margosis, one of my long-time friends, is one of the people at Microsoft making sure Microsoft Windows is securely configured.

Margosis currently has the hair of a rock star, and he is as excited about computer security as he is about baseball. He has been exploring thousands of security settings, making free configuration tools, and publishing articles on secure computing for almost two decades. He has written two of the most incredible, behind-the-scenes looks at how Windows really works along with co-author Mark Russinovich (profiled in Chapter 11) in their books on Windows Sysinternals utilities. Many Windows techies consider these books to be among their troubleshooting bibles.

Almost every day, Margosis is involved in either troubleshooting how a particular security setting works or trying to find out why some group, Microsoft or otherwise, made it their recommendation. Over the years, he has found dozens of very bad recommendations, many of which if followed would have caused their environments problems and hard-to-solve crises. Margosis has done more than anyone else I know to try to bring the various popular recommendations groups on the Internet, like the Center for Internet Security (https://www.cisecurity.org/), to a common security baseline supported by all the major groups. Through it all, Margosis has written, blogged, and presented everything he knows. These days he's working with Microsoft's AppLocker and Device Guard features, which seek to stop malicious programs from executing, as they apply to large enterprises. It's a natural extension of what he has been doing for his entire career.

I started our interview by asking how he got into computer security. He replied, "I got my undergraduate degree in Psychology from University of Virginia, but I had always had an interest in computing. I had started programming in BASIC when I was 12 in the 1970s. I took some graduate-level computer science classes while I was at UVA as an undergraduate, but I didn't major in computer science because that would have meant changing my major to Engineering. Later, after I started working in computers, I went back to UVA and got my Masters in Computer Science.

After college I worked for several different companies, including two companies that made hearing testing equipment, an accounting software company, and a company that worked in cellular infrastructure. In the middle of that, I worked at Maynard Electronics, which made the NT Backup program that came with the first version of Windows NT, and the 'Backup Exec' product sold by a series of acquiring companies (currently Symantec). I was personally concerned with keeping people (like my co-workers) out of my computer, and that got me interested in computer security. I ended up at Microsoft in 1999 and I've been there ever since."

Margosis was one of the first people I knew who told people not to run as administrator all the time. Not running as root was becoming pretty popular on Linux and Unix software, but the same type of security was not picking up in the Windows world at all. In fact, nearly every developer expected that the end-user would have full control of their system for their software to run correctly. Microsoft, with a great deal of informal influence from Margosis, finally decided that Windows Vista (released in 2006) would be the Windows version that finally drew a line in the sand. It introduced a feature called User Account Control (UAC) that forced all users out of running as admin and into being standard users by default. There was a ton of push-back, and there were tens of thousands of broken programs. Trying to get vendors and developers to change their mindset at the time was a huge undertaking. Some people thought the security change would mean the end of Microsoft Windows. It was that controversial.

I asked Margosis what his involvement was. "At the time, Microsoft as a whole didn't think the switch from always-administrator to standard users was the way to go. Some people did, like Michael Howard [profiled in Chapter 7]. He spoke about it and inspired me to try to run as a standard user all the time. I started running as a standard user full-time during the Windows XP beta, and it broke a lot of things. It was a delightful challenge. I started to think about how I could stay productive as a non-admin, and so I started coming up with tools and techniques that worked for me, and I shared them with the world. My first public conference presentation was at Microsoft TechEd in 2005, with more than 1500 attendees, and was about running Windows XP as a non-admin. My blogs, tools, and talks had a great impact on the Windows team that was developing Windows Vista. There was a struggle going on at the time and it wasn't clear whether pushing for a default of non-admin was going to win, but Jim Allchin and the UAC team held the line. And I'm glad to have been a part of it. It benefited the entire customer base and now it's an expectation, not an issue."

I asked Margosis how he got into releasing all his cool, free, secure trouble-shooting and configuration tools, like LUA Buglight and the Local Group Policy Object (LGPO) utility. He replied, "It started from all my work promoting non-admin. The government mandated a Federal Desktop Core Configuration (the FDCC) that included a large set of security settings and required that end-users not run with admin rights, which was a natural fit with what I was doing. Because of that, I learned a lot about security settings and Group Policy and developed tools to automate tasks that weren't well-covered before. It turns out that bringing well-researched, well-tested, and widely used baselines is a huge benefit to customers in terms of time and quality. If we didn't have those, every customer would end up having to do the same work themselves, which would take a long time and probably end up with suboptimal results. It's easy to make mistakes and incorrect assumptions."

I asked Margosis what he was working on now besides baselines and security configurations. He replied, "I'm working a lot in application whitelisting using Microsoft's AppLocker and Device Guard technologies. It will be a powerful and necessary defense in the enterprise against ransomware and other types of malware. It's harder for home users because home users have to administer their own systems so they have to make trust decisions. In the enterprise, end-users shouldn't make trust decisions or be expected to, so whitelisting is feasible in a well-managed enterprise.

"I see similarities in what I'm doing now in application control and what I did with standard user years ago. Both things are needed for better computer security, and both break software because the assumptions developers used to make no longer hold. Software vendors had to stop assuming their programs could store data in the Program Files directory, and they'll have to stop expecting to be able to execute from the user's profile or other user-writable directories. In the meantime, it will be an interesting application-compatibility challenge."

I asked what he wished he knew more about in computer security. He hesitated a minute and then said, "I wish I knew how to convince people to do the right thing more quickly. I don't think I've learned how to do that as well as I could. I know what I'm doing is right, but knowing how to convince people more quickly would help."

I think a lot of people profiled in this book would understand Margosis's pain.

For More Information
on Aaron Margosis

For information about Aaron Margosis, check out these resources:

- *Troubleshooting with the Windows Sysinternals Tools (2nd Edition)*: https://www.amazon.com/Troubleshooting-Windows-Sysinternals-Tools-2nd/dp/0735684448
- *Windows Sysinternals Administrator's Reference*: https://www.amazon.com/Windows-Sysinternals-Administrators-Reference-Margosis/dp/073565672X
- Aaron Margosis's Non-Admin, App-Compat and Sysinternals Weblog: https://blogs.msdn.microsoft.com/Aaron_Margosis
- Aaron Margosis's US Government Configuration Baseline (USGCB) Tech Blog: https://blogs.technet.microsoft.com/fdcc
- Aaron Margosis's Microsoft Security Guidance blog: https://blogs.technet.microsoft.com/SecGuide

33 Network Attacks

In Chapter 2, "How Hackers Hack," the various ways attackers try to exploit a computing device were discussed. These included physical attacks, zero-days, unpatched software, social engineering, password issues, eavesdropping/man-in-the-middle attacks, data leaks, misconfiguration, denial-of-service, user errors, and malware. All of these attacks can be accomplished on either the computing device itself or the network connecting to the computing device.

Types of Network Attacks

Network attacks can be anywhere along the Open Systems Interconnection (OSI) model (https://en.wikipedia.org/wiki/OSI_model). The OSI model is a very commonly known and used construct showing the different layers of interconnection along a network and to a networked computing device. The OSI model has seven abstraction layers:

- Physical
- Data-Link
- Network
- Transport
- Session
- Presentation
- Application

All layers could be applied to a network and its controlling devices (because network devices run applications, too), although many could be applied directly on the computing device as well. A physical attack could be any scenario where a network or network equipment is physically accessed, damaged, or stolen. The Data-Link layer often applies to Ethernet bridges, network switches, and protocols and standards at those layers like a device's MAC Address (https://en.wikipedia.org/wiki/MAC_address). The Network layer refers to routing. The Transport and Session layers refer to upper layer protocols, and the Presentation and Application layers are within the device or application. If a network medium is being shared without any other protections, it is always possible for one node on the network to interfere with another node's communications. The following sections explore some popular approaches for network attacks.

Eavesdropping

Eavesdropping is unauthorized viewing and/or recording of an otherwise intended private conversation. Although it isn't as successful now, years ago you could plug a network-sniffing application into any network and be able to see plaintext conversation streams and authentication information. There are many free tools available on the Internet that you can install and then click a single button to start capturing plaintext passwords. There are other tools that allow you to capture other people's website cookies and take over their sessions. In most cases it requires no particular expertise, just the ability to run software.

Man-in-the-Middle Attacks

Man-in-the-middle (MitM) attacks can be accomplished at any layer of the OSI model as well. A MitM attack breaks into an unauthorized communication stream and pretends to be an authorized party to all the other authorized parties. Most of the time the involved original, legitimate party is impacted and often kicked out of the communication stream. MitM attacks are done for all the same reasons as eavesdropping, including to view and steal private data. However, they can also manipulate the communication stream to change communications and data, like changing a "yes" to a "no" when someone asks a question or misdirecting one or more listening parties to an unauthorized location.

Today, many network protocols and applications have protection against MitM attacks, but sometimes they aren't always turned on by default, often because of performance or interoperability concerns. For example, the open DNSSEC standard was created in 2004 to prevent DNS spoofing attacks, but more than a decade later fewer than 1% of the DNS servers in the world run it.

Distributed Denial-of-Service Attacks

Distributed denial-of-service (DDoS) attacks are arguably the most common and easily the largest volume of attacks on the Internet. On any given day, there are terabytes of data being sent to interrupt legitimate sites and services on the Internet. DDoS attacks can attack at any layer of the OSI model.

Network Attack Defenses

There are many defenses against network attacks, including the ones discussed in the following sections.

Domain Isolation

Domain isolation means creating a secure border between authorized and unauthorized network traffic. This can be accomplished using a variety of tools and methods, including firewalls (both network-based and host-based), virtual private network connections, IPSEC, routers, software-defined networks, and other types of switching fabrics. If a network attack can't reach your device or network, it's not going to be able to hurt you, normally. There are edge cases like when a DDoS attack attacks an upstream or downstream network dependency, which in turn impacts the intended target anyway. But domain isolation can only help.

Virtual Private Networks

One of the best things any device can do when on an open, shared network service is to use a virtual private network (VPN). VPNs can be accomplished using software, hardware, or a combination of the two. At the very least they encrypt all the traffic between the sender and at least the first node of their intended receiver, if not the entire transmission path. VPNs aren't perfect. For example, a DDoS attack can interrupt them.

Use Secure Protocols and Applications

Nothing beats a secure protocol and application that includes defenses against known threats. Users should use secure protocols and applications when they are offered (such as SCP and SSH) and avoid knowingly using insecure protocols (such as FTP and Telnet). Also, no application should store plaintext logon credentials on disk or in memory or transfer them across a network.

Network Intrusion Detection

Network attacks can be detected by network sniffers (manually) or by look-ing for predefined patterns of maliciousness. When network maliciousness is detected, it can be dropped or an actionable alert can be created. Network protocol analyzers (such as network sniffers) are a great way to capture and decode network anomalies. Sniffers allow manual analysis and many include automated methods, too. Many firewalls contain network intrusion detection features as well.

Anti-DDoS Defenses

You can defend against distributed denial-of-service (DDoS) attacks by hard-ening network equipment, allocating more bandwidth on the fly, and utilizing specialized anti-DDoS services. Dozens of anti-DDoS services exist today, and they can help protect a company's assets against very large DDoS attacks. The only issue is that they can be very expensive, and every now and then it is an anti-DDoS service vendor causing the problem in the first place. Unfortunately, there are number of unethical competitors that will do anything to get a cus-tomer's business. If you are considering using an anti-DDoS service, do your research to make sure you only go with a legitimate, unquestionably ethical firm.

Visit Secure Web Sites and Use Secure Services

Many network attacks, like easy-to-steal web site cookies and authentication tokens, only occur because the web site or service is not using the secure development lifecycle (SDL) in their programming. A properly coded web site or service, appropriately threat-modelled and using SDL to close known vulnerabilities, will be more resistant to network attacks than ones that do not.

Unfortunately, it's difficult for the average web surfer to know whether the web site they are visiting or the web service they are using is follow-ing secure practices. Some web sites contain security attestations from well-known, trusted security vendors and if verified as legitimate should give the casual user some additional level of comfort.

Network attacks are a daily occurrence on the Internet and some of them have caused huge damages for their victims. There are many network attack defenses that users and companies can avail themselves of to lower the risk of attack.

The next chapter will profile Laura Chappell, one of the world's best net-work analyzers.

34 Profile: Laura Chappell

Scientists say that if we ever meet an alien civilization the likely language used to communicate will be math, because math is the only truly universal language that is likely to be understood by advance civilizations. To understand what is going on with a networked computer, the only true way to understand it is to sniff the network. No one does that better than Laura Chappell. She is like Dr. Louise Banks (played by Amy Adams) in the 2016 movie *Arrival* or Dr. Ellie Arroway (played by Jodie Foster) in the 1997 movie *Contact*. She's very intelligent, focused, especially good at what she does, and respected by her peers.

Her classes and presentations are always well attended and well ranked by participants. I first met her over 20 years ago, when she was teaching a network sniffer class to a local IT group in Virginia Beach, VA. Being a woman in IT was a rarity at the time, and Chappell was used to IT guys hitting on her by trying to show how much they thought they knew about network packet sniffing. She ended her introduction speech to our group by saying, "If you think you're going to come up here and impress me by trying to alpha-male me with your knowledge of network packet sniffing, don't waste your time. I know more than you do." The crowd loved it. Then she proved she was right and we became life-long fans.

She has used most network packet sniffers, although her current favorite is the very popular Wireshark (http://www.wireshark.com), which comes in both free and commercial versions.

I asked Chappell how she got interested in network packet analysis, and she replied, "Back in the late 1980s and early 1990s, I worked for Novell (the powerhouse in network operating systems at the time). I was a member of Novell Technology Institute, a geeky team that researched, wrote, and lectured on all the hot networking technology at the time. When Ray Noorda, the CEO of Novell, purchased Excelan Corporation in 1989, I was fortunate to sit in on a presentation of the Excelan LANalyzer. Watching this early network analyzer tool tap into our Novell network and delve into Novell's request/reply communications and pop up user names and passwords on the overhead . . . I was hooked! I said to myself (and everyone around me who would listen), 'I want to do that the rest of my life.' Geez . . . Here I am all these years later, still listening in on network communications!"

I asked Chappell how she got into computer security. She said, "I first entered the arena of network forensics quite by accident. In 1993, I started my company and spent most of my time performing onsite analysis of various corporate networks. Back then, companies were solely interested in troubleshooting, optimization, and capacity planning. They never called me in to talk 'security' at that time.

"Over the years, however, I would tap into a company's infrastructure only to find tremendous security issues screaming across the network. While keeping an eye on the primary goal set by the customers, I had to start bringing up the issue of security to my customers. I was seeing some packets and communications that just shouldn't be on their networks. There were quite a few instances where I felt poor network performance was the *least* of their worries—they were being robbed blind right under their noses (or across the wires). It became very apparent that I needed to weave 'security analysis' into my network analysis tasks. The world of network forensics came to the forefront. Here are a couple of general examples:

"In the midst of doing an onsite analysis of a customer's poorly performing network, I witnessed a sudden stream of rapid-fire traffic headed towards the egress point of the network. It was coming from a system that should have been relatively quiet at the time since no one was logged onto that machine. Taking a closer look at the stream of traffic, I noticed there were a lot of dollar signs and dollar amounts in that stream. After reassembling the stream, I realized I had the complete payroll of the company in my hands.

"During an onsite [analysis at] a hospital, it appeared students from a major university were accessing the prescription database system—a system that contained not only the names, addresses and social security numbers of patients, but complete details on the various medications prescribed to them and why. This onsite was designed as a live analysis session to identify the cause of slow login processes. Once the suspicious traffic was detected, everything changed. It became a training session on malicious traffic detection." And the rest is history.

I asked Chappell what most interests her in computer security right now. She said, "This is a big question. There are so many fascinating areas in network forensics. The top two for me right now are: Catching automated background processes (lots of 'phone home' stuff) as they send confidential and personal information out unbeknownst to the users, and teaching folks to customize Wireshark to quickly detect the most common symptoms of network reconnaissance and attack. The Wireshark customization project is a hot topic for me. Building a Wireshark profile that can quickly alert a forensic analyst is a great feature. Teaching folks how to use Wireshark as a network forensics tool is tremendously fun."

I asked her what the biggest problem in computer security is. She said, "Coming from a network forensic standpoint, I'd have to say that not enough companies understand how to integrate security through the various departments of the organization. I will often find that the folks who install software on the clients are not encouraged to learn network security—they just install the software and that's it. They don't do a baseline of the traffic to/from the newly minted system. They don't realize what 'normal' traffic is and so they can't spot the abnormal traffic. They certainly aren't given access to an IDS system to run the trace files through. It would be a blessing if the security folks at the companies would do some internal cross-training on how systems get breached and how to prevent future problems. I know these folks are busy, but they need to spread the knowledge through other departments."

Finally, I asked what she recommended that people interested in computer security as careers do. She replied, "First, learn Wireshark, of course! Just kidding … well, actually, I'm not kidding. Wireshark is a perfect tool to use when you really want to understand how the network works, and it's free! It is ranked #1 in security tools over at sectools.org for a reason. (Seriously, it's a lot more interesting to watch a TCP handshake than read about it in an RFC!)

"Secondly, learn TCP/IP really, really, really well. Take the time to capture your own traffic while you connect to a web server, send email, upload a file using FTP, etc. As you are learning how the protocols work, *watch* the protocols using Wireshark. Watch the TCP handshake, the request/reply nature of many applications, the connection teardown process, and more.

"Thirdly, put together a simple attack lab. The computers don't need to be big or fancy—just tie a few together with a switch and grab some of the free scanning/penetration testing tools available today. Capture and analyze the traffic as you launch attacks on your other systems. Most of us are visual learners—being able to see an idle scan is way more interesting than just reading about it. Network security is like a two-sided coin—you need to get a feel for how various attacks work in order to know how to defend against them.

"It's a game. Playing problem-solving games is a great way to prime your brain for networking and security analysis."

Laura Chappell is a woman who found her niche in the network packet sniffing world, became a world-wide expert, and more than 20 years later is still the best at what she does.

For More Information on Laura Chappell

For information about Laura Chappell, check out these resources:

- Chappell University: https://www.chappellu.com/
- Laura Chappell's LinkedIn profile: https://www.linkedin.com/in/chappelllaura
- Laura Chappell on Twitter: https://twitter.com/LauraChappell
- In Laura's Lab Blog (dated material, but still relevant): http://laura-chappell.blogspot.com/

35 IoT Hacking

he world of computers is no longer just computers. It's cars, houses, televisions, refrigerators, toasters, glasses, wristwatches, sneakers, lights, baby monitors, medical devices, and almost any other object that some salesman thinks will appeal to buyers more if it had a computer or sensor in it. Most of these items are connected to the Internet and have an Internet Protocol (IP) address. It's known as the Internet of Things (IoT). Unfortunately, many, if not most, IoT devices are very insecure and can be successfully hacked—some quite easily.

How Do Hackers Hack IoT?

The same way they do regular computers, by picking one or more vulnerabilities along the Open Systems Interconnection (OSI) model layers (Physical, Data-Link, Network, Transport, Session, Presentation, and Application). The only difference is that the IoT device may not use traditional hardware or a well-known operating system (or it might not even have a traditional operating system at all). Hackers have to learn as much as they can about the device, research its components and operations, and look for vulnerabilities.

For example, suppose a hacker wants to see if they can hack an IoT toaster. The first order of business is to get one and study all the accompanying documentation. They then attempt to determine how it connects to a network and what it sends over the network by enabling a network sniffer and turning on the device. You can learn an incredible amount about a device by listening to what it does or tries when it starts up. They might port scan it, looking for listening ports and trying to enumerate what operating system and services are running. If there is an admin console, they try to connect to it. They try to find out what language the device's code was written in and look for application programming interfaces (APIs).

Physical hacking is also a common method of IoT hacking. Hackers take the device apart and see what components it has, noting individual chips and chip numbers. Most devices use common chips, and those common chips are often well-documented. Sometimes the chip's vulnerabilities are well-known and can be similarly exploited across a range of devices. Hardware hackers cross wires, join chip pins, and even create their own custom chips to get around the device's authentication and access control blockers. They pay special attention looking for input and output ports and see whether they can connect some sort of debugger to the device.

They use man-in-the-middle (MitM) attacks on communications to try to see information being transmitted and whether they can change those values and what happens. They often share the information they learn in general IoT forums or even device-specific IoT forums. They even create virtual groups dedicated to a particular device, synergizing the expertise of the different members.

Here are some examples of publicly shared IoT hacks that make interesting reading:

- https://blog.avast.com/2015/11/11/the-anatomy-of-an-iot-hack/
- https://www.rapid7.com/docs/Hacking-IoT-A-Case-Study-on-Baby-Monitor-Exposures-and-Vulnerabilities.pdf
- https://securelist.com/analysis/publications/66207/iot-how-i-hacked-my-home/
- http://resources.infosecinstitute.com/hardware-hacking-iot-devices-offensive-iot-exploitation/

In general, if you can penetration test regular computers, you can penetration test IoT devices, except IoT devices sometimes take a bit more creativity and research, especially if you aren't familiar with the operating system or chips. But not only can they be hacked, they are far more likely to be hackable because most IoT vendors don't understand the risk and don't allocate enough defensive resources—at least for now.

IoT Defenses

It's not like plenty of people aren't working on better securing IoT devices. Most vendors at least think they are addressing it appropriately. Dozens of independent groups like the IoT Village (https://www.iotvillage.org/) are working to help vendors better secure their devices. Unfortunately, hacker forums like San Francisco IOT Hacking Meetup (`https://www.meetup.com/San-Francisco-IOT-hacking-Meetup/`) are just as active and are having more success. When an IoT vendor tells you that their device is very secure, they are probably wrong. Most likely very wrong.

So what can an IoT vendor do to better secure their device? Well, treat it like you are defending a regular computer. Threat model the device from the very beginning, and make sure the programming includes security design lifecycle (SDL) considerations from the very start to the end of the product's life. Make sure the device uses the most up-to-date software with the latest patches applied, and make the device self-updating. Remove any unnecessary software, services, and scripts. Close any unneeded ports. Use good cryptography in a reliable way. Ensure customer privacy. Don't collect information you don't need. Securely store customer information you do need. Require strong authentication to access and conduct multiple penetration tests during the product's creation and beta testing. Offer bug bounties. Don't punish hackers for reporting bugs. Essentially take all the computer security lessons learned in the world of computers over multiple decades and apply them to IoT devices.

Unfortunately, most IoT vendors aren't doing this, and we are probably doomed to have decades of very hacked IoT devices.

The next chapter profiles Dr. Charlie Miller, who is considered one of the world's best car hackers.

36 Profile: Dr. Charlie Miller

Most people who recognize Dr. Charlie Miller's name and his work know him as part of a hacker duo who can completely remotely control your car like a kid's toy. For a few years if you saw a news report about hackers making a car or Jeep suddenly speed up or even run off the road, remotely, it involved Dr. Miller. A *Wired* magazine author described his experiences (https://www.wired.com/2015/07/hackers-remotely-kill-jeep-highway/) with Dr. Miller and his partner in crime, Chris Valasek.

Miller and Valasek wrote a detailed whitepaper called "Adventures in Automotive Networks and Control Units" (http://illmatics.com/car_hacking.pdf) that describes how many of a car's components, critical and non-critical, could be controlled including the emergency brake, air conditioning, indicator lights, transmission, entertainment systems, brakes, and even steering. For many of us, this paper was the most insight we had into how a car's network of computer systems worked and communicated. In later iterations, they figured out how to do it remotely. It was car-hacking nirvana! They even released their custom tools to help make car hacking easier for others.

The idea that hackers could remotely control your car wasn't completely shocking, but seeing two guys do it from their laptop 10 miles away as cameras recorded the action brought home the potential threat in a way that theories on a paper just cannot. Dr. Miller didn't need to actively promote the idea that these techniques, in the wrong hands, could be used to cause accidents and fatalities. Up until Dr. Miller's frequent public disclosures, the car companies hadn't really done a lot to prevent car hacking maliciousness. (Security by obscurity was the biggest protection.) Miller and Valasek's research and adventures changed all of that. Car manufacturers began to take notice of all the adverse publicity and began to take car computer security more seriously. There were even rumors that the testers might be sued by the big car companies in an effort to stymie additional research and disclosures.

When I interviewed Dr. Miller, he assured me that he and the others he worked with were never sued or even threatened to be sued, "Anyone can be sued, but we were very professional. It's a credit to them and us. They did ask us not to show certain details in one of our future presentations, but we did anyway, and no one sued." This is not to say that the car companies loved what he was doing. Despite Dr. Miller doing some of best public research in car hacking, he was never once invited to give a talk about his findings, private or otherwise, to a car company. And once during a conference when he asked the car companies about more future transparency to help car hackers find and eradicate more bugs, the result was a loud, resounding, "No." For reasons that sadly tend to repeat themselves over and over in different industries, the very companies that could have benefited the most from their research simply saw them as irritants, if not outright enemies. Luckily, times have changed, and Dr. Miller is working for Uber—one assumes to better secure their future autonomous self-driving cars.

I first met Dr. Miller nearly a decade ago when he was trying to become a high-paid professional bug finder. He held a bachelor's in mathematics from Northeast Missouri State University (now Truman State University) and a mathematics PhD from the University of Notre Dame. Although he is all right with you calling him doctor, you're more likely to see Dr. Miller goofing off in public spaces filled with lots of people, wearing Elton John–style sunglasses and using physical comedy to make friends. If you thought about what a car-hacking, PhD-holding professional might look and act like, it's probably not Charlie Miller.

Prior to his current employment, he spent five years working for the National Security Agency (NSA), three years at Twitter, and further years consulting and at various companies. Dr. Miller's background and love of mathematics made him interested in cryptography, and the combination of the two made him interesting to the NSA. For those that don't know, the NSA (https://www.nsa.gov/) is the United States foremost encryption/decryption agency, if not the world leader. The halls of the NSA are full the brightest cryptographers our universities have to offer, which is how Dr. Miller ended up there.

I asked Dr. Miller how he became a broader computer security person and professional car hacker, and this is what he said: "Prior to the NSA, I never thought I could do it [computer security]. I didn't study it. The NSA hired me as a cryptographer and I thought that was my field. At the NSA, you're expected to move around to different offices (i.e. departments) every six months to get exposed to a broad range of technologies that the NSA is interested in. You're supposed to choose different topics, but I sort of tricked them into training me in just computer security, and mostly not about cryptography. Other computer security topics seemed so much more interesting than the crypto stuff. I would trick my supervisors into thinking each office was a completely different new topic, but instead they were fairly concentrated on a few, more narrow computer security topics. After three years, I had been exposed to a lot of cool computer security stuff. I was lucky to be in a place where I was expected to learn and to get paid for it."

I asked Dr. Miller how he got interested in hacking cars. He said, "I'd been hacking phones and computers for a long time. But showing the hacking of a computer or phone to regular people just didn't readily elicit understanding and excitement. But people understand a steering wheel turning by itself or a brake applying on its own. It was a hack that I didn't have to promote or sell. It promoted itself and was accessible to ordinary people. We weren't even the first people to hack cars. Others did it first, but we built upon what they discovered wanted to exploit the limits of where it could take us."

Early on, Dr. Miller made quite a name for himself by winning several Pwn2Own hacking contests in only minutes. Pwn2Own (https:// en.wikipedia.org/wiki/Pwn2Own) was a conference based in Vancouver, Canada. It was focused on giving cash and other prizes to anyone who could hack different operating systems and software that were not previously publicly known to have a bug. Each successfully demonstrated hack was a new "zero-day," which is coveted in the hacker world and is worried about the most by vendors.

For a few years, the biggest highlight of the Pwn2Own contest was Dr. Miller showing up and within less than a few minutes using his exploits to walk away with one or more grand prizes. He did this so much that eventually the contest became known as the place where everyone's product would fall within a few minutes after Dr. Miller or one of his competitors sat down. For a few years, this is what Dr. Miller's name was synonymous with, not hacking cars. It was because of his success with hacking some of the most popular operating systems, browsers, and devices at will that people paid more attention when he started talking about hacking cars. His reputation preceded him. We knew that he knew what he was talking about and was probably going to be successful.

The secret to Dr. Miller's early hacking success was due to fuzzing. There are plenty of ways to find software errors. You can manually test the software by trying all combinations of operations and manually changing the inputs to see what happens. You can statically analyze the code using source code review software (or by manually reviewing source code) that looks for predefined coding errors. Or you can accidentally stumble upon a bug while using the program in a normal way. For decades those three traditional methods were the way most exploitable bugs were discovered.

Starting in the late 1990s, fuzz testing became an incredible source of bugs, and any software developer's program will likely be doomed to multiple zero-days if they don't fuzz test their own programs before they release them. With fuzz testing, another software program (the fuzzer) automates the process of injecting all sorts of different inputs, usually unexpected by the programmer or programming language in some way (for example, being extra long, containing random control characters, containing "reserved coding words," and so on) into an active version of the target program, looking to cause an error. Each error found is then inspected, either by the fuzz-testing program or manually by a human, to see if the error condition can be used to exploit the program or underlying operating system.

Here's how Dr. Miller describes his fuzzing successes: "I learned about fuzzing at the NSA. I liked fuzzing because it found bugs quicker and is really easy to do. I'd turn on the fuzzer, go watch TV, then to sleep, wake up, and look at the findings. Around 2010 at the Blackhat conference (http://blackhat.com/), I did live fuzzing on a stage against some other guys in a contest (somewhat modeled after the *Iron Chef* TV show) to find bugs. They used a static analyzer and I used a fuzzer. It took me a few minutes to get my fuzzer working, but then I literally kicked up my feet on stage and after an hour went by, I won."

NOTE If you're interested in using fuzz-testing software, there are lots of free and commercial products available. Microsoft even offers a decent fuzz tester for free at: https://www.microsoft.com/en-us/springfield/.

I asked Dr. Miller why his earliest exploits were mostly targeted at Apple products. He said, "Back then Apple didn't have a lot of computer security protections, especially memory protections in their code. And they didn't do their own fuzz testing. I did it for them and found lots of bugs that I could use in Pwn2Own and other findings. Microsoft and Microsoft Windows did fuzz testing and their programs have built-in memory protections. I wasn't targeting Apple just to find bugs in Apple and make a point. They were just easier to find and I like hacking easier."

In 2007, he was the first person known to remotely hack an iPhone, and he remotely hacked an Android phone on the day it came out in 2008. Later in 2008, Dr. Miller found a zero-day in a MacBook Air's Safari browser and won $10,000. In 2009 and 2010, he cracked Apple's Safari browser again, and he continued successfully hacking iPhones. In 2011, he found iOS security holes in iPad and iPhone devices. He essentially showed how an approved Apple app could maliciously steal information or otherwise hack Apple device owners. He created a demonstration program that he placed in the Apple App Store.

At this point, Dr. Miller's bug-finding exploits evoked the wrath of Apple. They accused him of violating the terms of his Apple's developer agreement (which was technically accurate) and took away his right to develop and publish Apple software. He told me of the incident: "They said they were taking my Apple developer ID away for a year. After I re-applied for reinstatement, it wasn't returned. I still don't have an Apple developer ID to this day." Much of the observing world thought Apple learned the wrong lesson and should have embraced Dr. Miller and his bug hunting by paying or hiring him.

When I first met Dr. Miller, he was desperately trying to get a great paying job finding bugs. At the time, very few people made a real living that way. Most people, like Dr. Miller, didn't get paid at all. There were very few "bug bounty" programs offered by vendors in the ubiquitous way they are today. In fact, the only people getting paid large sums of money for new zero-days were malicious hackers, often paid by bad guys and criminal groups. Occasionally whitehats could sell their bugs to legitimate companies who paid for bugs and then redistributed them to the highest bidder or to the originating vendor so they could examine the bug and fix it. That still goes on today.

But Dr. Miller was looking for Apple, Microsoft, or some other company to see the value of his excitement and expertise. For the most part it didn't come to pass, at least the way he initially had hoped it would. But ultimately it did lead to his high-profile jobs at Twitter and Uber. Along the way, he brought to the forefront the need for professional bug finders to get reimbursed for their efforts. He wasn't the leading advocate, but he was a very vocal part of it. He even started the "No More Free Bugs" campaign. Today, nearly every big software developer has a cash-based bug bounty program, and good bug finders can find full-time, good-paying, legitimate jobs.

I asked Dr. Miller about the frustration of those days when he was having to chase consultant work instead of finding a full-time job commensurate with his expertise and talent. He said, "I ended up being a traveling consultant, and at the beginning of your career it's a good thing. It exposes you to lots of companies, their problems, and cultures. I only got paid one time for finding a bug, in 2007, for a bug I found outside of Pwn2Own. I quickly found that I liked talking at conferences even more than getting paid. It was more important for me to talk about, to share it with people, than getting paid and maybe having to be silent."

If you have attended any of his presentations or conferences, it's obvious that Dr. Miller loves to have fun, entertain, and teach audiences. It's clear he is also in it for the intellectual curiosity as much as the fun and the money. If history is any gauge, once he has mastered something, he moves on to the next field, to another target. He told me, "Once I find five bugs in something, it becomes less interesting and I move on." Along the way, he has found other security vulnerabilities, in fields such as Near Field Communication (NFC). He has also published three books (https://www.amazon.com/Charlie-Miller/e/B0085NZ1PS/) that cover Mac hacking, iOS hacking, and fuzz testing.

I finished my interview with Dr. Miller with one last question: Did he think that cars would be fairly secure any time soon? He replied, "Cars aren't different than computers, and we still don't know how to perfectly secure computers. Cars are more like attacking networks and networks of computers since they contain a lot of computers. The thing about cars is the special physical safety issues. It raises the stakes. I may not be able to stop you from attacking a car, but I can mitigate the worst attacks a lot of ways. You may be able to mess with the entertainment system, but if we do our jobs right we'll stop you from talking with the brakes and other critical systems."

True to his early secretive NSA roots, he wouldn't tell me what he is working on at Uber, but you can guess that Uber and all its passengers are going to benefit.

For More Information on Dr. Charlie Miller

For information about Dr. Charlie Miller, check out these resources:

- Dr. Charlie Miller on Twitter: https://twitter.com/0xcharlie
- Dr. Charlie Miller's books: https://www.amazon.com/Charlie-Miller/e/B0085NZ1PS/

- "Adventures in Automotive Networks and Control Units" whitepaper: `http://illmatics.com/car_hacking.pdf`
- "Car Hacking: For Poories" whitepaper: `http://illmatics.com/car_hacking_poories.pdf`
- "A Survey of Remote Automotive Attack Surfaces" whitepaper: `http://illmatics.com/remote%20attack%20surfaces.pdf`
- "Remote Exploitation of an Unaltered Passenger Vehicle" whitepaper: `http://illmatics.com/Remote%20Car%20Hacking.pdf`
- "CAN Message Injection" whitepaper: `http://illmatics.com/can%20message%20injection.pdf`

37 Policy and Strategy

I was a guy who hated policies and procedures. I had no use for paperwork. All it does is slow you down. Or so I thought.

After toiling away for decades as a computer security professional, I finally realized that without the appropriate policies and frameworks nothing will ever get done. Anyone can perfectly secure a few computers and devices. I haven't been exploited in nearly two decades. But you absolutely cannot protect more than a few personal devices, and certainly not an entire company's computers, for long without the "right" paperwork. I've come to appreciate standards, policies, procedures, frameworks, and those who toil to get them right. They really are the true behind-the-scenes heroes, and without them we would not be able to make computers significantly more secure.

In this chapter I break down the paperwork that manages computer security into standards, policies, procedures, frameworks, and laws.

NOTE You'll also see the terms "guidelines" and "practices" frequently used, but I included their traits in the other terms presented here.

Standards

Standards are documented minimum norms, conventions, protocols, or requirements. In the computer security world, standards are often communicated as statements such as the following examples:

- All critical data will be encrypted during transmission and storage.
- Minimum public key cipher key sizes will be 2048-bit for RSA and Diffie-Hellman and 384-bit for ECC.

- Passwords will be a minimum of twelve characters long and will contain at least two non-alphabetic characters.
- After three bad passwords within a five-minute period, the logon account will be locked out until reviewed by an administrator.
- All critical security patches must be applied within five business days after release by the vendor.
- All computers must be protected by a host-based firewall with deny-by-default inbound rules.

A standard is often represented as a policy and further supported by procedures.

Standards sometimes become regulations, laws, or requirements that must be followed by every managed device. In the United States, one of the largest standards that must be followed by tens of millions of computers is the United States Government Configuration Baseline (`https://usgcb.nist.gov/`). Standards can also be developed by a vendor, like Microsoft's Security Compliance Manager baselines (`https://technet.microsoft.com/en-us/library/cc677002.aspx`). Sometimes the standards become so respected and trusted that they become national or worldwide standards. A great example of this is nearly anything the National Institute of Standards and Technology, or NIST (`https://www.nist.gov/`), produces. And many companies spend large sums of money and resources trying to get certified as following the ISO/IEC 27001 standards (`http://www.iso.org/iso/home/standards/management-standards/iso27001.htm`).

Policies

Policies are documented principles that guide decisions to achieve intended outcomes. Oftentimes they can be written declarations that could not be easily enforced by other means. An example of this is "Employees should not re-use their password on any other network." Although a company cannot easily ensure this never happens, just having it written and communicated to employees decreases the chances that a violation will happen. Additionally, if a violation is found, it can more easily result in punishment.

Procedures

Procedures are a documented sequence of steps designed to support standards and policies around deployment and operations. Procedures, if followed, will ensure the timely and satisfactory application of those previously stated standards and policies. Procedures can change independently of policies and standards, for example, if a new software program requires different procedures.

Frameworks

Creating standards and policies for the entire spectrum of computer security from scratch can be very difficult. Frameworks assist by demonstrating commonly supported standards, policies, formats, and a set of inclusive topics. A great example of a cybersecurity framework is NIST's Cybersecurity Framework (https://www.nist.gov/cyberframework).

Regulatory Laws

Standards and policies can be codified into legal regulations and laws. For example, companies wishing to process many common credit card types must follow the standards covered in the Payment Card Industry Security Standards Council's Data Security Standard (https://www.pcisecuritystandards.org/). Failure to follow the PCI DSS standards could result in suspension of credit card processing use or even legal consequences. Healthcare-related organizations in the United States must follow Health Insurance Portability and Accountability Act (HIPAA) guidelines. All U.S. publicly traded companies must follow the Sarbanes-Oxley Act requirements, and so on.

Global Concerns

And for multinational companies, each country can have its own, sometimes conflicting, set of standards and policies. Some countries may highly value personal privacy while others may legally require no guaranteed personal privacy.

One country may require that computer systems used in another country use lesser standards (like the United States crypto-export laws require). Global companies have exponentially more compliance issues to be worried about.

Systems Support

Many companies are under multiple, sometimes conflicting requirements. Trying to abide by one standard can be very difficult. For that reason, an entire ecosystem of companies and tools have been created to assist companies attempting to comply with one or more standards or regulations. Companies usually have dedicated teams and staff members, expensive software programs, and the attention of the CEO. Trying to meet all the compliance standards in a timely manner takes focused staff, the entire IT team, and every employee working toward common compliance goals. Compliance is big business. The consequences of not complying can be regulatory problems, legal procedures, and hackers exploiting known weaknesses.

If you just read this chapter and wish you had those minutes of your life back because it nearly put you to sleep, know that that used to be me, too. It took decades of seeing my incredibly technical, exacting recommendations being misapplied and ignored for me to understand the importance of policy-making and documentation. Without the compliance paperwork, there can be no true computer security. It's just that simple.

The next chapter profiles Jing de Jong-Chen, whose work focuses on improving international security standards and global cybergovernance.

38 Profile: Jing de Jong-Chen

As the previous chapter discussed, you cannot obtain real, long-lasting computer security without policies and strategies. Some of the "invisible" heroes of computer security are the people who drive corporate and global computer security strategies. Jing de Jong-Chen, Partner and General Manager, Global Security Strategy, Corporate, External and Legal Affairs Division at Microsoft, has devoted her professional life to pushing for better and more global interoperable computer security standards and cyber policy harmonization. She also serves as vice president of the Trusted Computing Group (TCG), a non-profit, international, industry standards organization focusing on security technology innovations. She is a board advisor of the Executive Women's Forum, an organization dedicated to promoting women in the security, privacy, and risk management professions. In addition, de Jong-Chen serves as an advisor to the Digital Futures project of the Woodrow Wilson Center, which champions technology thought leadership to shape public policy development. She received the "Women of Influence Award" from the Executive Women's Forum in 2014 for her professional contributions to cybersecurity. She holds a master's degree in business administration and a bachelor of science degree in computer science.

One of the things I noticed right away when I first interviewed her was how thoughtful and complete her answers were. She has spent decades successfully fighting for better global public policy and standards, and her experience and expertise shows. The length of her experience is a bit unique for both being a female and an Asian professional, something she readily acknowledges as she actively pushes for more diversity in the computer security field.

I asked how she first got involved in computer security. She replied, "I started working for Microsoft in 1992, specifically in Research and Development to tackle the challenges of producing Asian versions of Windows 3.1. There was no Chinese version of Windows at the time, and China was on its way to deepening its economic reform and becoming an important world economy. We successfully created the first Japanese, Korean, and Chinese versions of Windows 3.1, supporting 'double-byte' characters. To achieve our vision of democratizing computing with 'a computer on every desk and in every home,' our software needed to be designed with worldwide users in mind. Based on the challenges that we had to face while developing Windows 3.1, we realized that we must change our ways of creating software. We designed an approach to have a single codebase, to enable the Unicode standard, and separate resources (the language components) from the source code.

"This was far ahead of many software companies at the time when we released worldwide versions of Windows 95 with simultaneous release of many language versions. We shipped the Simplified Chinese version of Windows 95 within six months after the US release. That was quite an accomplishment given the localization involved. To comply with the national language standard, we included over 25,000 Chinese simplified and traditional characters. As you know, China prides itself on being the birthplace of the printing press, but before the availability of commercial operating systems such as Windows 95, publishing still required manual processes. We worked with Professor Wang Xuan, a pioneer at Founder Group (a Chinese information technology company), to create a Windows-based electronic publishing application, with immediate impact to not only China and but also overseas Chinese publishing communities. It was the beginning of China's entry into an electronic publishing era, after thousands of years' manual labor. It demonstrated the value of computing to significantly increase human productivity. It was very satisfying to me personally.

"Then in 1998, around the beginning of the ecommerce revolution, Microsoft started getting into the Internet space. I became a part of our online services division, and you can't be part of Internet services and software without security being involved. Within a few years, we had some pretty big challenges as hackers began to use viruses and malware to hurt our customers and the company—the Code Red worm and SQL Slammer to name two. All of Microsoft was trying to figure out how we could build more secure and trustworthy software. At the same time the attacks on 9/11 showed that the industries, such as financial services, that were more prepared for disasters recovered faster. Some of the lessons learned in the previous Y2K preparedness projects paid off for those companies. I saw where security was heading and joined Microsoft's Advanced Policy and Strategy Division under Craig Mundie. I became a part of the newly formed Trustworthy Computing Group led by Scott Charney, which focused on security, privacy, reliability, and business integrity. I was very fortunate to learn from both very seasoned leaders in technology and cybersecurity.

"I remember that during those early attacks, markets like Korea and Japan got hit very hard because they were early adopters of our technology and the Internet. Millions of users were affected. The governments were concerned. Microsoft had to respond very quickly. I devoted full-time to focus on computer security issues and government engagement. I started to conduct outreach and find ways to help create public-private partnerships to minimize risks and address security holistically. We were able to share our expertise and develop solutions to support government and industry partners to build technical response capacity. For example, many police departments in different countries did not have a cyber division and used very old systems. As more cybercrime investigations became a priority, law enforcement needed more experts who can handle incident response and forensic analysis. Microsoft stepped in to support this effort by providing much-needed technical training including in regions like Southeast Asia.

"My job is super-dynamic, and I am fortunate to work with great co-workers and thinkers who taught me a great deal. Microsoft became a champion in cybersecurity technology and strategy. We began by looking inward and outward, and working with partners. In some countries, it was not common at the time for competitors to work together, but we believed cybersecurity was bigger than commercial competition. We shared sensitive security information with anti-virus software providers and developed a Government Security Program to support cybersecurity efforts in both developed and developing countries. I eventually started working on hardware-based security solutions in 2008 and since then kept up with my involvement with the Trusted Computing Group, where I got to work with many talented people."

I wondered what types of issues she faces and solves as vice-president of the Trusted Computing Group (TCG). She gave me an example: "You know about TCG's Trusted Platform Module (TPM) chip, which helps to secure computers from the hardware layer on up. Version 1.2 of the TPM worked great, but its design lacked the flexibility to sunset encryption algorithms when weaknesses are found. At the same time, nations began to push for the use of their own algorithms in their security products. TPM 1.2 could not satisfy that requirement given only a limited set of algorithms were supported.

"There was a risk of competing by governments at the standards level before any global adoption began. If countries would start down the path of developing non-compatible standards only because of algorithm use, the overall security benefits to the users will be diminished. From an adoption perspective, this would certainly present a challenge of interoperability between the security chips that are based on an international standard and those with a local standard. The TCG made a decision to address this 'crypto agility' issue, among other improvements, with a new TPM 2.0 specification. With contributions from many security experts from different countries, the TPM 2.0 standard was approved as ISO/IEC 11889:2015. It is now a unified, global standard. This approval was remarkable because it required a consensus among many countries including the US, China, Russia, Japan, France, South Africa, Malaysia, and others. We achieved something remarkable. The new standard offers a much broader security protection not only for the users of PC desktops, but of the cloud and IoT devices." It was clear to me that de Jong-Chen's work decades ago in globalizing Windows 95 paid off when she was helping to develop a globally trusted computing standard and ecosystem.

I asked her what she thought was the biggest obstacle to significantly better global computer security. She replied, "Countries have very different belief systems, and that has to be considered when promoting international security standards and best practices. There are issues involving policy and technology. Naturally, the technical experts want to create the best technology, but that's only part of the challenge. There are ecosystem and cybergovernance issues to consider. Each country is worried about protecting its cyber sovereignty while competing to build stronger cyber capabilities. You can't just address the technology alone or just leave cybersecurity in the hands of politicians. You have to look for the best solution and balance requirements across a whole spectrum of concerns. And it's getting to be a pretty complex matrix of things that the policy makers and industry leaders need to consider before they take actions. Policy considerations include: security and privacy of the Internet users, critical infrastructure protection, social and economic stability, and global communications and trade. As more nations release more and more security regulations, the cost of enterprises doing business will rise. Any compliance will involve managing political implications, legal risks, technical design modifications, and business and operational model changes. There are challenges and opportunities, but you can't solve the big, shared cybersecurity issues without understanding how countries work and how things are interconnected. If we do it right, perhaps we can achieve the equilibrium required to improve cybersecurity and protect global cyber infrastructure while safeguarding users' privacy, maintaining fair competition, and gradually reducing the cost of doing business in support of global trade."

I asked about the lack of women in the IT field. De Jong-Chen replied, "Woman are rare in the IT field in general, but even more rare in the computer security field. I worked with [a large Internet company] where they aggressively hired women and saw them as the force behind its growth. Even though it has fifty-four percent of its workforce being women employees, I did not realize it when I interacted with their security team. There was only one woman, who was the liaison, and she was not a security specialist. We could do better as an industry. We need to increase the talent pool in the cybersecurity space, and we need to find ways to attract and retain women in the IT field and promote diversity in computer security. We need everyone's support to achieve that."

For More Information on Jing de Jong-Chen

For information about Jing de Jong-Chen, check out these resources:

- Jing de Jong-Chen's Microsoft blog: `http://blogs.microsoft.com/microsoftsecure/author/jingdejongchen/`
- Jing de Jong-Chen's LinkedIn profile: `https://www.linkedin.com/vsearch/p?orig=SEO_SN&firstName=Jing&lastName=Jong-Chen&trk=SEO_SN`
- "Governments Recognize the Importance of TPM 2.0 through ISO Adoption" (Microsoft Secure Blog post): `http://blogs.microsoft.com/microsoftsecure/2015/06/29/governments-recognize-the-importance-of-tpm-2-0-through-iso-adoption/`
- "U.S.-China Cybersecurity Relations: Understanding China's Current Environment" (*Georgetown Journal of International Affairs*): `http://journal.georgetown.edu/u-s-china-cybersecurity-relations-understanding-chinas-current-environment/`
- "Spotlight on Cyber V: Data Sovereignty, Cybersecurity and Challenges for Globalization" (*Georgetown Journal of International Affairs*): `http://journal.georgetown.edu/data-sovereignty-cybersecurity-and-challenges-for-globalization/`

39 Threat Modeling

hreat modeling is the process at looking at all the significant and likely potential threats to a scoped scenario, ranking their potential damage in a given time period, and figuring cost-effective mitigations to defeat the highest-priority threats. Threat modeling is used in all sorts of industries and in our particular case planning computer security defenses. Threat modeling is used in the security development lifecycle (SDL) efforts when programming and reviewing software and across computer devices and infrastructure. Only by using threat modeling can a defender quantify threats, risks, and mitigations, and compare the implemented plan against the reality of what occurs.

Why Threat Model?

Threat modeling reduces risk. At the very least it allows one or more people to consider the various threats and risks in a scenario. It allows multiple threats to be weighed against each other, mitigations to be developed and evaluated, and, hopefully, cost-effective, useful mitigations to be deployed. We know for sure that, over the long run, software programmed using threat modeling consideration has fewer bugs and vulnerabilities than software that is not threat modeled. If software is being threat modeled for the first time, modelers may discover more bugs and vulnerabilities than in a prior period, and that increased number of vulnerabilities may continue for some period of time, but eventually the number of newly discovered bugs and vulnerability should fall. And in the end, over the lifetime of the project or product, the number of total bugs and the total possible damage they might create should be reduced. Otherwise, why perform threat modeling?

Threat modeling even considers whether a very effective mitigation is cost-effective. It could be that a very good mitigation could be so expensive (in cost, resources, performance issues, and so on) that even though it might offset a particular risk, it isn't cost-efficient to do so. For example, suppose computer viruses cause $100,000 in damage ever year to a company. That company would not want to spend more than $100,000 to stop computer viruses. It might be that not using any computer virus mitigations could be the best decision they can make, in this super-silly, simple example.

Threat Modeling Models

There are nearly as many models for threat modeling as there are types of threats. They are normally known by acronyms such as STRIDE, PASTA, VAST, TRIKE, and OCTAVE. There are many software tools that have their own models or that base themselves on one of the existing models. Each model has fans and critics. It's far more important for developers and computer security providers to threat model, using any model, than to not threat model because they can't determine which model they should use. Simply doing threat modeling is a win.

Each model attempts to capture the processes of understanding what the project under consideration is in its totality. Usually this is done by brain storming, flow chart diagrams, and a detailed description of the involved processes. Then all the potential threats to the project, program, or service are considered. They are ranked for likelihood and potential damage. The threats and risks that are more likely to cause the most damage are considered first. Then mitigations are developed and evaluated for fitness and cost-efficiency against each particular threat.

All threat models must start with the concept of how much leftover (residual) risk the owner is willing or able to accept after all agreed upon mitigations are applied. For example, threat modeling offensive or defensive military weapons begins with the idea that there is very little acceptable residual risk. One company might allow some risk to remain, while another with strict resource constraints might be forced to knowingly accept many large, unresolved risks. Threat modeling helps users prepare for leftover residual risk scenarios. Some threat models even give time to the "known unknowns" and "unknown unknowns," for the same reason and to remind users that not all risks will ever be thought of and mitigated.

Threat Actors

Every threat model must also consider the most likely types of hackers that might target their project. There are a wide range of different types of threat actors, each with their own concerns.

Nation-States

Most industrialized nations now have teams of bright, capable, and resourced hackers, dutifully and patriotically hacking on behalf of the country's government or military. They are attacking and compromising other countries for strategies and targets deemed essential to their country's success. Cyberwarfare is also a huge component of this type of threat actor. Cyberwarfare attempts to harm an enemy's ability to wage war or mount a good defense by utilizing professional hackers and malware. A great example is the Stuxnet worm, which destroyed another nation's nuclear equipment. Other types of threats may come and go, but nation-state attackers are with us forever.

Industrial Hackers

There are hackers that focus on stealing other companies' secrets and intellectual property in order to re-sell them or to help another company or industry unfairly compete. This type of threat may operate from a competing company, act on behalf of a nation-state, or act independently as a freelancer.

NOTE Both nation-states and industrial hackers are known as Advanced Persistent Threats (APTs). APTs are human adversaries that hack in a professional way as part of a long-term, concerted effort against targeted adversaries. They usually have vast resources and are very, very difficult to stop from being successful.

Financial Crime

Financial cyber-attackers are represented by ransomware distributors, denial of service implementers, adware makers, and hackers who steal digital money, steal authentication information, or commit identity theft. Money has motivated criminals for longer than computers have been around, but the current state of computer security allows large sums of money to be stolen more easily and with far less risk than traditional, non–computer related crime.

214 Hacking the Hacker

Hacktivists

Politically-, morally-, and psychologically-motivated people often like to cause damage (to finances, reputation, or resources) to companies and organizations they disagree with. Some of the largest and most damaging attacks in history have been hacktivist-related.

Gamers

Computer games and gamers force software and hardware makers to push the technological and performance limits more than almost any other group. Today, not only do people pay money to play games, they pay money to watch other people play games. Gamers fill concert halls as quickly as yesterday's rock stars. Sometimes it seems as if half the television ads during the most watched television events (such as the Super Bowl) are ads for computer games. To say computer gaming is very popular is an understatement. Some hackers exist solely to hack computer games to increase their winnings (whatever that means), to give themselves competitive advantages, and to hurt gaming services they don't agree with.

Insider Threats

It's always been debated how big of a threat legitimate employees are to a company, but it's clear that they represent some non-minor percent of all attackers. Some insiders steal data and other intellectual property to sell to competitors or take on their way to another job. Others steal money or information, such as customer credit cards (for personal financial gain). Insiders doing unauthorized things are very difficult to detect and prevent, especially when conducting transactions using their legitimate authority. This is a threat that the computer security industry is still struggling with.

Ordinary, Solitary Hackers or Hacker Groups

Let's not forget the traditional hackers, who are hacking for their own individual needs, be it financial gain or just to prove they can do it. A decade or more ago, this group compromised almost all hacking. The hacking world wasn't filled by professional criminals. Most hackers were content to just write a computer virus that printed a funny saying on the computer or played "Yankee Doodle Dandy" at a predetermined time. A few caused real damage, like the Michelangelo boot virus did when it formatted hard drives. But most were just someone's vanity project, a way of saying that they were smart enough to do it. They didn't want to cause real, widespread harm.

Threat modeling is something developers and every computer security professional should do. It efficiently reduces risk by ranking threats based on the damage they are likely to cause. If you don't threat model, you're just guessing and wandering around in the computer security defense landscape.

The next chapter profiles Adam Shostack, a respected threat modeler and author.

40 Profile: Adam Shostack

One of my first encounters with Adam Shostack was at Microsoft when he was driving a new way of thinking around a type of problem. In this specific case, it was how to defeat the Conficker worm (https://en.wikipedia.org/wiki/Conficker). Conficker was a particularly nasty malware program that first appeared at the end of 2008. It had several ways of spreading (such as "vectors"), including guessing at weakly password-protected file shares, a desktop.ini trick, patched software vulnerabilities, and via USB drives using Windows's built-in Autorun feature. Conficker was infecting millions of machines a year and was showing no signs of abating. Anti-malware vendors were readily detecting it and Microsoft had put out several articles on how to stop it from spreading, but it was still prolific.

Shostack proposed using data analysis to look at the problem. He and Microsoft started looking at which attack vectors were allowing Conficker to spread the most. Our initial assumption had been that most of the people being infected had not applied a long-available patch. And that was indeed one of the most popular vectors early on. But now, nearly two years later, Shostack found out that it was largely due to infected USB keys. Using his collected data, he proposed that Microsoft disable the Autorun feature, which was a huge decision. It meant changing the way Windows worked and was going to force all users, infected or not, to now do something extra to make executables on removable media run. Autorun would no longer execute. But Shostack had the data. The powers that be agreed with the approach, and on our next Patch Tuesday, Microsoft pushed an update that disabled the Autorun feature. And just like that Conficker died. Well, it didn't die completely, but it stopped being the huge problem that it was and it hasn't been a big issue since. In fact, malware spreading via USB keys hasn't been a big problem since.

Shostack's, and Microsoft's, approach of using data to drive the response had a huge impact on me. It led me to writing what I think is the most important concept and whitepaper of my career, "Implementing a Data-Driven Computer Security Defense" (https://gallery.technet.microsoft.com/Fixing-the-1-Problem-in-2e58ac4a), which has since gone on to be recommended reading by many industry luminaries and groups.

Later on, I read Shostack's book, *Threat Modeling: Designing for Security* (https://www.amazon.com/Threat-Modeling-Designing-Adam-Shostack/dp/1118809998), by Wiley. It was clear that he really understood threat modeling and the errors in other models and implementations. It's still one of the top books I recommend to people interested in threat modeling. Shostack was intimately involved at Microsoft, helping with multiple projects, like pushing out the Autorun fix to stop malware like the Conficker worm, the SDL Threat Modeling Tool (https://www.microsoft.com/en-us/sdl/adopt/threatmodeling.aspx), and the Elevation of Privilege threat modeling game (https://www.microsoft.com/en-us/sdl/adopt/eop.aspx). He co-founded the Privacy Enhancing Technologies Symposium and International Financial Cryptography Association. He's also a prolific writer, blogger, and speaker.

I asked him how he got into computer security. He said, "Professionally, I was working as a sys admin in a medical research lab and security was a part of my job. This was in 1993 and 1994. I started reading several early Internet mailing lists, such as the original Firewalls and the Cyberpunks mailing lists. They had all sorts of interesting people saying interesting things. I started to participate and learned that I could contribute to the discussion. My next job was more security-focused. I became a consultant around Boston, and this was just as the Internet was really taking off. So, knowing about security and being able to contribute about Internet security really helped. I was able to find security flaws in a couple of things, and that helped my reputation."

I asked him for an example of what he meant. He replied, "I found a security vulnerability in a security key fob. It was the precursor of the RSA Secure ID before it was bought by RSA. The flaw was that information from the previous message was used to help secure the next message. Except they had a flaw in the algorithm that connected the prior message to the next that made the key that linked them predictable, and from that forgeable."

I asked him how he got involved in Common Vulnerabilities and Exposures (CVE), the dictionary of publicly known information security vulnerabilities and exposures. He stated, "One of my consulting clients was Fidelity

Investments. They had me doing secure code work, much like I would return to 15 years later at Microsoft. I was still staying very active in mailing lists and the Internet, sharing things and getting feedback from those sources. I'll always be thankful that the executives allowed me to do that because not all executives or companies allow that type of sharing. From Fidelity, I ran into a venture capitalist who owned a chunk of a vulnerability-scanning company, and I thought that it would be interesting, so I moved there. We were very competitive over how many vulnerabilities we could detect and making sure our product detected the most. I was working on a new fingerd vulnerability, and I couldn't tell if one of our competitor's products was detecting the same vulnerability or if it was something different. At the time, vulnerability information stank, and so did search engines. You couldn't find out information nearly as easily as you can today. I started out wondering how we could talk to other vulnerability management software people on what vulnerabilities we found or didn't find, and that thinking led me into thinking about how to communicate with sys admins so they could identify different vulnerabilities and figure out if they had fixed them or not. We needed a system to help bring different types of people together to talk about the same things in similar ways and understand each other. CVE did that."

I asked Shostack what he specifically contributed to threat modeling. He hesitated a brief moment and then responded, "I listened when people told me something wasn't working. Some people try to teach people around why something isn't working, but I see that it isn't working and it's the system that needs to change. For example, if someone is opening an email and getting infected all the time, even if you're telling them not to open untrusted emails, the problem is with the system, not the user. We've got to design systems that take into account what people do, because they aren't doing it wrong. The systems are. I'm reading about aircraft safety systems because in computer security we don't examine our failures very well. But in the aircraft industry they do. Even if all they have is a near miss incident, there's a form any pilot can fill out about the near miss and send into a common agency. The agency collects all these forms and examines each one. They can see common mistakes, even if it is at first being reported as human error. The agency can send a recommendation to a radio manufacturer and tell them how they can improve the radio issue by adding a light or tell a particular airport (or bunch of airports) how to fix a problem with the runway lighting. It's blameless root cause analysis. The computer security field doesn't analyze things well, so we end up repeating the same mistakes over and over and it takes longer to design better systems."

I ended our interview by asking what he would recommend to young people getting in the field of computer security. He replied, "Two things. First, I think students can benefit by studying the humanities (psychology, philosophy, etc.). Early on in my career, I was studying environmental science. I learned that our environmental issues are impacted by political, legal, and economic issues and if you don't solve those issues, you won't solve the environmental issue. The same with computer security. There are technical issues to be sure, but you have to understand the political, legal, and economic issues as well if you want to solve the technical issue. It isn't just a problem with the firewall. Also, learn how to write. Second, the technology skills you acquire aren't as important as learning how to think. The technology issues I faced when I first entered this field compared to now are not even close. The IT world changes all the time. But the approach I use stays the same. I try to look at the big problems and ask why something doesn't work. I want to find a big problem with a broad issue, but narrow the focus enough that I can solve that issue. You can't solve big problems immediately. Readers need to pick the right problems, the meaningful ones, ask the right questions, and then find the levers you can use to affect them."

For More Information on Adam Shostack

For information about Adam Shostack, check out these resources:

- *Threat Modeling: Designing for Security*: https://www.amazon.com/Threat-Modeling-Designing-Adam-Shostack/dp/1118809998
- *The New School of Information Security* (co-authored with Andrew Stewart): https://www.amazon.com/New-School-Information-Security/dp/0321814908
- Adam Shostack's web site: https://adam.shostack.org/
- Adam Shostack on Twitter: http://twitter.com/adamshostack
- Adam Shostack's LinkedIn profile: http://www.linkedin.com/in/shostack/

41 Computer Security Education

One bit of advice that has been consistent from almost every person profiled in this book is their belief that more and better computer security education is needed. No one thinks that any perfect technology solution will become available any time reasonably soon that will preclude people needing to be aware of computer security threats and how to handle them. Some computer security "experts" claim that it's a waste of time trying to educate end-users, but most serious security professionals know that education for end-users and staff can only help.

My current employer, Microsoft, forces all employees to undertake annual computer security training on multiple topics. One year, after we had been getting a lot of email phishing attempts, the mandatory training video included a well-respected Microsoft employee who had been tricked by a phishing email. He was well-liked and he worked in a field that required heavy computer security knowledge. In short, he should have been less likely to be socially engineered by a phishing email, but it happened to him. He shared his experience, including how he fell for the well-crafted, targeted spearphishing attempt. It was wonderful to see one our technological leaders share that he was fallible, that he made a mistake, and how that mistake happened. He then shared that although he was personally a bit embarrassed about his mistake, he wasn't too ashamed to call IT security to report the incident. It was a tremendously well-received educational video that led to significantly lower numbers of successful phishing. The education was so successful that the Microsoft IT security teams were inundated all year with people asking whether suspicious-looking but legitimate emails were actually phishing emails. Some people even said the education was overly successful.

Other education videos in prior years covered not getting tricked into giving your password away and making sure that people did not walk in behind you without having their own building access badge. Education can help to significantly reduce computer security threats.

Computer Security Training Topics

Computer security training comes in many varieties and approaches. The following sections examine some of the topics that people interested in computer security training can avail themselves of.

End-User/Security Awareness Training

This type of training typically prepares end-users for using their computers and devices more safely. It shares with them common forms of hacking they may be exposed to and how to detect, prevent, and report attacks. Everyone should get this form of security education, whether at home, going to school, or in an office. It should be taken at least once a year, if not more frequently, and should cover recent and most likely threats. This sort of training typically only requires dedicating 15 minutes to a few hours each year.

General IT Security Training

This is for IT and computer security staff members. It should provide a general overview of all types of hacking and malware and go into more detail on the most common and likely-to-happen threats. Typically, this type of training happens over many days or weeks and can recur with increasing maturation over time.

Incident Response

Computer security staff and particularly members of incident response teams should be trained in how to correctly respond to and manage computer security incidents. This should be required training for all personnel who share these responsibilities. This sort of training usually lasts several days and should be repeated as needed.

OS and Application-Specific Training

Many popular OS and application vendors offer general and product-specific security training. Vendor-specific training can supplement your general security knowledge, and if tested and/or used as part of a certification, it can attest to your knowledge of a particular product.

Technical Skills

Many training and certification entities offer security technical training. This includes learning skills around particular types of security products, such as firewalls, intrusion detection, malware analysis, cryptography, patching, backing up, and so on.

Certifications

There are dozens of computer security–related certifications. Every computer certification that a certification candidate studies for and/or takes a test for will contribute to their overall education. There are no right or wrong certifications. However, there are certainly some certifications that are more respected in the industry than others as a measure of computer security fitness. In general, any of the certifications from the following organizations are widely respected (in no particular order):

- International Information Systems Security Certifications Consortium (ISC)^2 (https://www.isc2.org/)
- International Council of Electronic Commerce Consultants (EC-Council) (https://www.eccouncil.org/)
- SysAdmin, Networking, and Security (SANS) Institute (http://www.sans.org)
- Computing Technology Industry Association (CompTIA) (https://certification.comptia.org/)
- Information Systems Audit and Control Association (ISACA) (https://www.isaca.org)

Well-respected, vendor-specific exams are also offered by Microsoft, Cisco, and RedHat. This list is not exhaustive, and there are certainly many other vendors that offer great exams and education.

For more information see my recent *InfoWorld* column on computer security certifications: http://www.infoworld.com/article/3115344/security/essential-certifications-for-smart-security-pros.html.

Training Methods

There are as many ways to learn as there are things to learn. The following sections explore some of the common ways.

Online Training

There is almost no test, certification, or topic that you can't master using online training. Online training can simply be teacher videos, or it can be fully immersive teaching experiences with text, videos, chapter reviews, and competency testing. Many have real-time teachers to whom you can raise a digital hand and ask questions. Some people prefer in-person teachers in a real classroom, but it is becoming more common for online training to give you nearly the same experience, usually for a far cheaper price.

Break into My Website

There are many online security education sites that primarily work by allowing you to break into, legally, their web site. It's a great way of teaching a skill and allowing a budding hacker to experience the thrill of breaking into something without the possible legal consequences of doing it illegally. One of my favorite sites of this type is https://www.hackthissite.org/.

Schools and Training Centers

Today, there aren't many major universities, colleges, technical colleges, or formal training schools that do not have a computer security curriculum. Although these are usually more expensive than other training options, and you do need to make sure that you are not just getting talked out of your hard-earned dollars (by diploma mills that don't really prepare you for good jobs), they can often give very a thorough and comprehensive security education. Many computer security professionals start off at technical schools or local community colleges and then eventually progress to full four-year college degrees or even further.

Boot Camps

Boot camps are places that offer accelerated training, usually focused on obtaining a specific certification. For example, a two-week boot camp could help you get the same certifications you could otherwise get in a one- to two-year technical school. I love boot camps and for two years even taught at some. If you're attending a boot camp, you have to be ready for intense study and should be the type of individual who can cram a lot of information into a short period of time. For many people with busy lives, boot camps are their best alternative for getting their education. Just make sure your boot camp offers money-back guarantees or multiple test-taking when going for a certification.

Corporate Training

As covered in the "Computer Security Training Topics" section in this chapter, many organizations offer and even require mandatory computer security education. Many large companies offer partial or full tuition reimbursement programs and have employee-led group meetings around particular security topics or certifications. Many employees consider the corporate-offered educational benefits to be one of the best benefits of working for a particular company.

Books

Of course, my book's chapter on education would not be complete without mentioning that books are a great way to learn about a topic at your own place and pace. Computer books are generally more inclusive around their topic, offer longer introductions to new material, and are usually professionally edited for technical detail and grammar.

Continuing, relevant education is essential for end-users, IT staff, and computer security experts alike. One of the most common threads I learned from interviewing all the people profiled in this book is that most of them are continuous learners, and the cream of the crop even reserve a specific time period each day dedicated to learning something new. Go forth and learn!

42 Profile: Stephen Northcutt

I've known Stephen Northcutt for almost 20 years. He's not only a vital part of the incredible computer security training organization, the SysAdmin, Networking, and Security (SANS) Institute, but he's an indispensable person if you're trying to locate a particular industry luminary. I don't know how many times in my writing career that when I needed to speak to someone all I had to do was call Northcutt and he set up the introductions. Sometimes it seems he has met, and impressed, nearly everyone.

Northcutt is a super-friendly and thoughtful deal-maker. He comes up with great ideas and has a way of motivating others around him to march off and make those plans happen. Some people have that special charisma that makes people want to be around them and to want to make things happen. Northcutt is that type of guy, and I'm sure that's why SANS got him involved early on when it was just a speck of the organization that it is today. Northcutt has also been an early investor in some of the most profitable computer security companies of our time, including Tenable (http://www.tenable.com) and Sourcefire.

The SANS Institute (http://www.sans.org) has been around since 1989 and from the start has taught some of the best computer security classes available. Their initial security conferences turned into industry-respected certifications, and their certifications turned into university-accredited curricula offering two master of science degree programs (in Information Security Engineering [MSISE] and Information Security Management [MSISM]), and three post-baccalaureate certificate programs (Penetration Testing and Ethical Hacking, Incident Response, and Cybersecurity Engineering). They have taught over 100,000 people and have some of the most sought-after instructors, many of whom have published best-selling books. As an employer, if you come across someone with a SANS certificate or degree, you know you have the cream of the crop. I consider their online newsletters (https://www.sans.org/newsletters/) to be must-read material for any computer security professional, and their Internet Storm Center is often the first place to notice a new attack.

Even though I've known Northcutt for almost two decades, I've never asked him the story of how he got into computer security, so I asked. He replied, "I was a network designer working in a Navy lab running a Sun workstation. I knew nothing about computer security. One day I discovered someone hacking my computer and I flipped out. The connection was coming from Australia, and they were compiling a program on my computer. I didn't know what to do, so I pulled the cord. That was my response. Afterwards, I felt so violated. I started to learn about computer security and eventually got funding. Back in those days if you had a good idea, it was easy to get funding. I learned a lot about computer security, and I eventually got the number two slot under Fred Kerby. [Fred Kerby was the Information Assurance Manager at the Naval Surface Warfare Center, Dahlgren Division, for more than 16 years and now is a SANS instructor.]

"I really got into intrusion detection. I wrote the Shadow Intrusion Detection system, which was really good for its time. I started an intrusion detection team, and we ended up monitoring over 30 military bases. [He ended up being Chief for Information Warfare at the Ballistic Missile Defense Organization.] I made the radical mistake of accepting a position at the Pentagon. I went from where I was heavy in technical detail to a place where I couldn't do anything technical. My job was to go to meetings and sign papers. I made it a year. This was in 1999."

Although Northcutt wasn't one of the SANS co-founders (those were Michele Gell, Dr. Eugene Schultz, Alan Paller, and Dr. Matt Bishop), he was frequently meeting with Alan early on. I asked how he got involved with SANS. He said, "In 1999, I was being goat roped into a special project at the Pentagon around the Y2K undertaking and fears that hackers would exploit it. I created a great team, including some of the best technical analysts in the world. I loved that part, but managing it was very political, which is something I didn't love. Alan [Paller] came in and took charge of the political stuff while I concentrated on the technical stuff. I attended and taught at a great SANS conference on intrusion detection in December of 1999, and I remember I really enjoyed it far more than the political stuff. So I went back to my office in the Pentagon and threw all my stuff in a suitcase and never looked back.

"I started with SANS officially on January 5, 2000. At the time, they only had two events, a Spring and a Fall event. Each event was four days long. There were some educational classes before the main conference, the main conference was two days long, and it was followed by another day of training classes. It was great, but I remember saying to Alan, 'This is a lot of work for just two events a year.' And so it grew."

I attended some early SANS classes, back before you could get certified in something. I remember each of those classes as being the best classes on their subject still to this day. I remember who taught them and what I learned. I even took a class on the Snort intrusion detection tool by its creator Marty Roesch back in 1998 or 1999. When I told Northcutt of my recollection, he said, "I remember Marty coming up to me . . . this young kid . . . and he said, 'I have built a new intrusion detection tool and it's better than yours [Shadow],' and he was right. I ended up being an early investor in Marty's commercial Sourcefire venture." Sourcefire was so successful that it was later bought by Cisco.

I asked Northcutt when the idea of moving from training to certification began to take place. He said, "It was Alan's idea. I understood what he was saying right away, about how companies wanted to make sure they were getting their money's worth for the training and a certification was one way of making sure they got the training. I remembered when I was still at the Navy Lab and I sent some people to the Unix LISA conference. I showed up at the conference, but I couldn't find them. I eventually found them kayaking in the ocean. So I understood the value of certifications.

"The idea of certification tracks came even before that. Alan had come down to see me at the Navy Lab in 1998 and challenged me to identify all the job areas that were in computer security. There weren't a lot of them at the time: IDS, firewalls, malware detection, and a few others. So when we started talking about certifications, we both thought making sure the education and tracks were based around particular tasks was the best way to approach it. We eventually made our more holistic GIAC Security Essentials Certification (GSEC,), which is sort of like our version of the CISSP. The GSEC is not very technically focused. It's a mile wide and two inches deep. But we decided that we had to prepare people about security in general before they began taking domain-specific tasks full of command lines."

As we finished the interview, I remembered one of our earliest meetings. Northcutt had a great idea he wanted to run by me in person at his house in Hawai'i. I told him that I was spending the week head-down, finishing up my first book (*Malicious Mobile Code* [https://www.amazon.com/Malicious-Mobile-Code-Protection-Windows/dp/156592682X]). I was already way behind the deadline, and this one week was all I needed to finally finish it and get it to the publisher. But he was persistent. I remember what he said as if it was the other day. He said, "Hey, you and your wife like scuba diving, right? Well, my next door neighbor and friend runs Dive Hawai'i, and I'll get you and your wife on some great dives." I again said thanks, but that I could not make time to fly to Hawai'i, meet, and dive. He countered, "What's your wife's name and number? I'll call her to let her know the deal and see what she wants to do!" I never did give him her name or number, I didn't fly to Hawai'i, and I got my first book finally done. But to this day I regret not taking him up on it. That's the type of guy he is—even the deals you don't take him up on, you remember forever.

For More Information on Stephen Northcutt

For information about Stephen Northcutt, check out these resources:

- Stephen Northcutt's LinkedIn profile: https://www.linkedin.com/in/stephenraynorthcutt
- Stephen Northcutt on SANS: https://www.sans.org/instructors/stephen-northcutt
- Stephen Northcutt on Facebook: https://www.facebook.com/stephen.northcutt
- *Network Intrusion Detection* (co-authored with Jody Novak): https://www.amazon.com/Network-Intrusion-Detection-Stephen-Northcutt/dp/0735712654

43 Privacy

Many people, including the author of this book, believe that personal privacy, especially in digital age, should be a guaranteed, innate right of all human beings. Unfortunately, much of our digital and financial privacy is long gone. Internet search engines, online advertisers, and software vendors often know more about you than anyone besides yourself. A few years ago, an enraged parent visited Target because the store's marketing department was sending unsolicited ads for baby supplies to his teenage daughter. He eventually had to apologize when he learned Target knew more about his daughter than he did (http://www.forbes.com/sites/kashmirhill/2012/02/16/how-target-figured-out-a-teen-girl-was-pregnant-before-her-father-did/#d84bcce34c62).

In most countries, and certainly on the Internet, your privacy is gone. Nothing you do is truly private. Even ultra-privacy–promoting apps like Tor and the "darknet," which claim they give you the best privacy possible, don't really work all that well for real-world applications. Don't believe me? Ask all the arrested criminals who thought Tor or their anonymity service was providing absolute anonymity. There are lots of ways to increase privacy, but as long as tracking you and your activities is legal, companies (and law enforcement) are going to do it.

This is not to say that some governments and companies aren't trying to give you some reasonable level of online privacy. For example, the recently enacted European Union's General Data Protection Regulation (https://en.wikipedia.org/wiki/General_Data_Protection_Regulation) can penalize firms for up to 4% of their revenues for violating the act. Most countries have some form of official regulations (or multiple regulations) that purport to protect citizens' private data.

Unfortunately, most laws and regulations are half-efforts that appear more likely to protect the governments and businesses that collect personal data than to protect citizens' privacy. And many countries, especially in the Asia-Pacific region, outright reject any regulation that would prevent the government from wholesale monitoring of their citizens. Culturally, the majority of their populations often accept it without complaint. They give up their privacy for purported security. It's often an easy sale in countries without a history of trying to protect citizen privacy.

Still, violating a country's privacy laws can be very expensive for violators. Government departments and entire governments have been found guilty of violating standing privacy laws (although they are almost never punished). Businesses, on the other hand, can get in trouble a lot more easily. It is increasingly common for corporations to have privacy divisions and even someone at the "C-level" whose job it is to protect customer data privacy.

Privacy Organizations

Luckily for the world, many organizations exist that fight for every world citizen's right to privacy. These include the Electronic Frontier Foundation (https://www.eff.org/) and the Electronic Privacy Information Center (https://epic.org/).

The Electronic Frontier Foundation (EFF) was founded in 1990 to promote government transparency, user privacy, and freedom of speech around the world. They do this through a combination of litigation, activism, policy analysis, whitepapers, and technical tool creation. They are very active in several court cases, including one where they are fighting for the right for companies to re-fill and sell vendor ink cartridges (https://www.eff.org/cases/impression-products-inc-v-lexmark-international-inc). Their privacy tools include HTTPS Everywhere (https://www.eff.org/https-everywhere), which is a Firefox, Chrome, and Opera browser extension to maximize the use of HTTPS and Privacy Badger, which blocks ads and other tracking tools.

The Electronic Privacy Information Center (EPIC) is a public research center founded in 1994 that focuses on protecting privacy, freedom of speech, civil liberties, and other democratic values, largely using litigation, publications, and other advocacy means. They use the court system even more than EFF does, and both are advocating better cybersecurity as well as not letting cybersecurity trample on their other goals. Their list of privacy issues is huge (https://epic.org/privacy/).

Reading about the policy issues contained at either EFF or EPIC usually shocks most people not previously well-versed in the topics. It's amazing how much of our privacy is already gone. There's almost nothing left. Both organizations are 501(c)(3) non-profit organizations that depend on donations. If you care about privacy and freedom of speech, consider donating to a privacy-advocating organization.

A special shout out must go to Bruce Schneier (https://www.schneier.com/) for his untiring efforts to educate us and protect individual privacy. Schneier has been speaking publicly against our privacy erosions for as long as anyone, and his books, especially *David and Goliath* (https://www.amazon.com/Data-Goliath-Battles-Collect-Control/dp/039335217X/), are must-reads for people concerned about where our privacy currently is and where it is headed. You can read more about Bruce Schneier in Chapter 3.

Privacy-Protecting Applications

None of the prior dire warnings about our diminishing privacy should be construed to mean there is nothing we can do to make our privacy better. Many excellent, freely available applications give you as much individual privacy as possible with a minimum of discomfort. Nearly every privacy advocate will suggest using Tor-enabled software (https://www.torproject.org/) to make privacy invasion harder for anyone other than the very well resourced. The privacy given by Tor may have its issues, but it's the best we're going to get in general-purpose software. Many privacy-minded people like to use the DuckDuckGo (https://duckduckgo.com/) Internet search engine instead of the more well-known engines that are funded by invading your privacy. There are many software vendors competing to protect your privacy. Please read the author's privacy application picks at http://www.infoworld.com/article/3135324/security/17-essential-tools-to-protect-your-online-identity-and-privacy.html for more privacy-protecting software.

We cannot have security and freedom without individual privacy. The next chapter profiles Eva Galperin, who works for the Electronic Frontier Foundation.

44

Profile: Eva Galperin

You've got to love a person who likes computers and cybersecurity and spends their free time hanging out performing aerial acrobatics at circuses for a hobby. The Electronic Frontier Foundation's (https://www.eff.org) Director of Cybersecurity, Eva Galperin, is such a person. Working for EFF since 2007, she became their Director of Cybersecurity in 2017. Prior to EFF, she earned degrees in political science and international relations from San Francisco State University. Her work primarily focuses on providing privacy, free speech, and security for everyone around the world, along with examining malware that threatens the same. Galperin is now known around the world for her work in the field, writing about the malware she has come across, and speaking at security conferences like BlackHat (https://www.blackhat.com /us-16/speakers/Eva-Galperin.html).

I asked Galperin how she got into computer security, and she replied, "I got into computers fairly early. My dad was a computer security guy and I asked him about hanging out on Prodigy [a precursor of AOL and other online services]. Instead, he created me a desktop on his Unix/Solaris computer. Age 12 … on a Unix machine, can you imagine? I was in the Usenet discussion areas about science fiction books, playing interactive text games, and when the web came along I got into building web pages. I put myself through college as a Unix system administrator, and back then being a sys admin meant it included computer security."

I asked her she got into EFF and malware analysis. She said, "I came to EFF in 2007 for the activism. I ended up doing cybersecurity research because no one else at EFF was doing it. My start in malware analysis goes back to 2011 and 2012 in Syria. Back then [Syrian President Bashar Hafez al-] Assad was the darling of the West. He promoted himself as the father of the Syrian Internet, and he opened access to Facebook, which had previously been blocked. Everybody thought he was great. Westerners thought that his unblocking Facebook was a sign of Assad's increasing openness towards free speech. They were really, really wrong. What he was really doing was man-in-the-middling conversations. I was working on Syria, doing research on free speech and censorship issues, when someone found malware that was created by pro-Assad hackers, targeting supporters of the opposition. It was RAT [Remote Access Trojan] installed on their machines to exfiltrate data, including passwords and screenshots, to a Syrian IP address. Together we analyzed it. Over the next two years, I helped write about a dozen reports on the two pro-Assad groups writing this kind of malware."

I asked Galperin what she saw as the biggest problem in computer security. She replied, "The biggest problem in computer security isn't security. It's privacy. A lot of companies prioritize computer security, but not protecting the privacy of their users. Many companies monetize user data, which incentivizes them to collect as much of that data as possible. Many companies have large amounts of extremely detailed user data, and once they have it, the data is subject to legal hacks (subpoenas and warrants) as well as the kinds of technical attacks that information security people usually spend their time thinking about. Even if a company is protecting their data from hackers, they have a harder time protecting it from law enforcement and government. Often, they're not even thinking about governments and law enforcement as attackers. I want to be clear that I'm not advocating that companies shouldn't collect data, but users should have the power over their own data. The user should know when it's being collected, what's being collected, how it's being used, how long it's being kept, how it's being secured, etc. User choice is extremely important."

I wondered with her experience with many different governments how the United States stacked up against other countries on protecting privacy, on a scale from 1 to 10, with a 10 being the best protectors of privacy. She said, "The US is maybe a 4 or a 5 on protecting privacy. The strongest digital privacy protections are in the European Union. On the other hand, the US has much stronger protections for freedom of speech, while free expression protections in the EU are much weaker."

I asked her if she thought privacy and free speech would get better or worse over time. She replied, "It would be easy to say things will get worse. Someone says that and when it happens they seem like a genius. But I'm going to take a different tactic. I think there is a chance things will improve over time, but as long as the user's information is the product and free software or service is what [they exchange for it], it's going to be very hard. We do know that users do value privacy and would often be willing to pay for it if you gave them a choice. But you have to give them the option, and I'm not sure if that will be the case because the big players are becoming more powerful and that's not compatible with the current business model."

Lastly, I had to ask Galperin how she got into aerial circus activities as a hobby. She replied, "I was a gymnast in middle school. My high school has a circus, so I did acrobatics instead of sports. After high school, I did some aerial acrobatics and I got back into in my 20s. It's great exercise, and when you're 30 feet up in the air swinging, you're not thinking about the Internet."

I don't know about you, but I like knowing that one of our biggest privacy advocates doesn't mind taking risks, in either her advocacy or her hobbies.

For More Information on Eva Galperin

For information about Eva Galperin, check out these resources:

- Eva Galperin on Twitter: `https://twitter.com/evacide`
- Eva Galperin's Electronic Frontier Foundation (EFF) profile: `https://www.eff.org/about/staff/eva-galperin`

45 Patching

Every day, millions of web sites and emails contain links to malware known as "exploit kits." Malicious programmers (or programming teams) create exploit kits and then use them or sell them. An exploit kit usually contains everything a wannabe hacker can need in the exploit cycle, including 24×7 technical support and auto-updating to avoid getting caught by antivirus scanners. A good exploit kit will even find and maliciously modify otherwise innocent web sites to ensure it gets executed whenever visitors browse to the infected web site. All the attacker has to do is buy the kit, execute it, and send it along its way to find victim web sites.

Exploit kits almost always contains client-side (programs that run on end-user desktops versus code meant to exploit servers) exploitation routines that check for multiple missing patches. They can check for anywhere from a handful of vulnerabilities to several dozen. Any unpatched, unlucky visitor gets silently exploited (by what is also known as a "drive-by download" attack), whereas fully patched web surfers usually get prompted by a social engineering trick to install a Trojan horse program. Exploit kit bad guys would rather exploit unpatched devices than use social engineering because not all end-users will automatically agree to install any program they are prompted to install. The involved vulnerabilities are routinely updated so that the exploit kit can be as successful as possible. Most exploit kits even contain centralized management consoles so the criminals can check to see what vulnerabilities are working and how devices are infected.

Even without exploit kits being involved, missing security patches are one of the biggest problems that allow successful exploitation. This may change one day, but so far this fact has been true for more than three decades. To give yourself or your computers the best protection against software vulnerability exploitation, all you have to do is apply security patches in a timely and consistent manner. That sounds easy enough to do. There are even dozens of tools that can help you.

Unfortunately, effective patching remains overly difficult and elusive. In my entire career, scanning hundreds and hundreds of thousands of computers for patching, I don't think I've ever found a fully patched computer. If I have, I can't remember it. It's that rare.

Patching Facts

The following sections describe some very significant patching facts that most people overlook.

Most Exploits Are Caused by Old Vulnerabilities That Patches Exist For

Most devices are exploited by malware that looks for vulnerabilities that were patched a year or more ago. Survey after survey shows that most exploitation happens from vulnerabilities that the vendor patched two to three years ago. Some non-minor percentage of computers are never patched. If you enable an Internet firewall looking to detect and identify exploitation programs trying to infect your computer or network, you will detect exploit tries that are only possible from computers infected over 15 years go (things like Code Red, SQL Slammer, and so on). There are occasionally zero-days (threats that exploit unpatched vulnerabilities), but they are very uncommon and routinely comprise less than 1% of all successful attacks on the Internet.

Most Exploits Are Caused by a Few Unpatched Programs

In an average year, 5000–6000 distinct vulnerabilities are found in hundreds of different programs. But usually only a handful of programs are responsible for most successful exploitations. For example, the *Cisco 2014 Annual Security Report* (http://www.cisco.com/web/offers/lp/2014-annual-security-report/index.html) stated that unpatched Oracle Java accounted for 91% of all successful desktop web exploitations. If you included the other top four programs, they covered 100% of all successful desktop web exploitations. That meant anyone could patch just five programs and remove the majority of desktop exploitation risk in any environment. Java isn't exploited nearly as much anymore for a few reasons (including that the major browser vendors removed default Java interoperability from their browsers), but what is the number one most exploited software program always changes over time. Years ago, it was DOS, then Microsoft Windows, Microsoft Outlook, or Microsoft Internet Explorer. Today, the most exploited programs are usually browser add-ins because they usually exist across multiple computer platforms. The most exploited programs may change, but the fact that a handful of top exploited programs account for most of the risk probably won't change any time soon.

The Most Unpatched Program Isn't Always the Most Exploited Program

There is a huge risk gulf between the most unpatched program and the most likely to be exploited unpatched program. A good computer security expert understands the difference and concentrates on the latter. For example, for many years, one of the most unpatched programs was Microsoft's run-time Visual C++ Redistributable program, installed by many third-party programs. However, it is hardly ever exploited because it was installed and used differently by thousands of different programs, which made it hard to detect and exploit. Defenders need to focus on patching the critical security holes in the most likely to be exploited programs. Those programs are not always the most popular unpatched programs.

You Need to Patch Hardware Too

Most hardware runs firmware of some kind. Firmware is basically software programs implemented into silicon chips, or as I like to say "harder to update software." Computer security defenders must make sure to patch their hardware, firmware, BIOSs, and appliances along with their software.

Common Patching Problems

If patching were easy, it wouldn't still be the big problem that it is today. The following sections describe some of the issues involved with patching.

Detecting Missing Patching Isn't Accurate

No matter what program you run to check for missing patches, it will miss some percentage of devices. It's not always the patch management program's fault. Computer devices are complex machines with lots of moving, buggy parts, and any of those buggy parts can stop accurate patch checking.

On top of that, users may use devices or versions that aren't supported by your patch-checking program, or your network security boundaries might be in the way. There are many more reasons why patch-checking status may not be accurate, but it suffices to say that they are never 100% accurate. And if you can't detect it, you can't patch it.

You Can't Always Patch

Sun (and now Oracle) Java has long been one of the most exploited programs when left unpatched, and unfortunately most of the world left it unpatched for nearly two decades. Java programmers consistently write their programs (incorrectly) to rely on particular Java versions and features, and updating Java could break programs relying on a particular version. For that reason, most enterprises knew they had a high percentage of unpatched Java programs and that Java was the biggest reason for successful exploits in their enterprises, but they still were not able to patch Java. It turns out that causing operational interruptions will get you fired far more quickly than simply reporting that you can't patch something because the business owner won't let you.

Some Percentage of Patching Always Fails

As with checking for missing patches and for the same reasons, some small percentage of computers will never get the patch applied that you told them to apply. In my experience, that number of devices is around 1–2% on average, but sometimes it jumps way higher to something like 15–20%, depending on the complexity of the patch and the involved devices. One great way to defeat patching issues is to follow up and try to resolve the issues on computers that have poor patch detection and application rates.

Patching Will Cause Operational Issues

Vendors try their best to reduce the number of operational issues caused by a particular patch, but they cannot be expected to test their patch on every unique combination of hardware and software that the patch might be applied to. Sometimes applying a very reliable and safe patch can be undone by previously undetected malware or an untested third-party program. Most companies have been burned by one or more patches causing a significant operational interruption, and they are hesitant to apply future patches without lots of testing (which they often don't have the time or resources to do). Because of the fear of unintended operational issues, they either don't ever apply the patch or don't apply it in a timely manner. I understand the fear, but the risk of not applying critical security patches in a timely manner is higher than the possible, less likely operational issues. If you are worried about operational issues, just wait a few days. Most of the time the serious operational issues are found by other faster adopters and resolved by the vendor so you can safely apply the patch.

A Patch Is a Globally Broadcasted Exploit Announcement

When a patch is released to close a security vulnerability, if it wasn't already publicly known, it is now. Malware writers and exploit kit programmers will quickly examine any patch that comes out and reverse engineer it to find out how to exploit the now-solved vulnerability. Because it takes the best patchers a few days to patch and some people never patch, every newly released patch is another likely avenue for exploitation.

Some vendors sneak high-criticality bug fixes into patches that address other issues and do not announce the bug. Later, they formally announce the vulnerability and provide an official patch. By that time, thanks to the earlier patch, the bug has already been fixed across a majority of computers. One very popular OS vendor once deployed a critical patch fix over several months of patches. To the reverse engineers, it looked like unexplained garbage code segments, but once three months of patches had been applied, the whole bug fix was applied to close the huge hole, leaving happy (and mostly unaware) customers and frustrated hackers.

In the end, good patch management means one thing: timely, consistent patching of the most likely to be exploited programs. It's easy to say but hard to do. My advice is to turn on all automated patching or use a reputable patch management program that can handle all your software patching needs (and hardware too, if possible) and let critical security patches be applied within a few days. If you patch within a few days, you'll be among the most protected environments on the Internet. Perfect patching may not be easy, but patching the critical vulnerabilities of the most likely to be exploited programs is essential on any computer. Not doing so is effectively just asking to be exploited.

In the next chapter, Window Snyder, a woman in charge of helping some of the largest companies in the world patch their products, is profiled.

46 Profile: Window Snyder

Mwende Window Snyder has worked for a who's-who of industry powerhouses. Early on she worked at @Stake as the Director of Security Architecture. @Stake was a great vulnerability-finding and computer-security company that generated or acquired more than its fair share of computer superstars. It was eventually acquired by Symantec in 2004. Snyder went to work for Microsoft in 2002 and was a senior security strategist in the Security Engineering and Communications group. She was a contributor to the Security Design Lifecycle (SDL) and co-developed a new methodology for threat modeling software. She also was a security lead on Microsoft Windows XP Service Pack 2, which was basically Microsoft's first serious attempt at a secure-by-default operating system, and Windows Server 2003. She managed the relationships between security consulting companies and Microsoft and was responsible for its computer security community outreach strategy.

She joined Mozilla in 2006 and used the humorous tongue-in-cheek title of "Chief Security Something or Other" instead of the more formal Chief Security Officer (CSO). I remember many of us being quite jealous of the title. She eventually worked for Apple as a senior security product manager, developing security and privacy strategy and features for iOS and OS X. Today she works for Fastly (https://www.fastly.com/), a content delivery network that is quickly expanding into other services such as computer security. Snyder is the daughter of an American father and a Kenyan-born mother, and co-author, along with Frank Swiderski, of the book *Threat Modeling* (https://www.amazon.com/Threat-Modeling-Microsoft-Professional-Swiderski/dp/0735619913/). She is the only person I personally know who has worked inside three of the four largest companies that provide very popular browsers and software. She's been in the trenches so to speak.

I had to start off our interview by asking about her name. She replied, "I can tell you a story about when I used to work at Microsoft. Back then, by default, most people's email addresses began with their first name followed by their last initial. But a large distribution group, the Windows product group, already had Windows (which would have been my email alias if mine had followed the defaults). Over the years, many people would be trying to send something to me private or confidential ... maybe it was about malware or a new vulnerability report, and instead of sending it to me, they would accidentally send it to one of our largest email distribution groups. They might eventually realize their mistake when the email bounced off the locked distribution list."

Then I asked her how she got into computer security. She said, "I was a computer science major and got interested in cryptography and crypto-analysis. I was interested in the idea of secrets bound by the difficulty of a mathematical problem. It was around the same time I first had access to multi-user operating systems. I started thinking about the security boundaries between different users and their processes and what prevented them from interfering with each other or the operating system. What I found was that, back then, at best there were semi-permeable barriers. It was fun, like taking apart a puzzle or machine and finding out how it worked. It was an exciting time."

I knew she had been involved in the Security Design Lifecycle (SDL) while at Microsoft. I wondered how that happened and what she did. She replied, "When I first got to Microsoft it wasn't very mature in computer security at all. There were something like only eleven employees. I was the twelfth, concentrating at Windows security. And back then it was mostly reacting to what other outside people found. There wasn't a strong internal program. Then SQL Slammer and Blaster hit. I helped by co-creating the first core methodologies of formal Threat Modeling [and she co-authored a book on the same subject]. I helped start proactive bug finding and reaching out to the community. When I first got to Microsoft, if someone externally found a security bug, Microsoft called them a hacker. The media at the time conflated hackers of all sorts with criminals. The people reporting issues to Microsoft, even dropping them unpatched publicly, were not criminals. I helped to push an outreach program to make them our allies instead of our adversaries. One of those improvements was to call them security researchers instead of hackers, to focus on how their work was a valuable contribution. I also [helped create] a program within Microsoft to sponsor many small external hacking conferences, like Hack-in-the-Box. We were able to eventually change the perception that Microsoft didn't care about security or know about security, and these security researchers and Microsoft were on the same team.

"When I first got to Microsoft, there was no one representing security for the Windows product, so I stepped in. I represented security at the Windows 'war meetings' where all the different sponsors and stakeholders came together. We had a huge backlog of bugs that we were solving whack-a-mole style, and that was not efficient. As part of SDL we started to look at the larger causes of bugs, trying to find broader categories that if we fixed would mitigate a whole lot of bugs all at once. We took the lessons learned with the Windows security team and started to move them out to other teams and products, like to Microsoft Office."

I asked her to name another valuable lesson she learned and pushed. She replied, "There is an entire financial ecosystem behind today's malware. You have one set of people finding vulnerabilities, and another set of people who turn that vulnerability into an exploit and kit. You have another set dedicated to infecting as many web sites and hosts as they can with that exploit kit and then another set that uses it to accomplish some goal. But if you take a link out of that malware ecosystem chain, it makes it harder for the rest to do business. If you can do some things that make key points in the ecosystem more difficult or more expensive, then the whole chain is harder to build. Microsoft and Windows didn't catch that early enough. When I joined Microsoft, they were already experiencing an onslaught of malware, worms, and viruses. I later went to work on other platforms including iOS and OS X at Apple and used my experience to successfully put roadblocks that made the malware ecosystem less likely to develop and be profitable. If you can undermine the economics of malware, you can win that way, too."

Snyder worked at some of the most well-known big companies. I wondered what commonalities she saw in corporations that were so very different. She said, "In all the companies you have to make security work for the end-users. Security features that come at too big of a cost, that interrupt their normal workflow too much, aren't going to work. We need to implement more and better security but not get in the way of the user's workflow. Also, don't collect the data you don't need. If you collect the data, you have to protect it and give users control over their own data. The biggest problem in computer security is successfully executing the things we already know how to do."

Spoken like an experienced industry insider.

For More Information on Window Snyder

For information about Window Snyder, check out these resources:

- ■ Window Snyder's LinkedIn profile: https://www.linkedin.com/in/window
- ■ Window Snyder on Twitter: https://twitter.com/window

47 Writing as a Career

I failed high school English—twice. In grad school, while doing a hospital administration internship, the writing of my first corporate report was so bad that the boss questioned out loud our nation's entire education system. When I occasionally re-read that report to remind me of where I started, it physically hurts me. Almost 30 years later, I've authored or co-authored nine books and nearly 1000 national magazine articles on computer security, and I've been the *InfoWorld* magazine computer security columnist going on 12 years. All thanks to my brother (the first and best real writer in the family), my personal perseverance, and a slew of quality editors.

While I still have a hard time writing an email without a typo, my writing has improved enough that I make a very good living doing it. I frequently do writing assignments where I can earn up to $500–$1000/hour, and I make more in one year than the average American family income, and it's only my side job. Although I work full-time as computer security consultant, I've been writing about computer security even longer. It's nice supplemental income that I can make writing in spare cycles at home, while flying, and at nights in hotel rooms after consulting all day. Some people watch TV at night. I usually write while watching TV. My writing hobby has funded many a grand family vacation and allows me to spend way too much money on my hobbies. I'm not alone.

Hundreds of people around the world make their entire living writing about computer security. From the comfort of their home, with a decent Internet connection, they provide a good living for themselves and their families. Some work for established media giants, and others freelance, selling their articles and services to interested parties. Some write books, and most blog and write articles. They all have a passion for computer security, filtering out the vendor's marketing hype and revealing the truth to readers in a more understandable way.

Computer Security Writing Outlets

There are many ways to write about computer security, including those described below.

Blogs

Most computer security writers either have a permanent blog location or participate in several blogs. Blogs are essentially today's modern version of magazine articles. Blog postings may or may not be paid and may or may not have an editor to help check and correct the content before posting. Personal blog sites and posts are very easy to start, although the biggest issue is attracting readers and keeping up the work over the long-term. The vast majority of blogs are started and ended within a single year, when the writers either don't get the readership they desire or they've said everything they are passionate about. Blogging, like writing magazine articles, is hard work to do well.

If you are interested in a personal blog and don't know where to start, check out one of the many popular blogging sites, of which WordPress (http://www .wordpress.com) is the uncontested leader at this time. WordPress, created and maintained by a hip company known as Automattic, powers 27% of all Internet sites and something like 70% of all blog sites.

Social Media Sites

Most computer security writers have a Twitter site to which they post occasionally (or daily). Secondarily, they may have professional (and personal) sites at Facebook, LinkedIn, or Google Groups. Many writers maintain sites in all of these locations, in additional to their other professional publication locations.

Articles

Most professional computer security writers write "articles," which typically means writing content ranging from a few hundred words to many thousands of words. The average column length is somewhere around 1000 words. The articles may end up being published in print magazines, in online publications, or as part of a blog site. Article topics can be in the categories of news, opinion pieces, tutorials, or product technical reviews.

If you like writing and get lucky, you might even get a weekly or monthly column. Although before taking on a regular writing assignment, make sure you are up to the task. I remember how excited I was to get my weekly column with *InfoWorld* magazine back in August 2005. I couldn't wait to tell the world everything I thought and was passionate about. It turns out that you can tell the world everything you are really passionate about in about 12 articles. After that you have to figure out a rhythm of generating new ideas each time a column is due. Sometimes I wake up at 4 AM and write three columns. Other times I'm struggling to think of a new, interesting article or angle until well after my deadline. Most routine writers burn out, so if you want to make it a career, figure out a creative routine that works for you and your employer.

Books

Books are wonderful way of sharing what you know and even validating your own skills as a writer. I still haven't come down from the joy of getting my first book contract (after years of trying and more than 100 rejection letters) and the feeling of holding my first book in my arms. When you are a book author, there's a good chance your obituary will probably say "book author." No one can take it away.

With that said, unless you find a way to successfully marry international intrigue, vampires, zombies, and computer security, preferably with a teenage protagonist, you're unlikely to get rich writing a book. The vast majority of computer security books never earn their authors more than $10,000. This wasn't always the case, but it has been since Internet search engines became popular and people can just look up things for free. There are exceptions. I know a handful of computer book authors who made hundreds of thousands of dollars and were able to buy boats and beach houses. Just don't decide to write a book because you think you're going to get rich doing it. Do it because you think you have an interesting idea that will appeal to tens of thousands of readers in a way that can really help make their lives and careers easier, if not more enjoyable.

However, although writing a computer book might not make the average author rich, it does almost always lead to better paying jobs. Being a book author gives you credibility, much like a college degree or certification does, but often even more so. The average computer book author I know makes far more money than non-authors. And again, I can often make more in a few hours of work than most people make in a week or two of work. This from a guy who failed English twice.

Self-Publish or Publishing House?

If you're going to write a book, you will need to decide whether you want to self-publish or go with a publishing house, assuming you can get through the discerning process of getting selected by a publishing house. It can be difficult for first-time book authors to get a book contract, where there are guaranteed and ongoing shared payment arrangements. Many authors, first-time and otherwise, decide to self-publish, partly because they want a higher proportion of the profits for each sold book. More often, many authors decide to self-publish after not getting accepted at a publishing house. It can be very difficult.

If every author can be guaranteed to make a higher percentage of profit from each self-published book versus using a publishing house, I'm sure some readers are wondering why anyone would decide to go with a publishing house at all. Well, for a lot of reasons. The average book author spends roughly a year, some less, some more, writing a book. If you're not lucky enough to do it full-time for a living, it means sacrificing every spare moment you have for a year. You end up neglecting family members, missing fun parties, and in general, being stuck in front of a computer way more than you already are as a computer security professional. For all that effort, you want your book to be good. A book put out by a publishing house is far more likely to be a better product in the end. Self-published books rarely sell more than a few dozen copies (especially in the computer security field) and are usually just not as professional-looking as books published by publishing houses.

The very act of having to qualify for being accepted by a professional publishing house makes you, your writing, and the book better. Plus, the publishing house will take over the "non-writing" parts of the book, which can be substantial. Before writing this book, I wondered if I should self-publish for the first time, but then I realized that writing the chapters and handing them over to the publisher who handled the editing, technical editing, professional graphics, marketing and distribution, and actual professional creation of the final product meant that I could spend much more time with my family and doing things I loved besides writing and computer security. For example, instead of having to create a front and back book cover from scratch, the editor sent over several mockups, all done more professionally and creatively than I could have done. I simply chose the ones I liked and sent back a reply. It literally took one minute instead of days or weeks of work, and it came out better. On top of that, the professional editors you will get with a publishing house are probably way better than your loved one or friend doing it as an unpaid favor.

I think going with a professional publishing house probably saves you half the effort otherwise, and has a far greater chance of making a better product with more sales, than self-publishing. With that said, if you are a devoted professional and don't mind the extra effort, self-publishing is a viable alternative for those willing to put in the extra work. Unfortunately, the self-publishing world is full of half-crocked works with more typos than average. This is not to say that publishing house books don't have errors, but in general, they have far fewer.

If you're interested in getting a book at a professional publishing house, go to their web site and find their book proposal format. Take your time when filling it out. It should usually take you a few days. Submit it to their "acquisitions" email address or the person who handles such things. If you are a first-time book author and want to get accepted faster, hook up with a book agent who specializes in the types of books you want to write. They can help refine your idea and book proposal, and in my experience they are almost always successful in getting you a book contract. I haven't always used a book agent, but when I have (I use StudioB [http://www.studiob.com/]) it was well worth the small percentage cut they took from my book's (or other content's) royalties.

Technical Editor

Long before I was a published book author, I was a technical editor reviewing books headed toward publishing. I still do it today. A lot of computer security book writers start this way. It's a great chance to learn how the process works, what is expected of authors, and how to avoid the common mistakes that first-time book authors make.

Newsletters

There are dozens of daily, weekly, and monthly computer security newsletters you can write for. It can be hard to get accepted by some of the more established magazines and newsletters that have been around for a while. Many don't accept any new, unsolicited writings, while the other less established newsletters are begging for (free) writers. Newsletters can be a great place to build your writing chops and writing resume to help you get other higher paying gigs.

Whitepapers

In my experience, vendor-sponsored whitepapers are often where the easier, big money is. Vendors often offer top dollar for 5–10 page whitepapers. Some of the topics I have been paid for come easily to me, and I end up writing the whole whitepaper in a few hours. Others require more research and interviews and end up taking many weeks. But in general, you can earn the same money for a few whitepapers with far less effort than writing a book. The catch-22 is that many times it is being a published book author that gets you the whitepapers in the first place. Although remember that ethically, if you have ever gotten paid by a vendor to do promotional work for them, you must always disclose that in any other writing involving the same vendor or its competitors.

Technical Reviews

The toughest writing I've ever done is technical product reviews. This is where you review one or more products, looking to remove the vendor's ever-present hype, and report to readers about the capabilities of the real product. Product reviews take days or weeks to complete and often involve simulation test labs and interviews with real customers. For all that effort, they don't usually pay as much as easier-to-produce whitepapers. With that said, a good technical review can be far more fulfilling and helps more people. I try to do a few each year when I see either a promising product or overly hyped products that readers are interested in.

Conferences

Once you begin writing for a living, you might start to get involved in giving presentations at conferences. It took me two decades to get over my nearly crippling stage fright, but I can seriously say that presenting at conferences is some of the most fulfilling work I've ever done. You not only get to share your insights as an authority on a topic that you care about, but you'll meet tons of like-minded people, get additional job opportunities, and often discover facts you did not previously know. Of course, presenting requires additional skills, such as the ability to create good slide shows and developing a good presentation style. Many conferences have pre-conference workshops to help new (and experienced) presenters to improve their presentation and speaking skills.

Professional Writing Tips

After nearly three decades of writing, I can offer readers a few pieces of advice, including those described in the following sections.

The Hardest Part Is Starting

I've had hundreds of people come up to me over the years and ask how to professionally write. I always give them lots of information and recommendations. In that time, maybe a handful of people have followed through and even tried. Professional tech writing isn't easy, or at least not until after you've been doing it awhile. Simply starting is the hardest part. If you want to be a professional writer, part-time or full-time, you need to start writing and putting in the effort it takes to get published. Sure, you need to have the knowledge of your subject and be able to write decently, but as I have shared, some of that can be learned along the way. If you are not a strong writer, pick up some books on grammar and writing—more than one.

Read Differently

Much as a professional musician listens to music differently than a regular fan, writers should look at other writing to pick up ideas, hints, and tricks. Start reading articles, looking to see how the writer did what they did. What was the way they introduced the story? What was the opening sentence? How did they cover the material? Was it interesting? Did they use graphics, and when? How did they end it? If you're going to be a professional writer for a living, start noticing the bricks in the foundation of the house. Also, if you like a particular author's writing style, start following the writer to see what else they have done. One of the biggest clues that you're interested in a particular writing style is when you start to follow your favorite writers because you know they are above average for delivering information the way you want to read it.

Start Out Free

It is the rare writer who gets paid for their first writing assignment. Most of us have to put in our time in the trenches, so to speak. If you're hoping to be a new professional writer, look for the less obscure newsletters and blogs to see if they will take unsolicited articles and ideas, and make multiple pitches. As you build up your writing chops and experience, you can start to increase what you ask for, although remember different types of writing pay differently. It isn't always about the initial money. Each bit of writing gains you credibility.

Be Professional

Lastly, it goes without saying that in the professional writing industry, being professional goes a long way. That means being prepared and knowledgeable, but also meeting deadlines. Every editor and publisher in the industry has horror stories of people they gave a writing contract to who never finished the book or article. Early on I doubted my ability to write, and that led to missed deadlines. I've learned that simply meeting deadlines can get you lots of other paid work. Oftentimes when a publisher or editor meets you for the first time, they are trying to figure out whether you will be reliable and professional. If you can convey professionalism, you can become a professional writer. If you do it over time, you can do it for a career.

Be Your Own Publicist

Regardless of whether you self-publish or use a professional organization, you'll need to expend as much effort as you can on getting your work seen by more people. That's why most professional security writers have presences on many different social network sites. The more people know you, the greater the chance that you can make a living at writing.

A Picture Is Worth a Thousand Words

I give thanks to my long-time friend and best-selling professional IT author, Mark Minasi (http://www.minasi.com), for this hint: Try to get your profile picture included with your writing any time you can. Readers will remember you far more easily if you help them associate an image with your name. Early on, I told web sites that I would write for free (even if they were offering to otherwise pay) if I could get my picture next to the article. This helps to build name recognition and followers faster, which leads to everything else. The ego-fulfilling side effect is that sometimes complete strangers will walk up to you and say they enjoy your work. My books never overly impressed my daughters, but the occasional fan walking up to us in a restaurant or amusement park and recognizing and thanking me did.

As a full-time computer security consultant, I'm not only a writer, but writing has definitely made me a better consultant. When you write, you have to learn your subject really well and become a near-master. It forces you to learn and exercise your brain in ways that you otherwise would not. I like to think that being a computer security consultant helps me be a better writer and being a writer helps me be a better computer security consultant. At least in my case it isn't coincidental.

The next chapter profiles Fahmida Y. Rashid, a senior writer and colleague at *InfoWorld* magazine.

48

Profile: Fahmida Y. Rashid

I've been a technical computer security journalist for almost 30 years. While I'm not the best writer, I do consider myself one of the better technical writers, in that I live and breathe my subject. When I read other computer security writers' work, I don't usually learn much. That changed when I was introduced to a new writer at *InfoWorld* magazine by our Editor-in-Chief, Eric Knorr. Eric was very excited about hiring her and I soon knew why. Like computer security journalist Brian Krebs (profiled in Chapter 29), Fahmida Y. Rashid is an incredible computer security researcher, although in a different way. I've yet to read a single article of hers where I do not learn something new. She groks her subject in a way that continues to surprise me for someone who isn't doing computer security as their day job. She really understands the technical details and is able to ferret out the "BS" better than anyone in the game. She occasionally sends me technical questions about something she doesn't understand, to which I almost always reply "I don't know either," but a few days later after more research, she is publishing an easy-to-understand explanation. She finds her answers somewhere.

She is an experienced information security journalist. She has worked at eWeek as the senior technical editor for the CRN Test Center, covered network infrastructure for Forbes.com, served as Editor-in-Chief for an RSA Conference, and written for dozens of respected magazines and websites including: Dark Reading, PCMag.com, SecurityWeek, Tom's Guide, *InfoWorld*, SCMagazine, Dice.com, BankInfoSecurity.com, and GovInfoSecurity.com. She is currently a senior writer at *InfoWorld* magazine, and she also works at Pragmatic Bookshelf helping to guide authors through the process of writing technology books.

I asked Rashid how she got started in computer security. She replied, "I actually started out as a network technician and help-desk support for students, faculty, and administrators in a large urban university. I learned a lot about securing the network while juggling BYOD challenges even before the acronym became a security buzzword. I learned web server administration the hard way while working as a ColdFusion developer for a dotcom startup and someone hacked into the IIS server and deleted files. I spent six years as a management consultant for various financial services firms and pharmaceutical companies, developing Java applications, building large data warehouses, and manipulating large data sets. While I enjoyed the work, I wanted to take a step back, have a broader view of the technology world, and not just see the network of one company. I joined the journalism world as an enterprise technology reporter, writing about networking, storage, and hardware. All my technical experiences came in quite handy because I actually understood the technology I was writing about.

"Security became a logical extension of my focus because it is really difficult to write about networking and not think about security. After about five years, I started specializing in information security. A part of it was serendipity, as the increasing number of high-profile attacks, insider leaks, and the rise in online credit card fraud meant I had to spend more of my time focusing on security. I understood networking, so I could see the gaps which made the attacks possible. I started learning about SQL injection and XSS, and I really hoped that none of my code from my consultant days was still in production because I know I didn't sanitize any inputs. I've written for both business and consumer audiences and learned the groups look at security very differently. But over the years, I am pleased to see that more and more people are actually thinking about security and not just dismissing it as something the techies deal with."

I asked Rashid what she thought was the biggest issue in computer security. She replied, "I think the biggest issue is that being secure is hard. It requires new habits, and we don't have the time or patience to develop them. It doesn't have to be easy or convenient, but when security is confusing, the benefits aren't all that obvious, and we have people just looking for workarounds. Every single problem we have in security boils down to the fact that it's hard to do things the secure way and much easier to just keep everything open and unprotected. Some examples: Encryption makes sense, but it's still too difficult to use regularly. WhatsApp takes care of it automatically, so now people don't mind using encrypted chat. But secure file sharing and encrypted email are still too hard.

"We don't think twice about locking the door of our homes, but there must have been a time when people thought it was crazy. We are in that state right now, where people think all the security steps are crazy, but the mindset is slowly shifting. But to really make that change, we need better tools. On the other hand, I know too many people with iPhones who still don't use TouchID to lock their phones, so I don't know how much further we have to go on the 'not hard' path for people to care. Maybe we need to get to the point where iPhones automatically record the user's fingerprints without having to set up TouchID manually. We need security by default, where doors lock themselves automatically without our having to get the keys out. Skynet may be the answer to all our security woes."

As a long-time successful computer security journalist, I asked Rashid what she would recommend to other people considering a career in computer security writing. She said, "While I don't think you need to have a technical background to be a good writer, it helps. I am not saying to go out and become a CISSP, write code, or learn how to use Metasploit. But learn the basics of how networks work, how computers and other devices communicate, and what some of the common terms mean. If you are going to be looking at web application attacks, have a flow-chart–level understanding of how web applications, web servers, and databases interact. If you are going to write about DDoS attacks (or its smaller cousin, DoS), you need to have a basic comprehension of how a network works. You don't need to know the mathematics behind cryptography, but understand the difference between some of the different implementations and understand why some should not be used. Read. Look at the technology. Don't shy away from understanding how technology works. You can't explain to people why we need to have more security over our digital lives and to protect our tech if you are scared of the technology. Think about it this way—you don't need to be an airplane pilot to write about the aviation industry, but it would help if you've at least flown on some planes.

"Another important thing to remember is that technology tends to go in waves. What used to be old becomes new again, with a tweak or new feature. The number of young writers who don't know about mainframes or dismiss mainframes as 'no one uses them anymore' is frightening, because so much of our world still has mainframes at the foundation. Information rights management is making a comeback again. And every time I hear people talk about mobile devices and data in the cloud, I think back to the dawn of thin-client computing. Knowing the past is always important, but it really makes a difference when looking at security because you can then see patterns."

I asked her what she knows now that might have helped in her career if she learned it years sooner. She replied, "Don't be afraid to ask questions. I had this feeling that in order to have security researchers and experts take me seriously, I had to already be well-versed in the basics, so I spent a lot of time doing homework to try to get to the basic understanding. It took a long time to realize that experts are dying to be asked questions so that they can brag about their knowledge. You still need your basic knowledge—don't ask your source what a DDoS attack is—but you can ask for explanations, such as the difference between a Layer 4 and Layer 7 DoS attack. Much of my security basics started out as self-taught, and if I'd asked for help sooner, I could have learned much more thoroughly (as opposed to cramming) without nearly half the stress. Also, be skeptical of words like 'innovative,' 'first-ever,' and 'market-leading.' In fact, when looking at security announcements, cross out the buzzwords so that you can see the basic message."

I asked Rashid what she liked about writing about computer security. She replied, "I like computer security because it forces me to keep learning. There is always new research to read and new ways of tackling the problem to learn about. Security blends creative problem solving, curiosity about the world, and a willingness to break something to make something better. It's also about ego. Security professionals are the people who get up every morning intent on saving the world, one piece of data and device at a time. They may not get the millions that the Instagram founders get or the fame of Elon Musk, but the people who keep my data safe in corporate databases, make sure the SSL certificate on the web site is up-to-date so that my financial information is transferred securely across the web, and test code to make sure there is no gaping remote code execution flaw in the software are the ones saving the world for us. I like writing about information security because it puts me tangentially in the orbit of these heroes."

For More Information on Fahmida Y. Rashid

For information about Fahmida Y. Rashid, check out these resources:

- Fahmida Y. Rashid's LinkedIn profile: `https://www.linkedin.com/in/fyrashid`
- Fahmida Y. Rashid's *InfoWorld* articles: `http://www.infoworld.com/author/Fahmida-Y.-Rashid/`

49 Guide for Parents with Young Hackers

NOTE Some of this chapter originated from an article I wrote in 2016: "11 Signs Your Kid Is Hacking and What to Do About It" (http://www.infoworld.com/article/3088970/security/11-signs-your-kid-is-hacking-and-what-to-do-about-it.html).

As a computer security writer for over 20 years, a few times each year I have parents email to ask how they can tell if their kid is hacking—the bad kind of hacking—and what they can do to encourage their child's pursuit of a promising honest career. I know what they are talking about because years ago I had to have the same confrontation with my teenage son. He was starting to do some not-so-legal hacking and in some cases was getting into minor trouble. Luckily, my wife and I intervened early and, with a few wrinkles, successfully encouraged his exploration of whitehat hacking.

I think that many smart computer teenagers have the ability to turn to the blackhats if not appropriately guided. Often, they either aren't doing great in school or aren't deriving much satisfaction from their scholarly accomplishments. At school and likely at home, they are being told to do what they consider to be boring tasks without a purpose, and they feel like they are being harassed for not working toward their full potential. In the online world, they seek and get the admiration and respect of their peers. They feel powerful and mysterious at the same time. It's like a drug. I get the attraction. Most of these kids are good kids and will get over their blackhat hobby without getting into trouble. The problem is you can't be sure whether your kid will do so or not, so it's best to intervene before they have to learn how hard it is to get a job with a felony record.

Signs Your Kid Is Hacking

Before you can counsel your kid into using their hacking skills for only ethical and good things, you must first figure out if they are hacking maliciously in the first place. After you've ruled out that their secrecy is only related to pornography or a girlfriend or a boyfriend, there are some signs your kid is involved in malicious hacking. The following sections explore these signs.

> **NOTE** Obviously, there are many things that can concern a parent about what their kids might be doing online, such as viewing pornography, going into chat rooms with predators, and engaging in other activities that can be troubling, dangerous, or illegal. Each of those concerns is serious and can be addressed through various means, but our focus for this chapter is specifically on the dangers of hacking.

They Tell You They Hack

This one is pretty simple. Your child tells or brags to you about how easy hacking is. I know it sounds funny to read, but some parents hear this direct claim, often multiple times, and ignore it. They either don't understand what "hacking" really means in the way their child is using it, or they want to believe that their previously good kid isn't doing anything stupid or wrong. Unfortunately, sometimes they are.

Overly Secretive About Their Online Activities

Every teenager wants 100% privacy for everything they do, online and otherwise, regardless of whether that includes hacking. A kid who is hacking will go to even greater lengths than usual to hide everything they do. What I'm talking about is a complete erasure of everything they do online. Their browser history is always blank. Their log files are clear. You can't find new files or folders. Everything is hidden. The absence of any activity is a big sign that they are intentionally hiding something that might get them into big trouble. By the way, clearing the browser history could be hiding other types of activities, so I'm talking about doing more than just that.

They Have Multiple Email/Social Media Accounts You Can't Access

It is common for kids to have multiple email and social media accounts. It's the issue of inaccessibility that is important in this instance. If your kid has an email and social media account that they're comfortable with you reading, but you discover signs that they have other accounts and logons that they keep secret from you, something is going on.

You Find Hacking Tools on the System

If you find hacking tools like the ones described in this book or that are generally found on hacking web sites, then there's a good chance your kid is interested in hacking.

People Complain You Are Hacking

Several times during the period when my son was into computer hacking, I received emails and calls from strangers or my Internet provider warning me that if I continued my hacking activities I would have my Internet connection terminated or I would even face criminal and civil actions and fines. I was confused at first. I wasn't hacking anyone. But my son was.

You Catch Them Switching Screens Every Time You Walk into the Room

They could be switching screens when you enter the room to hide any of many things (like watching pornography or communicating with a girlfriend/ boyfriend), but if you catch them always switching screens when you walk into a room, investigate.

These Signs Could Be Normal

All of these signs could be normal. Your kid may not be a malicious hacker or any kind of hacker for that matter. I'm sure lots of readers and their children are reading this right now and saying that each of those things listed above happened and they were not involved in illegal or unethical hacking. I get that.

I'm just trying to share some of the signs that your kid might be hacking, so you won't be caught blindsided like my wife and I were, just as many of the readers who write me were. Awareness is a good thing.

Not All Hacking Is Bad

In fact, most hacking is good. Hacking is simply someone going beyond the standard confines of a GUI or what the average computer user does. I'm a hacker and I've never done anything illegal in my life. This applies to many of my co-workers (although a few did walk on the dark side for a while when they were younger). If you think your kid is hacking, you need to determine whether they are doing something unethical or illegal before tearing into them and taking away their computer privileges. Most of our most valuable companies and their leaders and employees have the hacking ethic. It's just a question of making sure it's ethical and legal hacking.

How to Turn Around Your Malicious Hacker

So, suppose that you discover your kid is engaged in unethical or illegal hacking activity. What can you do?

First, understand that these kids can be reformed. Most go on to give up illegal activities as they mature and find fulfillment with better paying, legitimate work. Only a few go on to make a career out of blackhat activities. The key is to help guide these kids, who know they are doing wrong, to use their newly found skills for good.

Second, let them know that you know what is going on and that it is unethical, illegal, and could lead to their arrest. The days when companies and authorities were clueless entities that rarely arrested someone are ancient history. Hackers are arrested and prosecuted all the time. It happened to some of my son's friends. I have talented, competent co-workers whose criminal record prevents them from accompanying me on certain high-profile engagements to this day.

Third, tell your kid that you will be monitoring their activities for as long as you feel it is necessary. Let them know that you won't give them details about what you'll be doing, but that that you'll be watching. And warn them that if you catch them engaging in the slightest unethical or illegal activities, every electronic device they have will go bye-bye for a long time. Threaten them with taking away whatever is their other favorite activity. Now is the time to scare them a little and to let them know there are consequences. And if they break the rules, be sure to follow up on your threats.

Move Their Computers into the Main Living Area and Monitor

If your kids had computers in their room, tell them they have lost the privilege, and move them into the main living area for easier monitoring. Tell them they can't use their computers when you're not home and not monitoring. Tell them these new changes will be permanent until you can trust them again. Make sure you monitor what they are doing, even when they are in front of you.

Give Guidance

In addition to the forfeitures and potential punishments, most of all give guidance. Have conversations with your kid about the importance of ethics both online and offline. Explain how any hacking activity is illegal without being granted explicit permission by the legal owner or custodian of the data. Explain to them that even questionable hacking activity, such as uninvited port or vulnerability scanning, can be illegal and even in the instances when it is legal, it is still unethical.

Give Legal Places to Hack

If your kid is interested in hacking, give them legal and ethical places to express that creativity and learn. There are a variety of places where they can do this.

HackMe Websites

There are all sorts of web sites on the Internet that allow and even encourage hacking. Search these locations out. One of my favorite sites is Hack This Site (https://www.hackthissite.org/). You can hack their web site, and it includes tons of groups and projects dedicated to hacking. Another site dedicated to hackers of all types, not just computer hackers, is Hacker Spaces (http://hackerspaces.org/wiki/).

Bug Bounty Programs

Many vendors offer bug bounty programs where legal hacking can turn into thank yous or big bucks. Some vendors pay several hundreds of thousands of dollars for the biggest critical bugs and have already paid out millions of dollars in bounties. Many young adults have earned thousands of dollars by reporting bugs, including this one (http://www.pcmag.com /article2/0,2817,2371391,00.asp&title=12-Year-Old%20Earns%20 $3,000%20Bug%20Bounty%20From%20Mozilla). Many prominent bug bounty programs exist:

- Microsoft's bug bounty program is here: https://technet.microsoft .com/en-us/library/dn425036.aspx.
- Google's program is here: https://www.google.com/about /appsecurity/reward-program/.
- Apple has an invitation-only program but will still pay for bugs reported by outsiders.
- Mozilla's bug bounty program is here: https://www.mozilla.org /en-US/security/bug-bounty/.
- HackerOne (https://www.hackerone.com) is the company that coordinates the bug bounty programs for many companies, such as Twitter, Slack, and Airbnb.

Not every vendor has a bug bounty program, but all the smart ones do.

Hardware Hacking

If your kid is more interested in hardware than software, there are plenty of hacking outlets. They can join some of the IoT hacking groups covered in Chapter 35 to learn how to hack real-life IoT devices or start with a basic hardware hacking kit like Raspberry Pi (https://www.raspberrypi.org/). Raspberry Pi is essentially a little tiny Linux kit computer on a single circuit board. Over 10 million units have been sold. Arduino (https://www.arduino .cc/) is another similar product. Long gone are the days where the best you can do is buy some circuits, wires, chips, and learn how to weld. With these products you and your kid can do millions of do-it-yourself projects.

Robotics Clubs

Look into any local robotics programs. Many schools and computer vendors sponsor robotics clubs specifically targeted at young hackers, and the leaders

are usually top notch. If you can't find any locally, RoboRealm (http://www
.roborealm.com/clubs/list.php) and Arrick Robotics (http://arrickrobotics
.com/clubs.html) are good places to start.

NOTE Another related hobby and club for budding hackers is amateur
HAM radios. Many hacker friends are also long-time HAM radio people.
There must be an intellectual link.

Capture the Flag Contests

Many schools, web sites, groups, and security conferences sponsor "capture
the flag" contests, where individual hackers or teams compete to see who can
successfully hack something first and get the prize. Just type "hacking capture the flag contest" into any Internet search engine, and you'll see dozens of
capture the flag contests you or your kid can join. The following site shows
many different upcoming capture the flag contests: https://ctftime.org/.

Training and Certifications

Getting training or a certification is a great way to direct youthful hacking
exuberance into the right channels. Challenge your kid to prove how good
they really are by obtaining a computer security certification (some of which
are covered in Chapter 41). Earning a respected all-around first-time hacking certification, such as EC-Council's Certified Ethical Hacker (https://www
.eccouncil.org/Certification/certified-ethical-hacker), is a great way
to learn and eventually move into a career. In my nearly 30 years of hacking,
I've learned something new and valuable from every certification I've earned,
which has made me a better hacker.

Connect Them with a Good Mentor

Lastly, try to hook them up with someone who has been through their experience and was able to transform their new-found creativity into a legal and
lucrative career. If you don't know anyone else, consider me (roger_grimes@
infoworld.com). I'll be happy to add your kid to the list of people that I mentor.

I usually give the same guidance that I provide here, but I can also intro-
duce them to the smarter, good hackers. Most kids mistakenly believe that the
blackhat hackers are the most clever, intelligent ones. But in any given year,
maybe one bad hacker is doing something new and interesting. Everyone else

is just following what they did. Unquestionably, the best hackers I've met have consistently been the defenders.

It's easy to take a sledgehammer and destroy a car, but it's much harder and more challenging to build that car. Want to impress me? Be the person who builds something that can withstand the constant challenges from hackers.

If you suspect that your child, or someone else's child, might be engaged in unethical or illegal hacking, show them this book. Teenagers who love hacking can always be turned around to the good side. For that matter, so can adults.

And my hacking son? He's doing great in life. He's got a great job working with computers making lots of money, he's a wonderful son, father, and ethical human being. I couldn't love him more. We look back and laugh about the days when it was us versus him in the digital world. He thanks me and his mom for stepping in and providing a little guidance to help him move away from the darker aspects of hacking.

50 Hacker Code of Ethics

If you do an Internet search for "hacker ethics," you are more likely to find a glamorized version of so-called "hacker rules" that embrace the idea that hackers can do anything they want, even perhaps without limits, in the pursuit of whatever they want. Best-selling author Steven Levy's 1984 book, *Hackers: Heroes of the Computer Revolution* (https://www.amazon.com/Hackers-Computer-Revolution-Steven-Levy/dp/1449388396/), introduced the world to one of the earliest versions of hacker ethics (https://en.wikipedia.org/wiki/Hacker_ethic). In a nutshell, almost word for word, it said the following:

1. Access to computers should be unlimited and total.
2. All information should be free.
3. Mistrust authority—promote decentralization.
4. Hackers should be judged by their hacking, not criteria such as degrees, age, race, or position.
5. You can create art and beauty on a computer.
6. Computers can change your life for the better.

Levy was sharing, not necessarily agreeing with, what many hackers felt about the early days of hacking. Unfortunately, many hackers took Levy's hacking ethics to mean that the ends justified the means and that even illegal activities were okay. That's like saying robbing a bank or taking someone else's property is okay as long as you give it away to change your or someone else's life for the better. Hacking without a moral compass can lead to unethical situations and illegality. But more than that, it would hurt us all.

Ignoring for the moment that Levy's proclamations were made more than a decade before the information superhighway came into existence, even Levy didn't promote outright lawlessness and unethical activities. Although some of the people in his book did do some ethically questionable things, the majority did not. Most made a better life for themselves and society without doing a single illegal deed. Many have selflessly dedicated their entire lives to enriching the lives of others for almost no monetary remuneration. Where some hackers saw Levy's hacker ethics as a lawless free for all—how else is "All information free" —most readers and budding hackers saw the beauty of ethical cooperation. The hackers in Levy's book may have started as decentralized, mistrusting free thinkers, but in the end what they learned, created, and invented changed the whole world for the better.

If all information was truly free, that would remove much of the incentive for most of the world's best artists and writers to create the wonderful things they create. Even Steven Levy wanted to be paid for writing his book. Most hardware vendors and software programmers would not do what they do without being able to make a living in some way. Someone ultimately has to pay the bills for the work that paves the information highway. If creators and owners could never charge for their information and creations, we would have far less information and fewer creations. If we took the original hacker ethic to its foremost strict interpretation without considering moral ethics in the process, we would have a less great society. Indeed, hacking without the ethical consideration for the greater good would simply denigrate society.

The culmination of this book is to demonstrate that the best hacking is ethical and legal hacking. Everyone profiled in this book took their amazing mental gifts and used them to better mankind.

The most important guiding principle for hacking is that you do no greater overall harm to the world even if it would give you greater fortune and fame. Put the best ethical outcome ahead of money and glory. This doesn't mean you can't make profit or gain fame, but do so in a legal and ethical way.

Today, many computer security training organizations have an ethical code of conduct that you must agree to abide by in order to be certified by them. The most popular hacker code of ethics I can find on the Internet is the EC-Council Code of Ethics (https://www.eccouncil.org/code-of-ethics/). It's a good code of ethics, but a bit too focused on penetration testing, and it's growing a bit long over time (with 19 statements at press time). With that said, the next section provides a solid, concise code of ethics to operate by, both personally and professionally.

Hacker Code of Ethics

This is my personal hacker code of ethics, one that I've lived by all my life. And I think it's a good starting point for any hacker looking for ethical guidance.

Be Ethical, Transparent, and Honest

It almost goes without saying that following a code of ethics means being ethical. Ethical means trying to do right versus wrong, good versus evil, justice versus injustice. When in an ethical conflict, decide to do what benefits society the most. Be transparent in what you do, being sure to allow either observation by or adequate communication with all stakeholders. Say what you will do, and then do it.

Don't Break the Law

Follow the laws that govern you and your activities. If an ethical issue is making you consider breaking the law, ensure that you have tried everything else reasonably possible and that your actions would likely be seen by most of society as being for the greater good. Most unlawful situations are unlawful because society has determined that everything works better in a particular way, even when you believe you have a powerful justification for breaking the law. Of course, be prepared for living with the consequences of breaking those laws should you be caught.

Get Permission

Always get prior, documented permission from the owner or their lawful representative before hacking an asset owned or managed by them. No exceptions.

Be Confidential with Sensitive Information

Society breaks down without trust. Part of being trustworthy, besides also being ethical, transparent, and honest, means not disclosing sensitive information without prior permission of the owner, especially when that information has been given to you in confidence. In general, the less personal and confidential information you share in life, the more trustworthy people will see you as. I always get a non-disclosure agreement (NDA) signed by new customers. It makes them and me feel better. If you're going to break someone's confidence, make sure it is ethical, legal, and better overall for society for you to do so.

Do No Greater Harm

The Hippocratic Oath should apply to society in general as well as any companies or customers you are working for. All hackers should follow it. Hackers and professional penetration testers should start every engagement by trying not to cause any harm. Minimize potential disruptions. Always start any operation that could cause disruption to an environment slowly, testing, testing, testing, first. And then use the least disruptive settings of your software if those types of settings exist. If you're performing hacking, always warn customers (in writing) that your activities could cause unintentional harm to their environment. Also, make no public disclosure of software vulnerabilities without first notifying the software vendor and giving them adequate time to create a patch. Doing otherwise just harms more customers.

Conduct Yourself Professionally

Strive to be professional in all activities and interactions. This doesn't mean you have to wear a suit, but it does mean that you should act in ways that ensure that people find you trustworthy, if not predictable. This all goes back to being ethical, honest, and transparent. Good communication is a big part of being professional. It also means using your real name (or easy-to-find real identity) and not harassing others or their resources.

Be a Light for Others

Finally, be an example for others by leading an ethical hacking life. Use your powers for good and for the overall betterment of society. Show others how your hacker ethics improve the lives of everyone.

Let your hacking behavior be driven by a combination of both Levy's "hacker ethics" and the truly ethical guidelines proposed in this chapter. Declare yourself an ethical hacker and be proud of it. Like all of the people profiled in this book, it's possible to earn a good living and do all the hacking you need to do in an ethical and legal way. The smartest and best minds aren't the hackers, but the defenders who hack the hackers.

Index